"A mosaic of a book, written by a ski accomplished storyteller. It is a memoir, a family history, a chronicle of Sicilian immigration to the United States, an incisive account of the Mafia's brutal impact on its homeland. It's also the record of a struggle to solve a family mystery—the murder of the author's great-great-grandfather 125 years ago. At all levels, it makes for absorbing reading."

—Nicholas Gage, *The Washington Post Book World*

Critical acclaim for Frank Viviano and
BLOOD WASHES BLOOD

"The book that lays out the origins of the Mafia, far better than the many Italian books I've read, has been written by an American—granted one of Sicilian descent. It's Frank Viviano's brilliant and profoundly moving memoir-cum-detective story. . . . In the course of the book we learn much of Sicily's history, as well as what village life is like today. We also get a crash course in the contemporary Mafia. . . . The book defies categorization; in the end, it's a beautiful exploration of the links between family and history, and of the secret histories that are often truer than the official ones."

—Michael Covino, *East Bay Express*

"Viviano's conclusions seem both well reasoned and enticing, as do the results of his inquiry into the story of his great-great-grandfather—a search that comes to a particularly satisfying surprise ending. And while, in its purest form, the book is a solid piece of storytelling and reporting, its greatest strength may be that while it begins as a personal search, it ultimately reveals the history of a people. Viviano's unsentimental but poignant close-up of one Sicilian family and the role of the Mafia—how it began and how different it has become—will appeal to fans of the equally unsentimental but courageous TV program *The Sopranos*."

—*Publishers Weekly* (starred review)

"Manages to unite in a single strong narrative three distinct strands—Viviano family history, secretive Sicilian folklore, and contemporary reality. . . . Throughout, Viviano writes with insight and poignancy of the complexities and burdens of Sicilians."

—*Time International*

"A great yarn about his search for his Sicilian ancestors, interspersed with the kind of reporting he has done for the *Chronicle* on the Mafia and other European blood feudalism."

—*San Francisco Chronicle*

"A glimpse into a world so many have heard about but so few truly understand. A book that cannot be forgotten. *BLOOD WASHES BLOOD* is written with style and grace, its painful tale told with a simple eloquence. Viviano has composed an epic work about a complex people, a story overrun with love, anger, and pain. . . . It demands to be read."

—Lorenzo Carcaterra, bestselling author of *Sleepers* and *Gangster*

"Bravo—unlike the fruits of some published research that are dry, distant, and only of interest to immediate family, Viviano's lifts his ancestors off the pages and creates living, three-dimensional characters. . . . The writing throughout is musical."

—*The Albuquerque Journal* (NM)

"Part memoir, part detective story, this probe should appeal to all readers interested in the origins of the Mafia, immigration stories, the differences between European and American connections to the past, and personal searches for meaning. Viviano's wide experience in international reporting and his honesty about his own self-doubts lend credibility to his findings, both historical and emotional. Fascinating."

—*Booklist*

"Suspenseful and well balanced, *BLOOD WASHES BLOOD* is an exciting and thoughtful page-turner, a remarkable story of family, mystery, and friendship. Viviano's writing is at its best when he follows the complicated trail of his family's past."

—Amazon.com

"A highly enjoyable memoir."

—*Library Journal*

BLOOD WASHES BLOOD

A True Story of
Love, Murder,
and Redemption
Under the Sicilian Sun

FRANK VIVIANO

WASHINGTON SQUARE PRESS
PUBLISHED BY POCKET BOOKS

New York   London   Toronto   Sydney   Singapore

WSP A Washington Square Press Publication of
POCKET BOOKS, a division of Simon & Schuster, Inc.
1230 Avenue of the Americas, New York, NY 10020

Copyright © 2001 by Frank P. Viviano

Originally published in hardcover in 2001 by Pocket Books

All rights reserved, including the right to reproduce
this book or portions thereof in any form whatsoever.
For information address Pocket Books, 1230 Avenue
of the Americas, New York, NY 10020

ISBN: 0-671-04159-2

First Washington Square Press trade paperback printing April 2002

10 9 8 7 6 5 4 3 2 1

WASHINGTON SQUARE PRESS and colophon are
registered trademarks of Simon & Schuster, Inc.

For information regarding special discounts for bulk purchases,
please contact Simon & Schuster Special Sales at
1-800-456-6798 or business@simonandschuster.com

Cover image by Richard Jenkins

Printed in the U.S.A.

For Alicia and Rosa and their angels in the desert

"So we beat on, boats against the current,
borne back ceaselessly into the past."

F. Scott Fitzgerald, *The Great Gatsby*

Lu sangu lava lu sangu. "Blood washes blood."
—Sicilian proverb, alluding to the torrent of
unforgiving vengeance that flows
from an unforgivable offense.

THE THREE FRANCESCOS

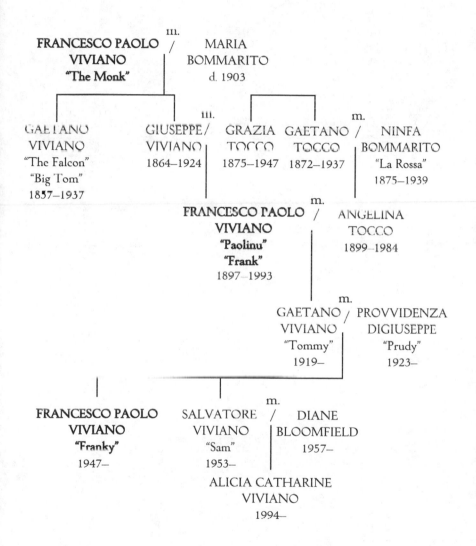

III.
FRANCESCO PAOLO / MARIA
VIVIANO BOMMARITO
"The Monk" d. 1903

GAETANO   GIUSEPPE /   GRAZIA   GAETANO /   NINFA
VIVIANO   VIVIANO   TOCCO   TOCCO   BOMMARITO
"The Falcon"   1864–1924   1875–1947   1872–1937   "La Rossa"
"Big Tom"   1875–1939
1857–1937

III.

m.

FRANCESCO PAOLO / ANGELINA
VIVIANO TOCCO
"Paolinu" 1899–1984
"Frank"
1897–1993

m.

GAETANO / PROVVIDENZA
VIVIANO DIGIUSEPPE
"Tommy" "Prudy"
1919– 1923–

m.

FRANCESCO PAOLO   SALVATORE /   DIANE
VIVIANO   VIVIANO   BLOOMFIELD
"Franky"   "Sam"   1957–
1947–   1953–

ALICIA CATHARINE
VIVIANO
1994–

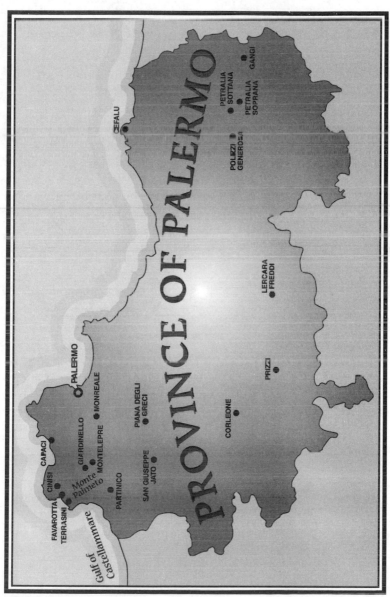

PROVINCE OF PALERMO

CEFALU

GANGI

PETRALIA
SOTTANA

PETRALIA
SOPRANA

POLIZZI
GENEROSA

LERCARA
FREDDI

PALERMO

MONREALE

GIARDINELLO

MONTELEPRE

PIANA DEGLI
GRECI

CAPACI

CINISI

Monte
Palmeto

PARTINICO

SAN GIUSEPPE
JATO

PRIZZI

CORLEONE

FAVAROTTA

TERRASINI

Gulf of
Castellammare

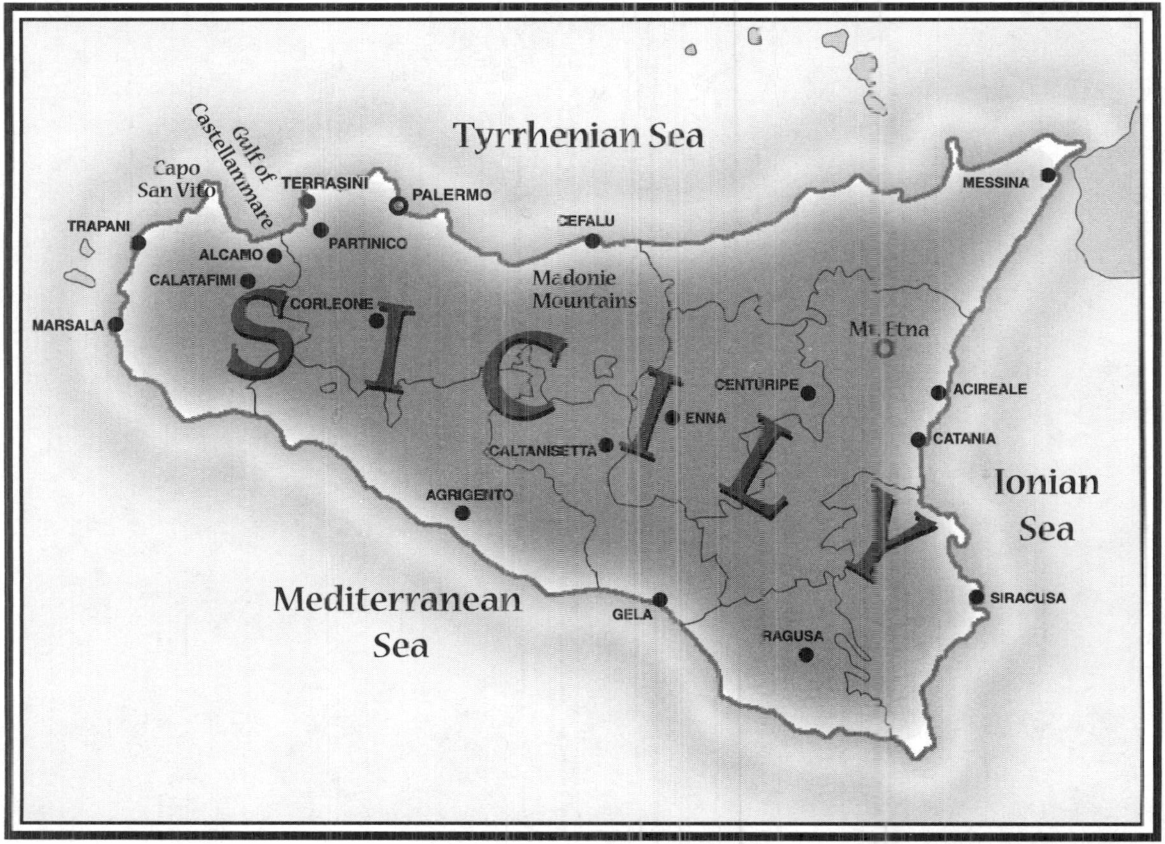

MAP BY SAM VIVIANO

Contents

Prologue *1*

PART I

ONE: A Stranger in the Village *11*

TWO: The System *21*

THREE: Mike *28*

FOUR: An Old Man's Riddle *35*

FIVE: Ano in the Desert *42*

PART II

SIX: A Map *61*

SEVEN: The Red Sash *71*

EIGHT: The Monk *80*

NINE: The Saint and the Beast *87*

TEN: A Burglary at Paternella *94*

ELEVEN: Dark Franky *106*

TWELVE: The Frenchman's Palace *116*

THIRTEEN: *Risorgimento 130*

FOURTEEN: A Parable *138*

FIFTEEN: Death on a Country Lane *151*

PART III

SIXTEEN: The Bandit Kingdom *161*

SEVENTEEN: Fable of the Chickpea *172*

EIGHTEEN: Antonina Randazzo *183*

NINETEEN: Festival of Bachelors *190*

TWENTY: A Parallel Universe *196*

PART IV

TWENTY-ONE: Family Portrait *209*

TWENTY-TWO: "Mafia" *219*

TWENTY-THREE: Domenico Valenti *228*

TWENTY-FOUR: A Secret Life *237*

TWENTY-FIVE: Blood Washes Blood *250*

TWENTY-SIX: Quattro Vanelle *256*

Epilogue *265*

Acknowledgments *269*

Prologue

-→→-←←-

IN THE BEGINNING, before the mystery, there is the killing. Four gun shots at a deserted crossroads. A highwayman in the robes of a monk. A face that he recognizes in the dusk.

There is his name, my name, scrawled into the death registry of a country church in Sicily: "Francesco Paolo Viviano, son of Gaetano, was buried this day." There is the raw fact that edges into fable, a bandit ancestor with a red sash tied around his waist.

There is the elemental drama, a betrayal and murder that my grandfather wraps in silence for more than eighty years, until a November morning in Detroit when he whispers another name to me.

I am an American, Sicilian-bred. Heir to a nation's pulp fiction, from *Little Caesar's* dying gasp to the baptisms, weddings, and funerals of *The Godfather*. I am the infant in a black-and-white 1947 photograph of a baptism at Holy Family Church in Detroit. An immigrant priest pours water over my brow. I am dressed in the same white lace christening gown that my grandfather wore fifty years earlier. In the photograph, he stands beside my grandma Angelina. Grandma has burst into song. My mother looks at her in alarm. I scream at the frigid sensation of December water on my skin.

"*In nomine Patri,*" the priest intones, "I baptize thee Francesco Paolo Viviano." My grandfather's name and *his* grandfather's name, the name in the death registry. The name of the Monk, echoing soundlessly through a century

* * *

THERE WAS NO MYSTERY to unravel before then, because there was no past in which to set it, no murder and no murderer. History, for our family, opened in 1910, when Grandpa stepped ashore at Battery Park in New York. Sicily was a featureless blur of generations. Yet its ghosts were always with us, adrift in the fables of Grandma Angelina. She began chanting them to the grandchildren when we were toddlers, in a delphic cadence that is still the metronome of my dreams.

"Figghiu miu, miu cori," she sang, "my child, my heart," and the tales were spun.

One of these tales obsessed her. She pursued it throughout our adolescence, and returned to it many years later, in that same mesmerizing chant, when she had fallen into a cruel and prolonged dotage. We came to think of it as the story of "Ano in the Desert."

There was once a man named Ano, in my grandmother's telling, who found himself without food or water in a vast desert:

"He had been on a journey lasting many years, under a sun so hot that it burned away his thoughts one by one. Ano forgot almost everything: Where he had come from. Who his people were. How he had wandered into the desert. It was all he could do to keep crawling, with no destination, until his soul began to crack apart and his last thought turned to ash. That last thought was his name. "I am Ano," he said, over and over. "I am Ano . . ."

Grandma would often pause at this point and look up from the mangle where she ironed three generations of sheets and diapers. She had a peculiar intensity in her eyes that told us we must not speak. The chant also intensified for a few moments, as she repeated Ano's dying words:

"I am Ano. I am Ano. I am Ano."

Ano's spare cry from our grandmother's fable terrified us. It foreshadowed her own last months, when she too could remember nothing more than her name and repeated it over and over: "I am Angelina. I am Angelina."

Eventually, she flattened a diaper under the mangle and continued the tale:

"Ano was near death now, and the sound of his name was only a sigh. "Ahhhhhhhnoooooo." The sigh made the Virgin Mary herself weep, because this Ano was no ordinary human being. Even when death came for him, he spoke his name without fear. So Mary asked God to send a beautiful angel to Earth, with a chalice full of cool wine. "*Vivi*, Ano! Drink!" the angel cried, hovering over the dying man.

"The angel saved his life, *miu cori*, and ever since that day the family has been called "Viviano" in his honor. For Ano was your ancestor, and the reason you are alive, and must never, never surrender to despair."

Many years passed before I recognized that Grandma saw herself as the angel; that in Ano's tale we were to read my grandfather's own escape from the desert of confusion and loss. To start over. To bury the past.

But the past never really dies. Family history bubbles and ferments under the surface of family rebirth. In a lock of hair or the angular tilt of a nose, we concede the work of heredity, even if the model who inspired our canvas is only a name to us, a ghost adrift in a grandmother's fables. Why not a legacy in character, mood, temperament?

The past is not another country. It is the country within, ruled by a bandit in the robes of a monk.

WHEN I WAS FIFTEEN YEARS OLD, I asked my grandfather for the first time about the man he referred to as *lu Monacu*. The name only came up in his private conversations with Grandma Angelina, and then very rarely. But I overheard, and one day I could no longer restrain my curiosity.

"This monk you talk about, Grandpa. Who was he?"

We were on the way to the produce terminal, trying to make out the center line on Gratiot Avenue through the frosted windshield of a January morning. For several minutes, there was no answer. I stared ahead into the darkness. The gavel fell on the Detroit fruit auction just after dawn. My grandfather liked to arrive early, so he could climb into the freight cars and pry open a few boxes of oranges and lemons. The word around the terminal was that Frank Viviano could tell, just from picking up an orange, feeling its heft and running his fingers over the skin, what it was worth. He was the founder and patriarch of our family business, a wholesale produce firm that employed all four of his sons and a son-in-law.

He leaned forward in the driver's seat and spoke very softly. *"Lu Monacu fu miu nannu.* He was my grandpa, Franky, like I'm yours. At the church, when he's a baby, they give him the same name as you and me. But after he's a man, everyone in Sicily call him 'the Monk.'"

"Why did they call him that?" I asked.

I remember that my grandfather paused again, a long time, before responding. "Because he wore priest's clothes," he said.

We stopped at a traffic light, the interior of the Buick bathed white in the headlights of cars bound eastward toward the General Motors and Chrysler plants. My grandfather didn't wait for me to ask another question.

"He robbed big people like that, Franky. He went out on the roads at night, dressed like a priest, and he fooled the people who was no good."

It was the only thing my grandfather said to me about the Monk until a November morning in 1992.

I WAS A MIDDLE-AGED FOREIGN CORRESPONDENT on that morning, a forty-five-year-old bachelor with no fixed address. In the past twelve years, I had covered two dozen wars and revolutions. My rootlessness was excessive, even for a rootless profession, and the contradiction of everything my grandfather found meaningful.

He had arrived in New York at the age of twelve in 1910, with a change of clothes and a straw basket. For two years, he peddled fish from the basket, on foot across Harlem from the East River to the Hudson. The basket led to a fruit and vegetable pushcart in booming Detroit in 1912, the pushcart to a horse and wagon, the horse to a Republic truck. That's how my grandfather chose to remember it. His pilgrim's progress from Battery Park was a methodical journey through the new world, broken by a cry from the old.

In March 1916, as he walked up East 116th Street during a trip back to New York, the sun lit a face in the rear car of the Third Avenue elevated train. My grandfather knew this face: Angelina Tocco looked back, and sang out his name through an open window. She was a cousin from Terrasini, his village, a sixteen-year-old seamstress in a Brooklyn factory. Their eyes met for an instant that was to last sixty-eight years.

These were the icons that tugged at our family memory: the basket, the pushcart, the horse, and the truck. Grandma Angelina on the Third Avenue el. Their six children and eighteen grandchildren in a big, raucous house in Michigan. My grandfather, the second Francesco Paolo, "Paolinu" to his boyhood friends, was a relentless builder. He encircled himself with offspring and dug deeply, permanently, into his adopted soil.

The third Francesco—I, the American "Franky"—was a loner, forever on the wing. The demons that drove me were shadowy but irresistible.

They were the legacy of the Monk, my grandfather believed. An echo that he first heard when I was still a boy, and that grew to haunt him as the years passed. An echo that he kept to himself until the final year of his life. Like the Monk, I was a wanderer, and in my own way a fugitive. I had even been a thief, kicked out of the Boy Scouts at the age of twelve for robbing a gas station, arrested at fourteen for breaking and entering and assault. A year later, I stole a Lincoln Continental. After it was returned to the owner, I stole it a second time. In my forties, I was still alone and on the run, without a family or home, when a whisper sent me to Sicily. In search of the bandit who gave me my name. In search of his killer.

*   *   *

I SAW MY GRANDFATHER for the last time in a small apartment in Detroit's eastern suburbs, two rooms with a studio bed, a Formica table and four chairs, a kitchenette. He had moved there the previous April. His daughters had been after him for years to sell the big house, with its memories of Grandma and too many rooms to heat in the long Michigan winter. Until 1992, he wouldn't even discuss it. Then, suddenly, Grandpa announced that he was ready to leave. He turned ninety-five the week I arrived in Detroit.

My grandfather was a very solidly built man who looked much larger than his five-foot-eleven-inch frame. In the photographs that recorded his progress from teenaged fish peddler to family patriarch, he seemed virtually unchanged. Even at the age of four, in the studio portrait with his mother and two sisters that was his sole memento of Sicily, he had the ramrod posture that would set off Frank P. Viviano in snapshots at the produce terminal in 1928, at my parents' wedding in 1946, at his and Angelina's fiftieth anniversary in 1967. His hair had silvered and he walked slowly now,

A 1901 studio portrait of Paolinu at the age of four in Sicily, with his mother, Grazia Tocco, and his two sisters, Angelina (left) and Maria.

especially in the mornings, fighting to keep his shoulders straight. But he was as sharp of mind as ever.

"Franky, *figghiu miu*," he said, when he opened the door. We embraced for several minutes, standing in the doorway.

He had been giving things away since June. Grandma Angelina's silk brocade couch to one of my cousins, her mahogany dining table to another. He wanted me to take his ring, a diamond set in gold. I refused. I wouldn't listen when he looked into my eyes and told me that we might never see each other again.

"Sit down," he said. There was a tremor in his voice, something more than the tremor of age. We took our places at either side of the table, and he talked about Grandma, about their years together.

He pushed a lock of hair from his forehead and turned his face away toward the wall. Then he looked at me again and began to speak about the Monk. "He was always alone. He never stay in one place. You too much like he was, Franky. You can't live this way. Listen to me, Franky. I don't want you to die like he did."

My grandfather didn't know my world. He couldn't read a newspaper. I doubt that he had ever heard of Nicaragua or Tiananmen Square, much less the distant river town in the Balkans where I had brushed too closely with death that August and lost my bearings. But he knew me. He knew that I was not in my right mind. He had been Ano once, and now Ano was me.

"How did the Monk die?" I asked.

Almost inaudibly, Grandpa sighed, *"Aiutu di Diu."* God help me. "The boss tell his men to kill him," he whispered. "The boss, Domenico Valenti."

The name meant nothing to me.

Six months later, my grandfather died. Those few words in 1992, along with Angelina Tocco's fables, were all that I carried to Sicily.

PART I

ONE

A Stranger in the Village

✦➤◆◄✦

Terrasini, Sicily
April 1995

THE BIRTHPLACE OF MY GRANDPARENTS, of the bandit Francesco "the Monk" and the blur of generations before him, is a fishing village on the Gulf of Castellammare, twenty-five miles west of Palermo. In the blinding Mediterranean noon, four elderly men play cards under a makeshift canvas awning as I drive slowly through the port. Their eyes closely follow my car, but nobody speaks. In the rearview mirror, after I pass, they are still watching. The harbor *caffès* are deserted at this hour. A trawler rocks gently on a northern swell. The spring air is ripe with the odors of saltwater, lemon blossom, and wild fennel.

Two years have passed since my grandfather's death when I arrive in Terrasini, almost three since his enigmatic words in a Detroit kitchen. I have a story to sort out, a riddle to unlock. Beyond that, I can't really explain why I've come here, to a village where I know no one and have no past of my own. There is only that riddle with my name on it, a dead man and his killer.

In the mirror, the card players have returned to their game. I park the car and walk out along a concrete wharf, carrying a tourist brochure. From the sea, Terrasini is a cubist jumble of pastel houses set on a cliff above the harbor.

The wharf rests on blocks of amber limestone cut from Monte

Terrasini, Sicily, viewed from the fishing harbor. Photo by Author.

Palmeto, a bare ridge two miles inland that rises nineteen hundred feet into a jagged mosaic of peak and canyon. Quarrymen, I read, have been sculpting the brow of Palmeto for thirty centuries, since a Bronze Age tribe built their chief city on the outskirts of present-day Terrasini. The limestone blocks in the harbor may be the vestiges of that city, or of the antique Roman settlement Terrasinus, the "land on the Gulf." The village fishermen, who moor their boats to the enormous old stones, insist that they are the ruins of Atlantis.

My grandfather passed his childhood on the Terrasini harborside. The Monk must have watched the shadows flee Monte Palmeto under a noonday sun. I recognize that a setting is unfolding, that the plot and characters of my story are hidden in this landscape.

The rectangular grid of streets immediately above the harbor is the fishermen's quarter, a dozen blocks of net-draped cottages tightly packed onto a knoll behind the chapel of Maria Santissima della Provvidenza, protectoress of seafarers. On a map posted in front of the chapel, the quarter is identified as Contrada Marina, the maritime district, but its residents have always called it "Favarotta," as did my grandparents.

It is an allusion to the secret language that murmurs under the visible surface of Sicilian life, a vocabulary of coded words and symbols riven from a tortured history. The island of Sicily has been sacked by nearly every conqueror to pass through the Mediterranean basin for three thousand years. Ten centuries ago, when the most recent invaders were North African, Arab galleys were moored to the amber harbor stones. "Favarotta" is derived from *fawar*, Arabic for "fountain"; it refers to a spring of cool water that gushes up from slabs of rose shale where Our Lady of Providence surveys the tuna fleet.

Favarotta occupies the narrow end of an elongated wedge that encloses the village. Its dimensions have barely changed since my grandfather's birth. Twenty-two streets climb the slope toward the base of Monte Palmeto, cut by ten that parallel the gulf shore. The map's focal point, stretching along an east-west axis for a full block between the fishermen's cottages and the rest of the village, is the broad Piazza Duomo, lined by shady ficus trees and the crumbling *palazzi* of minor nobles. Maria Santissima delle Grazie, the principal church of Terrasini, anchors the piazza's upper end with two bell towers.

Officially, eleven thousand people reside in Terrasini and its outlying countryside in 1995. At noon on the day of my arrival, the face of the village is a sun-washed mask: narrow cobbled streets interspersed with baroque churches and squares, houses shuttered to the meridional heat, a border of seascape and citrus grove. Its soul is the ancestral memory, a dark grotto of whispered names and archaic understandings etched in nearly impenetrable code.

SICILY WAS FAMILIAR to me from periodic assignments dating back to the late seventies, when I'd begun covering organized crime as a wire service reporter. I knew the general history, a few of the local tales, and a lot of what was directly connected to the murder trials and political scandals that brought me to the island on professional business. But I had never spent more than an afternoon in Terrasini.

The idea had materialized gradually in the year after my grandfather's death: I would take up residence in the birthplace of my namesake, a village where three of my grandparents had also been born and the fourth was raised. I would learn who killed the Monk, and why. I would find out what my grandfather's words meant.

For two and a half years I put off this trip and prepared for it at the same time. I had to make a living, I told myself; I couldn't drop everything to chase down a riddle. But I knew, at heart, that it was just a matter of time.

I bought books on Sicily wherever I found them, straightforward tourist guides and obscure academic studies in English, French, and Italian, until I'd accumulated a respectable library. I hoarded vacation days, letting them pile up until I could take off for a couple of months. Then I locked up my office at the San Francisco *Chronicle* bureau in Paris and headed south across France and the Italian border to Genoa, where I boarded a car ferry for the 750-mile voyage to Palermo. Not precisely my grandfather's voyage in reverse, but a symbolic approximation.

Three hours after I arrived in Terrasini, I checked into a dusty guest house just behind Maria Santissima delle Grazie. My room had a sagging, ornately gilded matrimonial bed, a small wooden desk, and one chair, and a shower whose temperature shifted unpredictably from scalding to ice cold. There was no phone. The windows opened onto a narrow balcony directly under the church towers; their bells struck every fifteen minutes around the clock, in great baritone peals that rattled the window frames. Four strokes at 4:00 P.M. One at each quarter hour, two at the half hour, three at three quarters.

The bell towers overlooked the western turn of Terrasini's *passeggiata*, the evening promenade in the piazza. By unspoken consensus, teenagers ruled it for two hours, starting at five. They strutted in unruly knots, clusters of boys shouting insults at each other and ogling clusters of girls. At the stroke of seven, the teenagers promptly disappeared and were replaced by young families and older strollers, the men still with men and the women with women, gliding arm-in-arm past the church and the piazza's five *caffes* and three social clubs.

The protocol was rigid. The first time I joined the *passeggiata,* swept along on a teenaged wave as the bells rang six, I noticed that the men sipping *amaro* outside of the Circolo Contadino and Di Maggio's *Caffe* remained pinned to their chairs. An hour later, one of the Di Maggio clients rose from his seat, introduced himself in English, and walked me through several circuits of the piazza, explaining the rules. He had spent seventeen years in Michigan and New York, learning the ways of life in the United States through trial and error, and felt sorry for me. His name was Michele Cortese, but he said he'd be grateful if I called him Mike.

"Reminds me of America," he explained.

Mike was to become my closest friend in Terrasini, my guide. I needed both. I was a stranger in the village, with a trunk full of books and a fuzzy agenda.

THE MOST SIMPLE biographical facts were missing when I began the search for the Monk. I knew that he had had at least two sons, my great-grandfather Giuseppe and his elder brother. But I had no idea where our family had lived in Terrasini, no idea when the first Francesco had married, no idea if there had been other children.

Indeed, I had no idea when he was born or when he had died—only that the murder occurred after Giuseppe was baptized in 1864, with his father in attendance. And I only knew that because the baptismal certificate from Maria Santissima delle Grazie lay amid the yellowed documents that Grandma Angelina had hidden inside the furniture upholstery during the early stages of her dementia. We found it after her death in 1984, along with a cache of unpaid bills from J. L. Hudson's Department Store and the sheet music from love songs she played on the piano.

My grandfather took the answers I sought to the grave, leaving me with an improbable hope that the Monk and his killer had not been forgotten on the Gulf of Castellammare.

So I took a step back and began the way a reporter should have, surveying the ground, taking notes, asking more questions. The who, where, when, and why that might bring a riddle closer to a coherent account, to a killing and its motivation.

The history was fresher in Sicily, in place if not time. That was clear from my first acquisition in Terrasini, a telephone directory. The reporter's most basic tool. Sixty-three family names were listed in its pages. They were, I would soon find, the same names that had filled the village's civil ledgers in 1850. There could hardly be a corner of Europe where the pace of change was more lethargic. The wealth of direct connections to the past, traced by sixty-three unbroken family lines, bore its enormous weight on every conversation.

Sicily, in this regard, was the antithesis of America. Ancestral memory was inescapable here.

TWO DAYS AFTER I moved into the guest house, I presented myself at the Palazzo La Grua, an austere eighteenth-century baronial mansion that now served as Terrasini's town hall. My credentials were a note of introduction from Mike, with whom I'd had dinner the evening before, and the 1864 baptismal certificate of Giuseppe Viviano.

The research ought to have been straightforward: assembling a complete family tree from the municipal records and filling in the biography of the first Francesco, the Monk. Once I knew the dates of his birth and death, I could undertake the much more complicated investigation of his checkered life, in the pages of police and court transcripts at the state archive in Palermo, and begin tracking down the records of Domenico Valenti.

"In principle, no problem," the village registrar told me.

She was Marianna Trappeto, a former Detroiter in her mid-thirties. Like Mike, she had spent many years in America and was anxious to help.

"But in practice," she added, "there is a certain obstacle."

In principle, the birth, marriage, and death of every Terrasini native had been inscribed in the civil ledgers by Marianna and her predecessors for four centuries. In practice, the bare-bones records annex on the opposite side of the town hall square, Piazza Municipale, held almost no death or marriage ledgers from before 1890, a trail that would lead me barely beyond my grandfather's departure for America. The oldest birth records in the annex were from the 1850s, the last stumbling decade of the Spanish and Bourbon kingdoms that ruled Sicily for six centuries.

The rest of the ledgers had not been lost, Marianna assured me. "They are packed in boxes somewhere. . . ."

She promised she would try to find out more, and walked me across the piazza to the annex. *"Tanti auguri,"* she said, parting with an expression that translated as "good luck" and implied that I'd need it.

THE ACCESSIBLE RECORDS were stored in the back room of the annex, in two open bookcases. On the far wall, a photocopy machine was buried under a pile of newspapers and magazines, next to the desk of a filing clerk in a rumpled cotton suit who was finishing up a pack of Marlboros as he carefully studied the day's *Gazzetta dello Sport.* The phone rang, stopped, and then rang again. He ignored it, offered me a chair, and opened a new pack of cigarettes, tossing the *Gazzetta* onto the pile.

"For the moment, I'm afraid, this doesn't work," he said, pointing a nicotine-stained finger toward the buried photocopier and shrugging his shoulders. It didn't work today (or any other day over the next year), and I'd have to transcribe whatever material I found useful into a notebook. The ledgers were not allowed to leave the room.

After our introduction, the clerk shook my hand with businesslike formality each morning at my arrival and each evening at my departure, and nodded during the *passeggiata.* But for weeks we never exchanged another word.

The ledgers, huge leather-bound volumes in an atlas-sized

format, were another exercise in the distinction between principle
and practice. In principle, they were organized chronologically,
opening with the events of January and closing with December's
entries and an alphabetical index of the ledger's infants, newlyweds,
or deceased. In practice, the index pages were often torn out or
shredded beyond recognition because the protective leather covers
had fallen off.

The entries themselves were frequently rendered indecipher-
able by a nineteenth-century registrar's sloppy hand or by a pen
that had spewed ink blots over the ledgers. In a single volume, there
might be three or four alternate spellings of a family name:
Valente, Walenti, Valenti, Vallenti. The record—which noted who
witnessed a birth, marriage, or death, as well as the date and site of
the event and the immediate lineage of the subject—might be written in formal Italian or a phoneticized rendition of Sicilian dialect,
depending on the education of the registrar.

Some of the archive officials had been quite precise in their
descriptions. The 1900 birth record of my maternal grandmother,
Caterina Cammarata, identified her father as "blacksmith, Via
Santa Rosalia, four children." Others were satisfied with a no-frills
class label. On his son Giuseppe's record, Francesco the Monk was
simply described as *"viddanu,"* the dialect term for a peasant. Many
records noted only the names of bridegrooms in the marriage
indexes and omitted the ages of mothers from birth certificates.

A misstep and I could wander into a genealogical maze, confronted at every turn by my own name. There was nothing remarkable in village Sicily about the existence of dozens of Francesco
Paolo Vivianos in the same generation. "One tenth of the men in
Terrasini are named Viviano, and one fourth of the Viviano men
are named Francesco Paolo," Marianna Trappeto had declared,
when I told her I was looking for information about my namesake.

Her hands were held close to her sides with palms turned
upward, a gesture that conveys the fruitlessness of a proposed task
and the folly of anyone who might undertake it.

It was the code. Sicilian parents name their first son after his paternal grandfather and their second after his maternal grandfather, just as a first daughter takes the name of her paternal grandmother and a second that of her mother's mother. In anthropological jargon, the tradition is referred to as "pappanomy," and Sicily is its textbook example. Only with a third son or third daughter is invention allowed to play a role.

This is more than custom; it has the force of fixed, immutable law. To violate it is to break ranks with centuries of ancestors. A name in Sicily is at the existential heart of identity: Ano's final thought in the desert, clung to as though it were life itself.

In my own family, there were three Frank Pauls and five Angelas on my father's side, four Salvatores on my mother's. My grandparents had nine children in America. Seven of the nine had found spouses in New York or Detroit who were also children of Terrasini immigrants, and dutifully baptized a new generation of Francescos, Angelas, and Salvatores.

As the first-born grandson in my generation, there had been no doubt about what my name would be. From the moment that a boy was presented to my groggy mother in the delivery room of Detroit's Providence Hospital in 1947, the family had automatically referred to me as "Franky." But as far as Grandma Angelina was concerned, my timing bespoke a miracle. For I had chosen in the womb itself, she declared, to make my appearance on December 3, which was nothing less than the feast day of my saint, San Francesco—and her own birthday. *"Figghiu miu, miraculu!"*

It was a wonder the label didn't stick to me. Acquired nicknames, known in dialect as *'nciuria*, are supplied for nearly every Sicilian; had I been born in Terrasini, I would almost certainly have struggled through childhood nicknamed "the miracle."

In Sicily's more remote villages, there is no point in referring to someone by a baptismal first name; only the local priest recognizes it. More effective is to ask after the likes of *Ammazza-Mugghieri, Ninfa la Rossa, Cicciu Cinque Mille,* or *Facci-Lurdda:* "Wife-Killer," "Red Nymph," "Cicciu Five-Thousand," or "Dirty Face." Poor Signore Wife-Killer, the barkeep of a *caffe*, was a Terrasini widower who had outlived several mates. Ninfa la Rossa, my great-grandmother, was a fanatically devoted Catholic, "red" with religious fervor. But the 'nciuria could also be ironic. Dirty Face was a man known for his excessive fastidiousness. As for Cicciu Five Thousand, he earned his name in the Detroit numbers racket, before returning to Sicily. Cicciu is a Sicilian diminutive for Francesco.

The word 'nciuria itself is derived from the Italian ingiuria, which translates as "insult," but its force in Sicilian dialect is not usually pejorative and its function is far more complicated. On the one hand, it is a practical way of distinguishing between the scores of identically named men and women in a family or town. Among the nineteenth-century plethora of Francesco Paolo Vivianos, the invention and use of "lu Monacu" was a necessary device, as well as a suggestive riddle.

When acquired in one's childhood, an 'nciuria can also carry the weight of a prophecy or a definition of character. Saro D'Anna, a friend of Mike's in Terrasini, had been dubbed Aceddu, "the Bird," in his infancy; at thirty, he was light in his movements and airy in manner—visibly birdlike, a fulfillment of the 'nciuria that his fellow villagers regarded as entirely predictable. Just as predictable, in their view, was the fact that he had married a talkative young woman known universally as Caccarazza, "Magpie."

Yet as much as the 'nciuria prevails in everyday usage, it never appears in a church or municipal record. The result is the archival maze that swallowed me in Terrasini, the endless march of identical names. There were hundreds of birth records for infant boys baptized Francesco Paolo Viviano in the municipal archives, a mind-numbing prospect. But I would know, more often than not, if I was on the wrong track in my research when a first son with that name did not lead back to a paternal namesake in exactly two pappanomic generations.

In principle, it ought to have worked. I buckled down to the search.

TWO

The System

❧❧

THREE INTERIOR MINISTRY HELICOPTERS made a low
pass over the harbor as I walked out of the records annex and across
the Piazza Municipale on a brilliant afternoon in late April. I heard
their engines first, a *wuup-wuup* throb that built to a roar. Then
they swung into view, hovering just a few hundred feet above the
village in a wide v formation. My stomach tightened and I looked
for cover. It was an occupational reflex that I couldn't shake, a nervous habit in the gut.

Mike and I had planned to meet for a glass of wine at the
Cortese family grocery, a couple of kilometers south of the piazza
near the old Bourbon road that follows the coast from Palermo to
Trapani. He'd left a message at Di Maggio's *Caffe*, saying that he
had some ideas about my detective work. I called from the *caffe*
phone and told him I would show up around 4:00 P.M.

But on the outskirts of Terrasini, traffic had been slowed to a
crawl by a series of roadblocks. They were manned by teams of uni-
formed officers from the Guardia di Finanza, government customs
agents who parked their squad cars sideways across the highway to
Palermo and ran spot checks on private automobiles and trucks.

The Guardia's commanding officer waved me past. I drove a
Peugeot with French plates, and the customs men, who were continental Italians on yearlong tours of duty in Sicily, assumed I was a
tourist. Everyone else was put through a ruthlessly thorough inspec-
tion for contraband: mothers ferrying children home from school;

elderly couples returning from the village market; plumbers and electricians making service calls; the fishmongers and vegetable peddlers who plied the Terrasini streets.

I pulled over at the third roadblock to watch. The customs agents yanked boxes and shopping bags out of the vehicles' passenger compartments, trunks, and truck trailers, ripped open the packaging and minutely examined the contents. For every object that was not visibly worn, not clearly in long use, it was necessary to produce an itemized receipt—proof that the driver, whether a mother with children in tow or an eighty-year-old on a cane, was not in the smuggling trade.

You seldom encountered these roadside shakedowns in northern Italy. They were peculiarly Sicilian, a normal part of the scene, with the Finanza descending on Terrasini and its sister villages half a dozen times in some months. The drivers waited wordlessly for the inspectors to finish. It was a matter of local etiquette not to speak to the customs men, as they tore my neighbors' cars apart looking for smuggled American cigarettes, French cognac, and Japanese electronics products.

The helicopters were engaged in their own game of contraband cat-and-mouse, but with immensely greater stakes. Every night, Interior Ministry choppers scouted the coast and countryside, training searchlights on the flanks of Monte Palmeto and the coves that honeycombed the seacliffs around Terrasini. Normally, they tailed motor launches that were fast enough to slip cargoes of guns or unprocessed heroin past a Coast Guard blockade after dark, or trucks large enough to transport arms. But it was rare for them to mount an aerial operation over the village in the plain light of day.

"They're looking for Giovanni Brusca," Mike told me, when I finally showed up at the grocery and asked him what was going on.

Everybody was looking for Brusca, and had been since the afternoon of May 23, 1992, when he detonated twelve hundred pounds of explosives under the center lane of the autostrada at Capaci, six miles from Terrasini. The bombing was allegedly ordered by Salvatore "Toto" Riina, Brusca's boss from the bleak mountain town of Corleone in the island's interior, from which he reigned as the single most powerful man in Sicily. Three police bodyguards were killed at the moment of explosion. Its chief targets, the crusading anti-Mafia judge Giovanni Falcone and his wife, Judge Francesca Morvillo, lingered on into the evening, when they died in a Palermo hospital.

I had flown to Sicily the next morning. In two decades covering the underworld, I'd never seen anything to compare with the bomb site. Half a mile of the autostrada was lunar rubble, as desolate as the blasted towns of Bosnia and eastern Croatia where I was to spend much of the next three years.

THE PROVINCE OF PALERMO, stretching west from the city along the Gulf of Castellammare and south into the mountainous interior, was the very birthplace of organized crime. Yet its inhabitants rarely used the terms "Mafia" or "Cosa Nostra." In Sicily itself, almost everything was explained with the phrase *sistema del potere*. The system. The power structure.

For the people of the Castellammare coast, the *sistema* and those who presided over it were the world's central reality.

Just south of Terrasini on the Bourbon road, the first self-service gas station in western Sicily had opened in 1990. It was owned by a branch of the Badalamenti family, Toto Riina's most powerful rivals. The Badalamentis also owned a supermarket, the sand and cement that went into the autostrada where Judge Falcone was killed, and half a dozen construction firms. Through marriage and blood relations to other local families, they were involved in the maritime and hydraulic industries, fruit and produce wholesaling, electrical installation, earth-moving, sewage treatment, bars, discotheques, hotels, and restaurants.

But the Badalamentis' most conspicuous business achievement, according to law enforcement authorities in Italy and the United

States, was to exercise a near monopoly over narcotics trafficking in America. Gaetano "Tanu" Badalamenti, the family patriarch, was the principal godfather of the drug trade. At its peak in the 1970s, his operation accounted for 80 percent of the heroin delivered to New York.

The links between the Castellammare villages and America reach back to the turn of the century, when thousands of immigrants from the region settled in East Harlem, St. Louis, and Detroit. The majority earned their way as ditch diggers and railroad workers or, like my own family, as street peddlers selling fish and produce. But others carried the *sistema* with them.

A statue of a winged angel, honoring Terrasini men who died in World War I, stands in the Piazza Municipale. The pedestal reads: "To our fallen heroes, from their fellow villagers in Detroit." The angel was commissioned by the commanding generals in America's bootlegging wars, which captivated Hollywood during the Depression. They inspired the gangster epics that made Edward G. Robinson famous as Little Caesar in 1931—leading a seventy-year trail of corpses to *The Godfather* and *The Sopranos.*

The bootlegging stakes were cigar money compared to the business of today's Castellammare dons.

In 1985, the Italian authorities launched a giant crackdown on Mafia heroin operations under Judge Falcone's direction. Testimony in the succeeding trials identified Tanu Badalamenti and Toto Riina as *capi di tutti capi,* managing what was by then a $20-billion-a-year international empire that stretched from southeast Asia to western Europe and across the Atlantic to the Americas.

Of 460 organized crime indictments that grew out of the 1985 crackdown, 382 were served on residents of Palermo and its provincial villages. Twenty-four of the indicted were from Terrasini or the neighboring village of Cinisi. Every one of them was related in some way to the Badalamentis.

In 1973, an ambitious young Russian named Mikhail Gorbachev, a rising star on his way to the upper ranks of the Soviet politburo, vacationed in Sicily with his wife, Raisa. They were guests of the Italian Communist Party, installed in a villa overlooking the Gulf of Castellammare. Two decades later, Gorbachev told a biographer that this seaside interlude had been a watershed in his life, a reverie in an earthly paradise that sowed the seeds of *perestroika*.

The villa that changed Mikhail Gorbachev's life and altered the course of the twentieth century lies half a mile from the Terrasini birthplace of my grandfather, on land developed by associates of Tanu Badalamenti.

BEFORE HE WAS MUSCLED ASIDE by Riina in the bloodiest underworld struggle in a century, Badalamenti was a "commissioner," Riina's colleague in a triumvirate that ruled the entire island. In mainland Italy, a severe urban crisis took hold in the 1970s, highlighted by a spectacular rise in drug offenses and juvenile delinquency. But in Badalamenti's western Sicilian countryside, it was the *Pax Mafiosa*.

On their home ground, the dons of the *sistema* were scrupulous family men, resolutely modest in their living habits and firmly committed to marriage for life. If Terrasini kids got into trouble—a pregnancy, shoplifting, a problem in school—it was discreetly resolved by representatives of the *sistema*. If a couple of merchants were involved in a business dispute, somebody was sent by the commission to negotiate a settlement that didn't involve lawyers or courts. The junkies and hookers who hung out in mainland cities were briskly escorted out of town if they turned up on the Piazza Duomo. A puritanical strain of Roman Catholicism was one of the chief points that distinguished the *sistema* from its American affiliates, which embraced secularism and made millions in the flesh trade.

That was the picture into the mid-1970s, the high point of the *Pax Mafiosa*, the apotheosis of Catholic, invisible order. Then Riina and Badalamenti declared war on each other, leaving carnage in the streets and the *sistema* in tatters.

The population of Sicily was roughly five million when Judge Giovanni Falcone met his end on the autostrada in 1992. Over the previous fifteen years, the island had seen more than ten thousand underworld killings and assassinations, almost all of them as a consequence of the power struggle between Riina and Badalamenti—and the efforts of Falcone and his officers to bring it to a halt.

Although the majority of the victims were themselves soldiers in the *sistema,* the war also took aim at virtually every major law enforcement, judicial and political figure on the island. By 1980, the casualties included the subcommander of public security in Palermo, the provincial secretary of the ruling Christian Democratic Party, the commander-in-chief of the police tactical unit, the vice commandant of Sicily's largest prison, the chief investigative magistrate of the island's criminal courts, and the president of its regional government. General Carlo Alberto Dalla Chiesa, the no-nonsense military officer who had crushed the terrorist Red Brigade in northern Italy, was dispatched to Sicily on May 1, 1982. Four months and two days later, he was fatally machine-gunned, along with his wife and bodyguard.

A decade later, eighty-seven leading public officials had been killed. They counted the latest appointees as chief law enforcement officer, chief prosecutor, and chief magistrate for the island—positions that had become nearly indistinguishable from death sentences—the regional secretary general of the Italian Communist Party, two deputies of the Italian legislature, two mayors of Palermo, and five more criminal court magistrates.

When I took up residence in Terrasini, shootings or bombings were a daily event in Palermo. Seven thousand heavily armed soldiers were bivouacked in its streets, dug in outside the apartment buildings of government officials and ready to start shooting at the slightest provocation.

A friend of mine, a Palermo attorney who himself lived in constant expectation of a bomb or a gun shot, called it *la mattanza.* The word refers to a traditional Sicilian fishing method, in which tuna are driven into a ring of nets by boatmen beating oars on the surface of the water, then bludgeoned to death with clubs.

Nobody was more adept at the *mattanza*, more enthusiastic about it, than Judge Falcone's alleged assassin, Giovanni Brusca. While on the run, he had personally liquidated the twelve-year-old son of a Riina enemy, strangling the boy with his bare hands and throwing the body into a vat of acid. Two other Riina opponents lost seventy-two relatives between them.

"*Lu sangu lava lu sangu*," Mike said of the killings. "Blood washes blood." It was an ancient dialect phrase for the vendetta, the torrent of unforgiving vengeance that flows from an unforgivable offense.

THREE

Mike

WESTERN SICILY was the Badalamentis and Toto Riina. It was a place where calculated violence was so habitual, so commonplace, that murder had its own extensive vocabulary, with precise definitions employed for varieties and methods. Sicily was children thrown into vats of acid, honest judges blown to bits, and the unsolved murder of the man who gave me my name. It was the *mattanza.*

But it was also a sun-washed mask over the darkness, the intoxicating scent of lemon blossoms in spring, wafted by the gentlest of breezes over an azure sea. Sicily was Mike Cortese and his family.

Mike was one of those men who are busy all of the time, and yet always hunting for something to do, nervous with anticipation and hope. He had thrown himself into my work from our first meeting at the *passeggiata,* bitterly disappointed, even angry, when a line of investigation didn't pan out. The search that brought me to Terrasini appealed to Mike on a deep, personal level; he had made both journeys, my grandfather's and mine, to America and then back. "You're telling my story, too," he often said.

I humored Mike's volatile moods, for the selfish reason that he had quickly become indispensable. He seemed to know every family in the village. He was also an adroit interpreter of the annex ledgers, staring down at them over my shoulder for hours and offering translations.

"Mike showed up before Maria Santissima rang eight," my

notes for May 5 read. Usually, I waited for those eight strokes of the campanile bells, then rolled out of bed onto the cold granite floor of the guest house and hopped to the bathroom praying for warm water. It is one of the peculiarities of Sicily that rooms are often bone chilling there, despite the balmiest daytime climate in Europe. The problem comes with the night, when temperatures from October to mid-May can drop into the high forties if a north wind blows. Central heating is virtually unknown, and the widespread use of marble and granite leaves most apartments and homes with the stony morning frost of a mausoleum.

By 11:00 A.M., everyone assured me, the sun would turn the wind around and it would be back in the seventies. "Heating is for Detroit and New York," Mike said, when I brought up the subject. "In Sicily, we don't need it." But on May 5, he was wearing a thick wool coat that came down to his knees, and kept it on while he watched me climb into my frigid clothes.

Out in the piazza, the *caffe* regulars were decked out in an assortment of parkas and trench coats, already seated at tables under the ficus trees, rubbing their hands to keep the circulation going and waiting for whatever the day would bring.

"Let's see if anybody has remembered a story about your ancestor or that Valenti guy yet," Mike said, heading for Di Maggio's. He had canvassed the village like a Brooklyn ward-heeler, explaining who I was and what I was trying to do. We decided, early on, that it was best to put all of my cards on the table. To announce that I was a writer, out to learn why my grandfather's grandfather had been killed, and who had killed him.

"No way we find out anything if you beat around the bush," Mike said.

But direct questions made the villagers nervous, I could see that. The entire Castellammare coast was in a state of extreme tension over the Brusca manhunt and the Falcone murder investigation. "Everybody's scared their own name gonna come up in a courtroom one of these days," Mike pointed out.

It was only a modest exaggeration. Very few residents of

Terrasini, including me, were without some tie to an alleged criminal. That was another of the *sistema*'s assets, the tentacles that reached into every household. The very mention of an unsolved murder, even if it had occurred a century ago, put people on their guard. On the rare occasions when they had something to tell me— a sketchy anecdote they'd heard, or a suggestion that I look up a certain Signore So-and-so, a mile down the Palermo road in Cinisi—it seldom led anywhere. Signore So-and-so would have died just a few years ago, and the anecdote would either be dismissed as sheer fantasy or embroidered beyond all credibility by the next person I spoke to.

This morning, like most, nobody remembered anything. I thanked Mike for his help, and headed off to spend a few hours on my own in the annex.

MIKE HAD BEEN a construction worker in Brooklyn from 1964 to 1972, a tile salesman for three years in Switzerland during the mid-seventies, and the manager of a catering service in Detroit for six years afterward.

The rough outlines of his biography gradually materialized as we made the *caffe* rounds and got to know each other.

By 1980, half a decade into their Michigan sojourn, he and his wife, Rosalia, had a ten-year-old son, Roberto, and a four-year-old daughter, Alice. From kindergarten on, Mike told me, Roberto had always insisted on being called "Bobby." With the birth of his sister in 1976, the Americanization of the Cortese family had seemed complete. She was baptized in Detroit as "Alice," and tersely corrected anyone who referred to her as Alicia. "That's not me you're talking about," she'd say in English, which she spoke fluently by the age of five and never ceased using.

But their mother was unhappy in America. She never learned more than a sprinkling of necessary words in English, never lost her distress at living so far from her parents and village. When Detroit's economy went into a nosedive in the late 1970s, Rosalia reminded Mike that he was always telling customers Sicily was the most beautiful island on earth. That "heat was for Detroit and New York, we don't even need it over there."

In Terrasini, the Corteses had inherited a home just a few blocks from the Piazza Duomo; the house in America was heavily mortgaged and would take another twenty years to pay off. But their equity in it was enough to launch a business of some sort in Sicily, she reasoned.

Rosalia won the day. In 1981, the family emigrated back to the village. Seven years later, she and Mike had a second son, Flavio. The household was rounded out by Maria Cortese, Mike's widowed mother, who had returned to Terrasini in 1983 from seventeen years of her own in the United States. She was always referred to as Nanna, dialect for Grandma.

THE RESULTS of these peregrinations were a melting pot within the confines of a single home, an *insalata mista* of languages, accents, and habits.

Bobby and Alice were native-born U.S. citizens and spoke perfect midwestern American—"No sweat," "Hang in there," "You gotta be kidding"—as well as the Sicilian dialect that prevailed in Terrasini. Mike himself was a naturalized American, in his early fifties when I met him, who had an accent all his own that crossed Brooklynese with Italian. Rosalia and Flavio were strictly Italian in citizenship, and almost exclusively Sicilian in conversation. Nanna's mastery of English, despite her nearly two decades in New York, was limited to "Thank you," "You are very welcome," and "Please, eat something." She spent twelve hours a day in the kitchen, emerging only to deliver enormous platters of food to the table, accompanied by bizarre monologues on the shenanigans of public celebrities, which she religiously followed in the pages of Italian tabloids.

Like families everywhere, the Corteses were also a bundle of contradictory personalities. Mike was ambitious and energetic to a fault, a compact, muscular man with the shape and drive of a small bulldozer and the sharp self-honed intelligence that made him so indispensable to me as an interpreter and guide. Bobby Cortese was

unmistakably Mike's son in his blocky muscular build and hunger
to succeed, but without the ferocious intensity that made people
uneasy around his father. Bobby was engaged to Sara Pippitone, a
delicate, soft-spoken blonde from the village of Montelepre, ten
miles south in the Castellammare hills, and so enamored that he
would stop speaking in mid-sentence when she entered a room and
drift to her side as though borne on a cloud.

Flavio, the seven-year-old December child, was the heir to
Mike's manic energy. He whirled around the house, karate-kicking
the couch and easy chairs, hurling himself from room to room. At
nineteen, his sister Alice was a perfect specimen of the tough but
tender American beauty. She took no guff and spoke her mind
without compunction.

Rosalia was maternally plump, patient, and serene, so long as
Mike was somewhere nearby. She agonized when he was on a buying trip, driving a succession of doomed used cars at breakneck
speed from the western end of the island to the east, in a compul-
sive search for bargains. They all found their way to the *Salumeria*
Cortese, the family grocery store and delicatessen: cases of linguine
from an unclaimed shipment in Marsala; a truckload of grapes that
had not found a market in Catania; slightly damaged lots of canned
tomatoes, pickled eggplants, or dried chickpeas.

The possibilities for cutting a few hundred lire off the usual
price of groceries were limitless, Mike was convinced, if only you
were stubborn enough to hunt them down.

I TOOK TO JOINING HIM when I grew tired of the records
annex, grinding out a hundred miles or more before 7:00 A.M. in his
latest workhorse, a fifteen-year-old Lancia. We would jam boxes of
pasta and crates of vegetables into every available square inch of
the car, until the springs and shock absorbers were flat and the
fenders scraped the tires on sharp turns.

If Mike heard that a nursery or terra-cotta factory was shutting
down somewhere on the mainland, we'd drive the Lancia onto the
ferry and go take a look. There was no law, Mike declared, that said

the *salumeria* had to remain a *salumeria* forever. After some of his impromptu trips, the store's parking lot took on the appearance of an open-air shopping mall, with mountains of discounted ceramics rising above forests of sale-priced fig trees and palms.

This was Mike's restless American side, in Terrasini's view. Before immigration fever struck in the 1890s, Sicilians seldom ventured more than a half day's walk from their birthplaces. The exceptions, of course, were nineteenth-century bandits like the Monk, who were obliged to keep on the move, or their *sistema* counterparts today, whose business interests were as far-flung as those of Microsoft and Exxon.

For most Sicilians, the road was to be avoided; the autostrada was so underused that its tollbooths had been shut down. Even the Castellammare fishermen hugged the familiar coast, trawling for sardines or tuna within sight of their villages. At heart, the novelist Leonardo Sciascia contended, Sicilians despise the sea, "which is only good for carrying away immigrants and bringing ashore invaders."

"Michele, he is crazy," one of Terrasini's *marinari* flatly told me, when I mentioned that Mike and I had been to the port of Trapani and back that morning, a three-hour round-trip on the empty freeway. At fifty-five, the fisherman had never in his life been to Trapani.

Mike was also the leading offender in a family of incorrigible pack rats. He had the habit of bringing abandoned institution-sized refrigerators and freezers home for repair, wheeling them into a large storeroom behind the kitchen, then promptly forgetting about them. Nanna and Rosalia filled the refrigerators' shelves with their own soon forgotten supply of old sweaters, pantsuits, dresses, and scarves.

The Corteses argued incessantly, controversies large and small raging around the table as Nanna piled on dishes of *pasta con le sarde* and *bistecca alla Palermitana,* with Alice dividing her time between the battle and the kitchen, and Rosalia trying to calm everyone down. Yet argue as they might, they were welded together, not only by the ties of blood, but by immigration and reimmigration and the demands of a family business that always tottered on the edge of disaster. They were bound to each other, inextricable even in their differences, and at times, a painful reminder of the gaps in my life. My solitary journeys. My parents' own terrible battles when I was a boy, the bitter screaming matches that left them exhausted and sent me and my brother off to "stay with Grandpa and Grandma for awhile."

I ate with the Corteses two or three times a week. It was almost impossible to turn down Mike's invitations, which were more in the nature of orders: "Lunch is at one o'clock, Frank. See you at the house."

FOUR

An Old Man's Riddle

➤➤◄◄

MAY EASED INTO A PREMATURE SUMMER torpor. I followed a numbing routine of sluggish afternoons in the municipal annex, expeditions to the libraries of other Castellammare villages, and aimless walks around Terrasini.

My schedule was punctuated by Nanna's gargantuan meals, with the television droning its way through a soccer game or a dubbed American sitcom as Mike plotted his next unlikely commercial venture and Flavio karate-chopped me from behind, trying to goad me into a wrestling match.

My efforts to find someone who remembered any details about the Monk's killing were at a standstill. He could have died anytime between 1864 and the first decade of the twentieth century. The 1894 marriage license of my great-grandfather, Giuseppe Viviano, identified him as "the son of Francesco Paolo Viviano"—the son of the Monk—but without specifying if the Monk himself was still alive. No one in the village seemed to know.

The *Chronicle's* foreign news editor had already given me a generous leave. With a major offensive underway in Bosnia, it couldn't be extended. A little over a week remained before I would have to head back onto the road for the newspaper, and the registrar, Marianna Trappeto, was no longer encouraging about the missing civil ledgers. She had spoken several times to the *sindaco*, the village mayor, to ask whether I might be given special access to a locked room into which several truckloads of old files, books, and

manuscripts had been carted two years earlier. The idea made the
mayor uncomfortable, Marianna said. He wanted to think about it.
In Sicily, where an outright "no" is regarded as crudely direct, "time
to think" is tantamount to polite refusal.

Marianna was baffled by the mayor's response. She was sure
that the room held the municipal records for the period when the
first Francesco Viviano had been born and wed, died and buried. In
Mike's opinion, the problem was sheer bureaucratic embarrassment. "The *sindaco* don't want you to see the mess they've made of
things," he said.

The stored documents were to have been installed in a new
municipal library, an abandoned palazzo below the Piazza Duomo.
It remained nothing more than an architect's drawing two years
after the old library had been closed and funds appropriated for the
move. To make matters worse, a critical step had been overlooked
in the relocation. No one had bothered to note the contents of the
storeroom's hundreds of containers, Marianna explained; it was
stacked to the ceiling with unmarked crates.

Marianna slowly shook her head when she decribed the situation. She was a hard worker, still unwilling, after eight years back in
Sicily, to rid herself entirely of the notion that a job was comprised
of tasks to be completed rather than an infinite succession of cigarettes and coffee breaks between paydays.

There were several hundred former immigrants in Terrasini,
enough to justify a dialect term for them, *'Meddicani*—
"Americans"—even when they were returnees from Germany or
Switzerland. They were a frustrated bunch.

"We learned the wrong things over there," Mike liked to say.
The things he had in mind were the acquired foreign habits that
fueled efficiency but eroded the patience necessary to tolerate the
roadblocks, literal and figurative, that cluttered Sicilian life.

"You just knock your head against the wall when you try to get
something accomplished," another of the eximmigrants said. "In the
United States, there's almost no limit to what a man can do. Here
there are only limits. I miss America every day."

He was a fisherman in his late forties, a one-time resident of Gloucester, Massachusetts, who spent hours staring somberly out into the Gulf of Castellammare from a stone balustrade above the harbor. Many local fishermen had passed a decade or so in New England, working the Grand Banks for cod in Sicilian-owned trawler fleets.

Quite a few of those who came back had encountered "difficulties," the code word for a spell in prison. Terrasini natives in the United States often were asked to perform minor jobs for Castellammare dons with American business interests—to sign their names to a suspicious contract, or allow their homes to be used for periodic meetings whose agendas were not disclosed to the homeowner. It sometimes landed them in jail, with the certainty of deportation as soon as they had served their terms.

The fisherman at the balustrade never told me his name. I assumed that he had encountered difficulties in Massachusetts.

THE 'MEDDICANI may have missed the efficient, modern lives they had led in Brooklyn, Detroit, or Gloucester, but their self-absorption was strictly Sicilian. Melancholy is the island's natural mood. Its people share little of the exuberance associated with other southern Italians; they are given to long, gloomy silences rather than spontaneous outbursts of song.

"The men here don't chase foreign women like the Neapolitans do. In fact they don't even talk to you," according to one of my friends, a shapely Parisian who'd vacationed on the island. "They just stare, with that deadly morose look in their eye."

Morose. Melancholy. It was pretty much how I myself felt after the mayor's stonewalling and my plodding trudge through the incomplete municipal ledgers.

Random trips into Palermo were as inconclusive as my afternoons in the Terrasini annex. The state archive had raised my hopes enormously at the end of April, only to dash them in a lengthy wild goose chase.

The goose was a certain Francesco Paolo Viviano, then aged

eighty-six, who had been reported dead in Palermo on August 22, 1907. His birthplace, the authorities believed, was Terrasini. A brief advisory note, which offered neither the cause of death nor its circumstances, had eventually been posted to the village records office and glued to a page in the mortality ledger for 1907. I had chanced upon it in the annex.

Any possibility of turning up a court or police file that detailed the assassination of the Monk depended entirely on knowing the year of his death. There was no name index to the criminal cases presented before the Tribunale di Palermo, Sicily's presiding criminal court before World War I. Their dossiers were arranged chronologically, in bulging folders stored at the Gancia, a monastic complex near the old eastern gate to the capital. "You could spend the rest of your life in the Gancia without finding what you are looking for, Signore," the archive's curator had told me. "Unless you have that date, unless you know when your ancestor died . . ."

A transcription of the 1907 advisory note in hand, I had rushed straight to the Gancia to look for the complete file on the last day in April, taking the bus in rather than try to thread the Peugeot through the narrow medieval lanes and jammed piazzas of central Palermo.

The curator ushered me into a former monastic dining hall equipped with six long wooden tables and a series of immense baroque cabinets. They held binders of official proclamations, vital statistics, and decrees dating back to 1503. On the wall of the adjacent cloister a vivid sixteenth-century fresco depicted a "tree" of celebrated Franciscan monks, growing from a root planted by San Francesco d'Assisi himself. I took his raised arm as an omen, about to bless the meeting of two other Francescos.

There was reason for optimism. In the 1907 *tribunale* death certificate—the curator located it in one of the cabinets in less than five minutes—Francesco Paolo Viviano was described as "the husband of Grazia Cusmano." The Cusmano name was one of the most common in Terrasini; two nineteenth-century pastors of Maria Santissima delle Grazie had been Cusmanos. The family's ancestral home stood near the present site of Mike's *salumeria*.

I knew that Maria Bommarito, my great-great-grandmother, had died in 1903. Elderly men rarely remained widowers in Sicily. There was always a spinster neighbor or cousin around, anxious to make a belated start on a household of her own.

The *tribunale* Francesco's end had come in Palermo, where he seemed to have been under supervision by the criminal authorities. That fit the mold of a bandit's life. There had probably been a term at the city prison, I concluded, and then a final few years with his second wife in the Borgu, an adjacent district notorious for its population of ex-convicts.

The stated cause of death in the *tribunale* document, "cerebral trauma," might have been provoked by an old man's accidental fall in a back alley. But it could also have been the result of a blow to the head by henchmen of the shadowy Domenico Valenti, for whatever reason he might have wanted to kill my namesake. Sicilian coroners were often, and understandably, circumspect on death certificates.

The recorded age of the deceased placed his birth in 1821, which was credible for a man who had fathered sons in 1857 and 1864, even if it made him a rather elderly candidate for assassination in 1907.

So I set out, in great confidence, to prove that the dead man in the state archive was the Monk. His faint trail led me steadily through the annex and *tribunale* files, until the demoralizing discovery of a wedding notice two weeks later. This Francesco Paolo Viviano had married Grazia Cusmano in Palermo in 1893, ten years before Maria Bommarito breathed her last.

The dead man in the *tribunale* records may have been a thief. But unless he was a bigamist, he was not the thief who gave me my name.

A SHOWER BROKE THROUGH the morning clouds as I made my way across the Piazza Duomo on June 4, setting out on one more trip to the state archive before my departure from Sicily. A frail, elderly man, who was wrapped up in a faded yellow coat and

looked to be in his late seventies, stood outside the tobacco shop
where the Palermo bus stopped.

On the ride into the city, we sat next to each other and chatted,
making small talk for an hour. He was visibly eccentric, a catalog of
nervous twitches and unsettling stares, and wandered into long solil-
oquies that had nothing to do with the rest of our conversation.

Just as we pulled into the Viale della Liberta in central
Palermo, and I rose to leave, he said, "You're the one who wants to
learn about the Monk, aren't you?"

His face was impassive. It was the first time anyone in the village had alluded to my ancestor as "the Monk." I sat back down,
and rode the bus another three blocks. "Who are you?" I asked. We
hadn't exchanged names.

"You won't find anything in the state archive," he said. "Sicily is
the book you must study."

I sidestepped the riddle—there were already more than enough
of them keeping me awake at night—and asked him who he was
once again.

"Viviano," he answered. "Giuseppe Viviano."

Not only did this strange old man know who the Monk was; he
had the same name as the Monk's son, my great-grandfather.

"I've got to talk with you," I blurted. "When can we meet?"

I told him that I had only a few days left in Sicily. "If you return
one day," Giuseppe Viviano said, "inform the barman at Di
Maggio's *Caffe,* and I will call you."

Then he stood up abruptly and got off the bus, the door slam-
ming shut behind him.

THE NEXT EVENING, I was booked on the return car ferry to
Genoa. The ship sailed at 8:00 P.M., which gave me an afternoon to
double-check some of the dates in the family tree, what there was of
it, in the annex ledgers.

In the absence of volumes directly relating to the Monk, most
of the entries that interested me were on the fringes of the family,
where I might find a reference to a Francesco Paolo Viviano who

had attended a marriage or baptism. I had also hunted blindly in the ledgers, so far without success, for some mention of Domenico Valenti. Although my grandfather's own birth certificate was on the annex shelves, there didn't seem much reason to consult it. I knew when he was born and who his parents were.

But he was on my mind that day, in part because of the chance encounter with the old man on the bus.

So I picked up the ledger for 1897 and turned to the page for the ninth of November. The entry was faded but legible. It recorded the birth of a male infant to Grazia Tocco, age twenty-two, and Giuseppe Viviano, age thirty-three. The infant's legal name, certified by the village registrar, was "Viviano, Paolo."

There was no mention of "Francesco."

Like everyone else in the family, I had always assumed that "Paolinu" was merely a childhood nickname, dropped and forgotten in an America where my grandfather was universally known as Frank. That's what the sign over our family business read: "Frank P. Viviano and Sons." That's what appeared on the American citizenship papers he acquired in 1955. On his driver's licenses and home mortgages. On the headstone of his grave in Detroit. Frank P. Viviano, 1897–1993.

Frank: It was what my grandmother called him. It was the name I had been given because it was his. Because I was his grandson, as he was the Monk's.

The name's absence on my grandfather's birth notice was a profound mystery in its own right, as though the central link—the "second Francesco"—had suddenly vanished from the pappanomic chain that bound me to the Monk .

But I was certain, instinctively, that it was also a clue to the larger mystery. To a sequence of interrelated mysteries, turning not only on a murder, but on the power and symbolism of names themselves.

I knew one thing for sure now. As soon as I could manage it, I would return to Sicily.

Ano in the Desert

→ ➤ ◄ ✦

East Harlem, New York
March 1910

I BEGAN PIECING TOGETHER the story of my grandfather's
name, the missing "Francesco" on the birth certificate, during a
month-long trip to America after a harrowing summer in Bosnia.
The stateside visit was meant to calm me down, but I couldn't
relax. My grandfather's words hung over me, in the same murky
shadows as a murdered highwayman and his accused killer.

My bags were loaded with hundreds of pages of photocopied
nineteenth-century memoirs and notes from my haphazard
research in the libraries and municipal records of Sicily. When I
wasn't interviewing relatives and family friends in New York or the
midwest, trying to assemble the American fragments of the tale, I
was translating the written minutiae in Italian and Sicilian dialect
that now weighed down my travels.

My sketch of the young Paolinu, drawn on a makeshift canvas
of notes, diaries, interviews, and remembered conversations, gradually assumed tones and colors. The confusion surrounding my
grandfather's name—his two names—acquired the force of a deliberate act.

By the most powerful of Sicilian traditions, the twelve-year-old
boy who fought off seasickness for two weeks on the steamship
Italia in the winter of 1910 ought to have been named Francesco

Paolo Viviano; and in the eyes of his own family in America, he always was. But in the archives of the Italian state, my grandfather was simply Paolo. And Paolinu he remained to his boyhood friends and fellow immigrants from Terrasini, until the day one year after the storm-tossed voyage to New York, when he threw his passport into the East River and became Frank P. Viviano by his own will.

This was the baptism of the second Francesco, I came to understand: a passport's splash in the channel between Brooklyn and Manhattan.

MY GRANDFATHER had always been proud of the fact that he managed to keep his stomach down through the stormy eleven-day Atlantic crossing, while other village boys lay prone on the fetid third-class deck between bouts of vomiting. Maybe that was because he was half-Tocco himself on his mother's side; most of the Toccos had made their livings from the sea in the old country and still did in America.

Joe Tocco, my grandfather's older cousin, had emigrated several years earlier to New York, where he had opened a fish store with his brother on First Avenue and East 114th Street. It was thanks to the Tocco cousins that Paolinu found himself on the sidewalks of Harlem in March 1910, peddling mackerel and calamari from the straw basket in which he had carried his few belongings on the steamship. The peddling was done as it had been done in the Castellammare villages, as though the air carried the scent of lemon blossoms instead of snow flurries, with the basket strapped onto his back as he cried out his fish and their prices.

The route led up and down the Harlem streets from East 114th to East 118th, starting at the East River shore. It crossed back and forth under the Third Avenue el, past wooden shantytowns that crowded the Fifth Avenue hillside at East 116th Street, and westward through the Jewish end of Harlem to the Hudson. The Tocco brothers paid him one dollar a week.

The Sicilian quarter, "Hell's Gate" in the popular idiom, was a dense cluster of five-story brick tenements that replaced the area's pre—Civil War brownstones after 1880, when real estate speculators sold off huge parcels of Harlem farmland to builders just as the great European immigration wave was breaking over New York. In 1850, East Harlem had fifteen hundred residents; by 1920, the Sicilian population alone exceeded one hundred and fifty thousand, the largest of Sicily's immigrant colonies in the United States.

The neighbors also counted thousands of Bavarians and Irish Catholics who moved north to the Harlem tenements from slums in lower Manhattan. To the Sicilian way of thinking, the Irish and Germans were a pampered class, despite their own immigrant origins and empty pockets. Leonard Covello, who became the first Sicilian-born principal of Harlem's Benjamin Franklin High school in the 1940s, arrived in New York as a child around the same time as my grandfather. Before 1920, Covello told me, Sicilian parishioners were not permitted to attend Mass at the main altar of Our Lady of Mount Carmel, Harlem's largest Catholic church. "We were sent down to pray in the basement," he said.

"The Italian comes in at the bottom," the photographer Jacob Riis wrote in *How the Other Half Lives* (1890), his pioneering study of New York immigrant life. "And in the generation that came over the sea, he stays there."

Poverty was one hallmark of the Sicilian image in America at the turn of the century. The *sistema,* inevitably, was another.

An article in the December 1896 issue of *Popular Scientific Monthly* vividly framed the contemporary view of New York Sicilians. After the animals at a touring circus were fed, the author related, the leftovers were thrown away "and the dagoes collected these bones and boiled them for their soup! What terrors have jails and prisons for such human beings? What have they to lose by pilfering, assaulting, robbing, and murdering?"

The article was entitled "What Shall We Do With The Dago?" It echoed widespread fears of racial contamination, from an irrevocably depraved underclass, that led to a 1924 federal law restricting Italian immigration to fity-eight hundred people per year. In the single year of 1913, the flow had exceeded three hundred thousand.

My grandfather's East Harlem bed was in a second-floor tenement apartment on First Avenue, a few yards away from the fish store. It was a railroad flat, four claustrophobic rooms opening directly into each other without a connecting hall. Only the front and rear rooms had windows, except for a small transom in the kitchen that vented cooking fumes into an eighteen-inch-wide airshaft. There was a single toilet in the outside corridor, serving five apartments.

In February 1910, the First Avenue flat was already home to nine people. After the Vivianos arrived—Paolinu, his father, Giuseppe, his mother, Grazia, and his two sisters, fifteen-year-old Maria and nine-year-old Angie—it sheltered fourteen men, women, and children.

"The Italian," Jacob Riis wrote, "is content to live in a pigsty."

AS A BOY, I composed my own imagined, cataclysmic account of our family's departure from the old world, my own fable of origins.

There had been a great timeless calm in my imagined Sicily, an enraptured stillness, and then an explosion: Ano flung into the desert. Into the pigsty. Ano expelled from the garden.

A vast explosion had hurled us into frantic motion, into a journey without end—to New York, to Detroit, to a dozen other cities in the United States where I counted cousins by the 1950s, and where "home" seldom meant the same house for more than a few years.

That was my reckoning with the neurotic pace of American life, I suppose. But it's also probable, given the nuclear brinkmanship of those years, that the picture borrowed heavily from the anxieties of the Cold War; cataclysm was the prevailing nightmare image of my childhood. Which is not to say that my fable was entirely off the historical mark.

Between 1876 and 1924, seventeen million Italians emigrated abroad; Italy's entire population in 1900 was less than forty million. The vast majority of the emigrants, like my grandparents, were from the south. In the decade before 1910, the year that my

grandfather sailed from Palermo, two million Sicilians—over half
of the island's population—abandoned their ancestral villages for
the uncertainties of an immigrant's life.

The certainties, in Sicily, had become unbearable.

A series of earthquakes, between 1904 and 1908, killed thousands and made the cities of northern Sicily uninhabitable for hundreds of thousands more. One tremor launched a tidal wave that
erased three hundred villages and drowned fifty thousand people in
the province of Messina. As though in some malevolent natural
chain reaction, the earthquakes were followed by a severe agricultural crisis. Olive trees, which had been cultivated intensely in
Sicily since the fifth century before Christ, were infested with a par-
asitic insect that destroyed entire crops. Another parasite laid waste
to the vineyards, cutting wine production in half. Exports of citrus
fruits, the backbone of what passed for a Sicilian economy, plum-
meted more than 50 percent in the 1890s when Americans began
marketing oranges and lemons from modern farms in Florida and
California and shipping them directly to Europe in refrigerated
cargo vessels.

By contrast, half of all Sicilian villages were not even accessible
by dirt road in the late nineteenth century. According to an Italian
government study in 1910, the year my grandfather sailed for New
York, many Sicilians had never even seen a wheeled cart.

Eighty-five percent of Sicilians were landless agricultural labor-
ers in 1900, walking up to ten miles per day to work others' fields.
Just under 90 percent of the island had passed into the hands of
absentee landowners. The population density of the island was 438
people to the square mile, ten times that of the United States and
greater than the population density of China or India.

Hence, the explosion, massive and unprecedented emigration,
the cresting of one of the greatest human floods in history: nine million Italians to the Americas; seven and a half million to northern
Europe; another five hundred thousand to Asia and Africa.

In 1903, Prime Minister Giuseppe Zanardelli paid the first
visit to Sicily by an Italian head of government, more than forty

years after the island came under the jurisdiction of Rome. "I greet you on behalf of the eight thousand people in this *commune*, three thousand of whom are in America and the other five thousand preparing to follow them," Zanardelli was informed by the mayor of the town of Moliterno.

The garden, the edenic Sicily of my childhood imagination, the timeless pastoral calm, was sheer fantasy on my part. As a boy, I had no idea what Sicily looked like. Only that it was not America. In my dreams, it was the Earth before the fall, an enraptured stillness before the explosion.

AFTER THE EXPLOSION came the shock waves. The voyage to New York. The tenements. The pigsty. The chaotic streets. The new diseases. The restlessness. The American itch: Go west.

In the Sicilian version, circa 1910, the wayfarers were children, the surplus commodities of families that were too large and too poor to remain whole in New York. The youngest were passed off by their own desperate parents as orphans and shipped to midwestern and California adoption agents. Many more, too old for the bogus adoption trade, were shuttled into a form of indentured servitude barely distinguishable from slavery.

Paolinu Viviano's parents couldn't feed him, and they couldn't simply marry him off as they did with his elder sister. The crisis deepened when autumn came and the fish market was no longer able to pay Paolinu his dollar a week. The number of peddlers on the Harlem streets was rising even faster than the number of immigrants. In any case, as my grandfather put it, fresh immigrants don't buy fresh fish.

As the immigrant waves rose and peaked, Harlem was swamped with contagious diseases, run rampant with malnutrition and crowding. There was every reason to believe, in the awful winter of 1911, that Giuseppe Viviano and Grazia Tocco had no choice but to put their only son on a westbound train.

"They want to keep me alive, and they can't think of no other way."

My grandfather told me this seventy years later, but the memory was an open wound. "When it's time to leave, my mother stay home. She won't go to train station. My cousin, he says Mamma cried for a month after I'm gone. People in those days, Franky, they go away and a lot of times they never come back."

The explosion sent Paolinu Viviano to St. Louis, Missouri, on that January morning, to his uncle Gaetano, who paid the train fare. To *Gaetano lu Faccune*, Gaetano the Falcon. The eldest son of the Monk.

IT IS IMPOSSIBLE to separate myth from reality in the life of Gaetano the Falcon. He was a notorious bandit in his day, the Monk's natural heir and the hero or villain of dozens of my grandparents' stories. More than half a century after his death, people in Terrasini spoke of him with nervous admiration. "The old folks say he was a very tough guy, very strong, and he always let you know it," Mike Cortese told me. The villagers still referred to him as "the Falcon."

But I couldn't find out much more than that about him in Sicily—that he was "tough," which was also Grandpa's description of him, and that he had done unspecified things to merit the reputation. There was a vague recollection in Terrasini that he'd pastured racehorses in the countryside west of the village. He'd left for the United States in a hurry around 1900.

This much was clear: My grandfather hated and revered his uncle. In Terrasini and America alike, the Falcon always provoked ambivalent reactions. He was a moral cipher in the grim Sicilian tradition, with competing measures of primeval justice and stark cruelty.

In his coded heroic persona, Gaetano Viviano made regular appearances in Angelina's fables, where he was recast as a brigand-rebel and chivalrous lover. His dark alter ego took shape in bleak, unsparingly violent exploits that were sometimes recounted by my grandfather. I have him on tape, in 1977:

> My uncle, he know every town in *Sicilia*. Nobody can make him stay in one place, and nobody can get in his way. One time, they say he held up a bank. It's true, he was a very tough guy, Franky. But he didn't rob this bank. Somebody lie about it, to set him up. The police from Partinico, they finally catch him. And one of the *sbirru* [a "cop," in Castellammare dialect] put chains on his feet and hands to take him to jail. He beat him like a dog and dragged him on the road behind his horse. Finally, after a long time, my uncle says, "I'm tired, Signore. Please, I can't walk no more." So the policeman stop whipping him and get down from the horse.
>
> Then, as soon as he sees his chance, my uncle says, "Nobody treats a Viviano like this," and he pick up the chains on his hands and hit the *sbirru* in the head with them until he doesn't move anymore.

The pride of name again, turned menacing. And in a distorted glass, where honor edges into sadism. The Falcon was a man who took pleasure in breaking other men.

In 1911, he set out to break his nephew, Paolinu Viviano.

THE 1903 WORLD'S FAIR and the 1904 Olympics had been staged in St. Louis just a few years before Paolinu's train pulled into Union Station. Flourishing with trade at the main junction of the Mississippi River and the transcontinental rail line, in the geographical heart of the country, the city was proclaiming itself the metropolis of the American future, the "Gateway to the West." It was agog at its own prospects in 1911, enthralled by the magnificent buildings that had been constructed for the fair and the Olympic games.

My grandfather had no recollection of that. He had scarcely

any memory of St. Louis, because he saw almost nothing of it but the raw clapboard building in Little Italy, the immigrant settlement a few blocks from Union Station, that hid his uncle's gambling operation. "Big Tom's," it was called, after the Falcon's Americanized nickname. And big he was, in a photograph that hung on my grandparents' wall, a strapping giant with a thick handlebar mustache and the same square jaw, bushy jet black eyebrows and broad back that had already given my grandfather the bearing of a man at the age of thirteen.

My father noticed that at the Falcon's funeral in 1937. Even in the casket, the old bandit looked powerful, and my grandfather, staring down at him, was his mirror image. By then, Grandpa had made a temporary peace with his uncle. That it was temporary only became evident decades later, in my grandfather's own final year, when his mind drifted over the past until it ground to an obsessive impasse at the months in St. Louis.

"I have no choice, Franky. I have to do something. I have to do something," he told me, telling and retelling the story—but only part of it, that need to act, without any details about the act itself.

"He beat him like a dog," Grandpa had said, recounting the Falcon's humiliation at the hands of the Partinico cop. They were also the words that the Harlem fishmonger Joe Tocco used, when he spoke with Paolinu's mother after a trip to St. Louis in the spring of 1911. "Gaetano Viviano beats your son like a dog."

They were the words of my grandfather in 1992, when the memory of his second year in America seized hold of him and wouldn't let go. "He beat me like a dog."

Paolinu was locked into a back room of the clapboard building at night. He was dragged out before the sun came up to groom Big Tom's horses. After that, there were crates of fruits and vegetables to carry into the grocery store that fronted the gambling operation. Big Tom's daughter, Maria, ran the cash register. She was nineteen and separated from her husband. Maria treated the boy well in the beginning, sneaking him extra food, even helping him get away one morning and out into the streets. He was promptly taken into custody by a truant officer and escorted to a local school under the officer's supervision for three days, the only formal education he ever received.

Maria was playing a double game, and Paolinu came to see through her small kindnesses. "My cousin, she put five cents in the cash box, and a dollar in her pocket all the time. She let Uncle Tanu think it's me, and he beat the hell out of me every day."

But the Falcon was a better teacher than he realized. *Nobody treats a Viviano like this.* One night, he went too far. Gaetano Viviano crossed the line with his nephew that the *sbirru* had crossed with him. At 3:00 A.M., he unlocked the door to the back room and staggered half drunk to the bedside "Get up, nephew, you lazy son-of-a-bitch. Clean my horses."

Joe Tocco, on another trip to St. Louis, was in the next room.

There were the sounds of a struggle, a blow, a heavy weight toppling to the floor. Had Paolinu hidden a weapon of some sort under his bed that night? A stable hook? A bridle bit? My grandfather never told anyone, not Joe Tocco and not me.

"I have to do something." That was all he said in November 1992, all he had said to Joe.

"The noise stopped, and then your grandpa come next door," Joe's son Alfonso told me many decades later, in a Harlem coffee shop. "He said to my dad, 'Okay, let's go,' and nothing else."

Joe bought two rail tickets to New York. On the train, my grandfather spoke again for the first time: "Cousin, don't call me Paolinu anymore." When they arrived in New York, he threw his Italian passport into the East River.

"He never explained anything," Alfonso said. "But after that day, he was always 'Frank,' like you."

Exile, salvation, and rebirth, the old family legend—the act of redemption that takes on a name. As old Alfonso spoke, I could hear my grandmother Angelina's cry: "Ahhhhhhhnooooo." And then the angel's: *"Vivi, Ano!"*

In my grandfather's case, the name itself is redeemed, the name that was his birthright and legacy by Sicilian tradition. He claims it half a world away from Terrasini, in the back room of a St. Louis gambling house, and two days later puts Paolinu to rest in the East River. Bearing the Americanized name of the Monk, the first-born son of Giuseppe Viviano and Grazia Tocco assumes his place in the chain of generations, as he ought to have on November 5, 1897, at the baptismal font of Maria Santissima delle Grazie.

I knew that there could only be one explanation for Giuseppe Viviano's refusal to name his son Francesco: a breech of some sort separated Giuseppe and his own father, the Monk. When I learned what had come between them, I would unearth a great deal about the Monk's inner life.

Gaetano the Falcon, Big Tom, survived the violent night in 1911 when Paolinu became Frank. The Falcon lived on to discover that Maria's hand was in the till; she fled St. Louis a month after my grandfather boarded the outbound train at Union Station and vanished forever from our family saga.

BY 1912, Frank P. Viviano was a self-employed businessman, peddling oranges, lemons, and vegetables from his own pushcart in Detroit. The Motor City. Henry Ford's city. The fastest growing city in the world.

Ford manufactured fewer than eighteen thousand cars in 1909, the year before Grandpa emigrated to America. In 1912, when he moved on from Harlem to Detroit, the company's annual production had risen 1100 percent, to more than two hundred thousand. But he wasn't drawn there by the factories, even though they paid the highest industrial wages on earth. After St. Louis, my grandfather couldn't work for another man, much less a man who employed thousands, standing shoulder-to-shoulder in the cavernous plants that rose along the Detroit River.

Frank Viviano recognized that the Motor City would be ever hungrier as it grew ever more prosperous, and that its tastes would keep pace with its salary checks. He explained his move to Detroit, when I asked about it, in terms that framed the same theory that drove Henry Ford to produce an automobile for the average America family: "People *need* something to eat when they poor, like we were in Harlem. Anything to fill the stomach. Potatoes. Carrots. Pasta with a little greens and onions. Then they have money, and everything changes, Franky. They don't *need* anymore. They *want*. Something fancy. Oranges. Plums. Bananas."

By 1916, average Americans were driving cars and Ford's workers were eating oranges, plums, and bananas. Grandpa sold the pushcart to another immigrant, bought a horse and wagon, and had his name painted on it: "Frank P. Viviano, Fancy Fruits and Produce."

One year later, on a moonless September evening, four men abducted Angelina Tocco, the Brooklyn cousin who had cried out to my grandfather from the Third Avenue el.

THE TERRASINI ARCHIVES had provided no simple solution to the mystery of the Monk's death. But from the very first day, they were valuable in a more subtle way. They supplied a rich narrative backdrop, the village's collective story told in births, deaths, and marriages.

The ledgers described invisible borders that separated the upper village of Terrasini from the fishing hamlet of Favarotta and the surrounding rural countryside. On a conventional map, the three districts were knitted into the illusion of a single community. In reality, they were distinct social worlds. They had their own dialects. They observed the feast days of their own saints. And they had married by those divisions, until very recently, as though the Piazza Duomo and the municipal limits were unbreachable ramparts.

Buggisi cu buggisi, viddanu cu viddanu, marinaru cu marinaru, the village code proclaimed. "Merchant with merchant, peasant with peasant, fisherman with fisherman."

This was also the law of marriage in Sicilian America on September 18, 1917.

Sitting at the kitchen table in 1992, Grandpa had spoken of it for an hour. "In my head, I hear Angelina calling my name for a year and a half," he told me. Her cry from the el had sounded through a dinner in Brooklyn, where my grandfather came courting and Angelina's father, Gaetano Tocco, refused to look him in the eye. It continued through the first eight months of 1917, when the Toccos themselves emigrated to Detroit, as my grandfather waited for an invitation that never came.

Gaetano Tocco was a shoemaker, a de facto member of the Terrasini *bourgeoisie,* the French term from which *buggisi* was derived. Angelina had been born above the Piazza del Duomo, among tradesmen and artisans, and she understood that marriage to Frank Viviano, the son of a cart driver and stablehand, was unthinkable: "My father said the Vivianos had horse manure in their hair and black dirt under their nails—*viddanu cu viddanu.*"

But she paid him secret afternoon visits, behind Gaetano's back.

Seven decades later, my grandfather's eyes closed as he remembered her footsteps in a Detroit hallway; he was nineteen years old again, and lost in an amorous daze: "My mother, she knows you can't stop some things. She tells your grandma's daddy, 'Angelina belongs to my boy.' But he won't listen to nobody."

He had no choice. He had to do something.

The kidnappers grabbed Angelina just after dusk, rushing through the door of the cobblery that her father had opened just above the Detroit River on Fort Street. Two of them forced their way into the flat behind the shop, while the other two pinned Gaetano Tocco to his worktable. Angelina was stirring a pot of spaghetti for dinner as they burst in. "She fought like hell, throwing the pasta water into their faces, kicking and biting until she drew blood," one of my aunts always added, whenever she told the story.

The struggle had to be convincing; it was the custom in abduction marriages, which were common enough in Sicily, despite the code, to have their own rituals. Angelina knew all along who had sent kidnappers to Fort Street. "That's how it was handled back then," my aunt said. "As soon as they were a few blocks away, she calmed down."

My grandfather was waiting for her at a cottage ten miles south. A cousin rowed them across the river to Ontario, where they were married by a Canadian justice of the peace. They returned to Detroit at the end of the month.

Angelina was ruined now by Sicilian standards. A church wedding was hastily arranged. Two bridesmaids, two ushers, and a ring-bearer were recruited. The Toccos saw to it that the groom wore a rented tuxedo; Angelina appeared at church in a white lace gown and veil.

That afternoon, September 29, 1917, they posed for a studio photographer a few doors down Fort Street from the cobblery. My grandmother presses a bouquet of white roses against the embroidered flower petals that cascade down the bodice of her gown; her face in the portrait is radiant with calm purpose.

My grandfather's tuxedo is a size or two too small, its sleeves

The author's paternal grandparents, Frank P. Viviano and Angelina Tocco, at their second wedding in Detroit in 1917, a month after her abduction to Canada.

bunched in tight wrinkles around his upper arms. His eyes are defiant. There is nothing of Paolinu left.

LONG BEFORE I KNEW its details, I was aware of my grandfather's self-creation in America, even if I didn't know that it extended to his very name. It was his defining act, his escape from the desert, his claim to a birthright. But it was also his legacy to me, a morality play to reject or embrace. Identity, in the end, rests in the tension between conflicting plots, a lasting tension between the dramas we inherit, consciously or not, and the drama we choose to write for ourselves.

Consciously or not. These words frame a signal difference that separates my generation from my grandfather's, a distinction that explains much of what it means to be born in a nation of immigrants.

The dramatic narrative of ancestry is not erased by immigration. It is driven into a clandestine realm where setting and characters are only dimly recalled, or transformed into fairy-tale heroes and villains in the landscape of fable. The Monk, in this sense, had withdrawn into my grandparents' tales and the isolated recesses of my imagination, into hidden canyons where I could not directly confront him.

In a quarter century of wandering, I have been struck over and over by this gap between the old world and the new, between the breakneck spontaneity of American life and the slow-motion dance of the generations in Europe. Between unnerving restlessness and paralyzing custom.

I know a woman in France whose every change of address was dictated by an eighteenth-century oil painting of her great-grandmother. The portrait is enormous, roughly eight feet high and five feet wide, and meaningful only to her, the last surviving sibling in her family. Whatever the state of her finances, she is obliged always to reside in apartments with very high ceilings and a large vacant wall.

If this woman is an extravagant case, she is not far from the norm. In European homes, entire rooms are often given over to fragile heirloom tables and chairs, to chests bulging with moldy First Communion dresses and bridal gowns. The walls are covered with the foggy images of deceased relatives, captured on the tin-types and daguerreotypes of village photographers who have them-selves been gone a century or more. The faces in those images the eloquent souvenirs of an inner life that a taut smile or cocked eye-brow imparted—are the index of family history. They are allusions to what came before, harbingers of what is to come.

In my parents' home in Detroit, there was a single Terrasini photograph of my grandfather, the four-year-old Paolino posed with his mother and two sisters, to remind us that a world before Ellis Island even existed. That the drama had earlier acts.

But the old world did exist, and as I dug into its foundations I came to understand that the drama was unfinished. If the conscious memory of Sicily had neared its vanishing point in America, the resonance of that memory lived on. How could it be otherwise? How could patterns of behavior and temperament that defied the passage of countless centuries stop dead at the ocean's edge? The new world is not simply a blunt contradiction of the old, but also its latest chapter.

PART II

SIX

A Map

Terrasini, Sicily
October 1995

SOME DEFINING MOMENTS in life can never be explained.
No plausible sequence of events accounts for them. Yet "coinci-
dence" is no explanation at all and says nothing of their tenacious
power. They occur and they unsettle, jarring intruders in the rational sensibility.

It was such a moment that brought me to a citrus grove two
miles west of Terrasini, in the outlying Contrada Paternella.

The grove was the Corteses' summer retreat. Mike and Rosalia
leased the house from its present owner, who had inherited the
grove as a child and now lived in Detroit. They used it from May
until mid-autumn. The rest of the year, like most of the properties
scattered over the rural hillsides, the house was empty. Rosalia formally referred to it as "Paternella," and more often simply as *la
campagna,* "the country." She loved its cool shade and the low,
rhythmic moan of the gulf waves as they waxed and waned in a
rocky grotto a hundred yards away.

I had called Mike from Paris ten days earlier, when I'd finished
making arrangements with my editors for an extended stay in
Terrasini. I would sort out my random notes on the Monk, track
down the elusive municipal records, and talk to Giuseppe Viviano,
the eccentric old man I'd met on the Palermo bus. I had learned in

Detroit that he was a distant cousin of my grandfather, which explained why he knew about the Monk. He might well know about Domenico Valenti, too.

Mike was delighted. "My friend, I got just the thing," he had said, when I asked if he knew of a place I could rent.

In the last week of October, I rolled ashore from the car deck of the ferry to Palermo and followed Mike's instructions to a small lane that sloped off toward the sea from the Bourbon road. The house was about half a mile down the lane, behind an iron-wrought fence. Rosalia and Alice were on the terrace, setting the table for a lunch that was certain to last into dinner. Mike beamed from the garden, where he and Bobby were stoking a wood-fired brick oven, readying it for a platter of fresh sardines that sat on the table. Flavio ran out the door, yelling, "Franky! Franky!" then leaped into my arms.

I was supposed to yell back, to swing the boy over my shoulder or wrestle him to the ground; roughhouse had always been the language of our affection. But I didn't have it in me now. Flavio looked bewildered when I set him back down, not sure what to say, and the two women looked up at me from their silverware.

Mike had told them where I spent the summer. I was on the front in Bosnia, with a small medical aid mission, when United Nations troops guarding the embattled Muslim enclave of Srebrenica surrendered and the town fell to the Serbs. An immense flood of young women and children had poured across the Bosnian government lines, in the midst of a downpour that sent rivers of mud coursing through the forested valleys. There were almost no men or elderly women among the refugees. The men had been disarmed by the Serbs and shot on the spot, thousands of them. The older women had been too weak to keep up; many had simply sat down in the mud and waited for the incoming artillery.

In America, preoccupied with the riddle of my grandfather's name, I had managed to push Bosnia from my mind. The nightmares of reporters are often postponed. My colleagues spoke of the same experience, the nauseating emptiness months after an assignment. The postponement allowed you to negotiate a catastrophe, to observe and write; it seldom absolved you from a distant reckoning. My reckoning with Srebrenica, the chronic nightmares and cold sweats, came as soon as I returned to Europe.

I didn't tell Mike exactly what I had seen in the Srebrenica forest. But he had warned the family that I might be shaky. Something he sensed, rather than heard, over the phone. Rosalia walked across the terrace, took me in her gentle embrace. "Is okay, Franky," she said. "You home now."

Home. I had come home, in more ways than any of us knew that afternoon.

THE PATERNELLA HOUSE was quite modest by the usual standards of contemporary Sicilian immigrant architecture, which ran to swollen reproductions of Long Island trilevels, suburban ranches, or displaced Alpine chalets inspired by their owners' sojourns abroad.

Most of these houses were built personally, their foundations laid and cinderblock walls erected over a decade or more of summer vacations, by Sicilians employed as construction workers in New York, fishermen in Massachusetts, or truck drivers in Düsseldorf. In the local idiom, their overblown creations were known as "immigrant castles"; no one else could have afforded them, with the exception of the local dons, who carefully avoided all such ostentation. The castle owners were often *'Meddicani,* those melancholy, Americanized returnees who tried to wall themselves off from the inefficiencies of Sicily in gilded memories of Brooklyn or Gloucester.

If the Cortese place fell short of a true immigrant castle, it was nevertheless a far cry from the tiny mud-walled cottages that stood in the citrus groves when my grandfather and the Monk were born. Its plan was an unadorned rectangle, about fifty feet long by thirty feet wide, with an indoor kitchen at the seaward end and the porticoed terrace and brick oven at the other. Along one side of the interior, there were three modest bedrooms and a bathroom. The rest

of the house was a single spacious living area, with an enormous dining table and fireplace in its opposite corners. The floors were polished granite, and the walls a flat whitewashed plaster.

The casa Paternella was as plain Jane as a home ever could be.
But it was set, gloriously, amid more than six hundred citrus trees.
They blossomed or fruited year around; there was seldom a month
when the air wasn't perfumed with lemon or orange. The bedroom
windows opened into the grove, as did the terrace.

To the south, beyond the Palermo-Trapani rail line and the
autostrada—the light traffic a barely audible growl in the distance—Monte Palmeto soared majestically above the trees, its
limestone face etched faintly with the zigzag of a trail. East of the
citrus grove, a pasture stretched to the sea, accommodating a flock
of sheep, a dozen milk cows, and several horses. The animals sheltered at the lower end of the pasture, in a row of cavernous stone
buildings that had once been the stables of a French duke.

The original ducal residence was gone, Mike told me, replaced
with a red-and-gold-striped Art Nouveau mansion commissioned
by the late Baronessa Fassini, who had acquired part of the
Paternella estate at the turn of the twentieth century. Known now
as "Villa Fassini," it had attracted brief notoriety in the early 1970s
as Terrasini's one and only hippie crash pad, the scene of "wild
orgies and psychedelic drug trips," according to Mike. The party
ended almost as soon as it came to the attention of the hyper-
Catholic bosses of the *sistema*, who saw to it that the municipality
acquired ownership of the property.

Then inertia took hold. The villa had been abandoned in the
midst of a reconstruction project that ran out of money in the
1980s. A rusted crane stood motionless over the site the entire time
I lived in the grove. It had been there for more than ten years.

On the sea cliff's edge, about fifty yards from the villa gate, was
the Torre Paternella, a stone watchtower built in the sixteenth century to spot raiding pirate vessels from Africa. It too had been
abandoned to the weeds.

I had budgeted most of a year for research, alternating between two-week road assignments for the newspaper and two weeks in Sicily. It would not be easy. Getting to most datelines required a time-consuming, inconvenient first leg from Palermo to Rome or Milan, and then a connecting flight. But I was determined to make some progress in my hunt for the Monk.

THE EFFORT BEGAN inauspiciously, with the Terrasini mayor's final unexplained refusal to let me see the stored municipal archives. I had written him several letters, carefully outlining how important the documents were to my work. He never bothered to reply.

The bad news was delivered over the telephone by the village registrar, Marianna Trappeto, when I called her in frustration. It was no use coming to City Hall to argue, she said. The *sindaco* just wouldn't change his mind.

"A very big fuck you, *sindaco,* and fuck all of your descendants until kingdom come," I said under my breath as she hung up. It was the loose translation of a Sicilian expression that my father used when he was seriously rubbed the wrong way. I was glad I had restrained myself while Marianna was on the phone; she was embarrassed enough.

The phone rang. It was Marianna again. I cringed. Had the line still been live?

"You know, Franky," she said, a light quiver in her voice, "there is an architect in town who writes history books about Terrasini. You ought to look him up. He spent months and months in the records before the old library closed."

I wrote down the name and sketchy address that Marianna provided: "Signore Orlando, Via Archimede," somewhere above Maria Santissima delle Grazie. No street number.

The next morning, I surveyed mailboxes along the Via Archimede until I reached one with a business card affixed to it that read "Giovanni Orlando, *architetto.*" The first four times I rang the doorbell during the business hours indicated on the card, there was no response.

The same experience awaited me at the Favarotta end of the village, in the Via Cataldi, when I rapped on Giuseppe Viviano's front door. Mike had pointed out the house.

The windows on both buildings were always shuttered, and at first glance, Giuseppe's seemed entirely unoccupied. The walls were thickly encrusted with dirt, and several layers of exterior paint had peeled away, leaving faded streaks of color all over the facade. It looked like an expressionist canvas that had been left out in the rain. But a votive candle, set before a small statue of the Virgin Mary in a window alcove, was lit without fail each evening. I wedged letters into the space between the statue and the candle, reintroducing myself and pleading for an opportunity to talk, and dropped half a dozen notes off for him at Di Maggio's *Caffe*.

Mike was dubious. "Giuseppe don't like to talk to anybody, not if he can help it. He only leaves the house to go to church on Sunday or catch the bus to Palermo. Those messages you leaving all over town for him are a waste of time."

I knew that already. Giuseppe was dodging me. But I also knew that this elderly recluse with my great-grandfather's name had given me sound advice. "Sicily is the book you must study," he'd said.

READ LITERALLY, its pages were half a world's history in microcosm, reaching back more than three thousand years, as conquering armies swept westward into the Mediterranean Basin or eastward toward the Orient. Sicily had been put to the sword by three millennia of rampaging soldiers, converted by a thirty-century parade of militant priests and mullahs.

There was no understanding the violent tensions of the Monk and his world, there was no understanding my grandfather's journey or my own postscript to it, outside the context of that tumultuous book.

Before the birth of Christ, the empires of Phoenicia, Greece, Carthage, and Rome had swallowed the island in majestic succession, raising temples to Baal, Zeus, and Jupiter. Afterward came the

Vandals and Goths, Christian in name, Teutonic-pagan in practice. They were followed by Byzantium's satraps and monks in A.D. 535, who were in turn routed by the Arabs and Islam three centuries later. In 1061, the crusading Normans stormed ashore, returning Christ to the Sicilian throne. Next, one after the other, were German-speaking Schwabs and Francophone Angevins, the inquisitorial kings of Aragon and Spain, the dukes of Savoy and the emperors of Austria. They all had their moments in the Sicilian sun, culminating in the suffocating two-century rule of the Bourbons.

The Italians, who took power after a secular revolution in 1860—a scant thirty-seven years before my grandfather was born—were positively newcomers.

Older customs and beliefs survived each invasion, finding voice in grandmotherly fairy tales and refuge in isolated mountain villages, while new gods arrived on one wave and left on another. Always someone else's god, always an outsider.

Vestiges of all these gods are still evident today, cropping up in feast days for a gamut of strange saints whom no other Catholic community recognizes, and imparting a phenomenal syncretic chaos to the island's architecture. In the same densely populated valleys, Sicily's Greek and Roman temples jostle for position with Eastern Orthodox basilicas, Islamic mosques, Norman gothic cathedrals, and Spanish baroque chapels.

The sum effect is a bewildering lack of coherence, a landscape of extraordinary monuments that seem entirely divorced from the people who live and die in their looming presence. Prehistoric dolmens, Roman villas, and medieval watchtowers are crumbling into the soil all over the island, ignored or idly plundered by farmers who use two-thousand-year-old temple cornerstones to wall off zucchini and tomato plots.

"These monuments of the past are magnificent but incomprehensible, because they were not built by us, yet stand round us like lovely mute phantoms," the Prince of Salina tries to explain to a northern Italian official in Giuseppe Tomasi di Lampedusa's *The*

Leopard, the archetypal Sicilian novel. "They recall all of the rulers who landed by main force from every direction, were at once obeyed, soon detested, and always unfathomable."

But it is in the island's gene pool that the legacy of endless conquest is most striking, and oddly, most benign.

The evening promenade in any Sicilian village, even one as apparently homogenous as Terrasini, scans the chromosomal imprint of those many invasions, as the identifiable progeny of blue-eyed Norman blondes parade by, arm-in-arm, with the scions of dusky Spaniards or curly-haired Arabs and Greeks. Often, they are siblings, case studies in the vagaries of recessive genes.

Sicilians take great pride in this promiscuous racial stew. Unlike monumental architecture, which speaks of blunt conquest, miscegeny is evidence of gradual sabotage—the conqueror's identity slowly and relentlessly diluted by the conquered. There is no particular advantage to being mostly one thing in Sicily, no shame attached to being mostly another. Straight blond hair is no more highly valued than North African curls.

Mike Cortese was pleased that both his family and mine had collateral Terrasini branches with Sephardic Jewish and Arab names, respectively Lopes and Cammarata in my case, which were signs that we'd been Sicilian a very long time. In that, there was an advantage: the edge of the insider, an heir to the ancestral codes, on an island where a new wave of outsiders might storm ashore at any moment.

I MUST HAVE presented an odd sight in the first two weeks of November, caroming back-and-forth between the Via Cataldi, Di Maggio's *Caffe,* and the Via Archimede, sticking envelopes under the arm of a plaster Virgin and peering forlornly between the slats of window shutters. In the Virgin's case, the effort was as futile as my pleas to the mayor. But on the fifth day, just before noon, a short, balding man in baggy blue jeans and a polo short appeared at the entrance to Orlando's office.

"The architect is occupied for the moment," he said.

I told him I was in no hurry, and sat down on a hard wooden chair in the foyer. The bald man went into the next room, closing the door behind him.

Ten minutes later, the door opened and the same bald man reappeared, a suit coat thrown over his polo shirt and a tie looped around his neck. He motioned me in.

"Signore, I am the architect Orlando," he announced. "What am I able to do for you?"

He looked crestfallen when I said I wanted to talk about the village history. Hearing my slipshod and American accented Italian, he had probably taken me for a son of the 'Meddicani, about to unload a fortune on plans for a mock California hacienda or Cape Cod bungalow.

We exchanged a few pleasantries about our respective sorties into the past. Orlando was especially interested in an eighteenth-century conflict over religious jurisdiction that pitted Terrasini against the Benedictine friars of San Martino delle Scale, a wealthy monastery in the cathedral town of Monreale. Yes, he had written several books on Sicily, he said, five of them to date. They were very, very difficult to find, he added, nodding his head with satisfaction, as though this was the ultimate confirmation of his work's value.

I had inquired at nearly every bookshop and village library in the Province of Palermo since Marianna's call. The publications of Giovanni Orlando were indeed nowhere to be found, not even in the three newsstand-bookshops of Terrasini itself. The booksellers had never heard of them.

There was a long pause in our conversation. Then Orlando cleared his throat and said, "But it just so happens that I have the last copies in my study. In the interest of scholarship, I would like to put them at your disposal."

With that, he jumped to his feet, backpedaled through an inner

door, and returned in less than a minute, clutching five slim paperbacks, hardly more than pamphlets. "With my sincerest compli-
ments, from one historian to another," he announced.

We struggled through another long pause, until I asked if there
was some way I could thank him.

"One hundred thousand lire," Orlando immediately answered.

The price, which amounted to seventy dollars, was clearly
plucked from thin air. The books were self-published, and so redundant that they offered little more than the same essay rewritten five
ways, inflated with blurry illustrations and documents of no con-
ceivable value ("The Bylaws of the Terrasini Mutual Aid Society").
But there were enough oddball details and anecdotes to be worth
the cost, I decided, and handed Orlando two fifty-thousand-lire
notes.

IT WAS ONLY OUTSIDE in the Via Archimede, as I leafed
through one of the paperbacks, that I realized what I had purchased. There on page thirty-one, by way of illustration for a short
history of the construction of the Bourbon road from Palermo to
Trapani, was a detailed nineteenth-century military map of the area
between Monte Palmeto and the Gulf of Castellammare. Every
peasant farmstead, every aristocratic manor house, every pasture
and orchard was identified.

I took a long, slow look at the map—it was obviously of value
to my research—and gasped.

In the citrus grove just above the site of Villa Fassini, which was
identified as "Villa Carolina" on the old map, two *viddanu* households had faced each other across the Bourbon road a century ago.
A small stylized black box to the north of the road, floating in the
precise stretch of citrus grove where I was now living, was labeled
casa Viviano.

Its immediate neighbor, on the mountain side of the Palermo
road, was *casa Valenti.*

SEVEN

The Red Sash

THE OLD MAP was the boost I needed after the archive debacle. It provided a nineteenth-century frame for the village and its rural surroundings, for the rampart of Monte Palmeto and the citrus groves, for the stables beyond the lemon and orange trees and the Bourbon road that led to Paternella. A shadowy curtain parted, and characters stepped forward from my scribbled notes to take their places on the stage.

The gaps in my knowledge remained enormous. I was still without the date of the Monk's assassination, still without the means to bring my reconstruction of his drama to its fatal climax. But in the euphoria of my chance discovery of the map, I was certain that the rest of the drama would unfold, a narrative carpet unrolling steadily ahead of me. It was confidence of the sort that often generates its own good fortune, a self-fulfilling prophecy born of naïve faith.

Possibilities that should have been obvious to me long before, new roads along which to pursue the Monk, were opened by those two modest black boxes on a hundred-year old map.

ONE OF GRANDMA ANGELINA'S FABLES, set in this very countryside, featured a romantic outlaw who was sometimes presented as an unnamed ancestor. More often, he was explicitly Gaetano Viviano, the Falcon, the same demonic uncle who had whipped a policeman senseless with iron chains in the Castellammare hills and driven my grandfather to a brutal confrontation in St. Louis. Angelina must have known those tales, but she never repeated them.

The pairing, in one man, of Grandpa's psychopathic tormentor and Grandma's romantic hero was a classic Sicilian paradox, the paradox that labeled killers "men of honor" and helped ensure the *sistema*'s lasting power in Sicily. It was the paradox of American pulp fiction and film, which betrayed a similar urge to paint hitmen as heroes and dons as tragic, misunderstood King Lears.

"The Falcon was very handsome, the handsomest man on earth," Grandma always told us, pressing down hard on the mangle for emphasis, "and like your grandpa, he was stronger than any other two men."

At this, she would smile, or even giggle. My grandparents were among those rare and fortunate human beings who are shamelessly in love for a lifetime. Physically in love, long after the 1917 abduction to Canada, which had been followed by six children in ten years. Well into their seventies, Grandma and Grandpa would embrace at unexpected moments—in the kitchen when the pasta water was coming to a boil for our Sunday family dinner, at a relative's wedding or baptism—pinching and grabbing at each other while the rest of us laughed with pleasure.

Grandma had "filled out," as she put it, after her children began having children of their own. The trim waist of the seventeen-year-old girl in the Detroit wedding photograph was gone. But the spark was still in her dark flashing eyes, the mercurial disposition was intact.

"The Falcon could not stay in one town, because his strength was so great that it made other men jealous," she said.

"The strength made him a famous warrior, with an army of loyal friends. But it was also a curse. When there was a war, he was a hero. When there was peace, he was feared. So he had to spend most of his life hiding with his followers, *mischinu,* far from the sea in a mountain canyon."

If my grandmother pitied someone, she always referred to him as *mischinu,* "the wretched one."

"A man like that has no family. He can never rest. The Falcon knew every village in Sicily, every hill and valley, and he knew many, many beautiful women. But except for a single moment with the most beautiful woman in the world, he never knew genuine love . . ."

The woman, in my grandmother's account, was "the Queen of Naples." She noticed the Falcon for the first time at the marketplace in Terrasini—to which he returned weekly in disguise, leaving his brigand army behind in the mountains—and was unable to take her eyes off him.

"The queen fell instantly in love with the Falcon, and he fell in love with her. They watched each other every Saturday for three months, always from a distance, over the crowd, so her guards would not notice. They shared not a single word in all that time. Then, one morning, she nodded, just a little tipping of her head."

Grandma stood up at the mangle and tipped her head toward one of the boy cousins, her eyes closed and her lips pursed in a coquettish grin. That moonless night, she said, the Falcon climbed to the queen's balcony, "and they both experienced genuine love for the first and only time.

"She gave the Falcon a red sash to remember her by. He wore it always, to the end of his days. And he was buried with it wrapped around his chest."

THE RED SASH was a seminal prop in our family legends, my earliest subject as a writer and my subject still four decades later. From the time I could write a complete sentence, I was constantly reframing that fable of my grandmother's. It was a personalized nursery tale, complete with the innocently erotic undercurrents that course through so many children's stories.

Yet something beyond that, something more universal, moved me: the contradictions of violence, the defiance of convention, the seductive power of a glance—the idea that the resonance of an act could outlive its actors for more than a century.

In my freshman year at college, I unrolled the red sash for a writing assignment in English 101; the Falcon was recast as my own fictitious uncle, a natural storyteller who understands the reveries of a dreamy child and weaves the fable of a romantic outlaw ancestor into them. The actual sash, in this version, is seen only at the uncle's funeral, where it serves to vindicate the child's dreams. The story wound up in an anthology of student fiction, my first publication.

Nonetheless, my cousins and I laughed at Grandma's version of the story when we reached our teenage years (even if the laughter made me secretly uneasy). The thought of a queen turning up in our dirt-poor country village was only slightly less preposterous than the notion that Grandpa's uncle was her lover.

But we knew, too, that Gaetano the Falcon was buried with a faded red sash wrapped around his torso. The old bandit had been killed in an improbable accident in 1937, falling off of the tailgate of a truck and breaking his neck at the age of eighty. He died in Los Angeles, where he had moved abruptly in the 1920s, no doubt because of "difficulties" in St. Louis.

My father, then eighteen, had gone to the funeral with my grandfather. He told us that that red sash was real.

IN FACT, it was the Monk, and not his son, who earned the red sash. The bolt of scarlet cloth had nothing to do with Uncle Gaetano's exploits as the Falcon, much less with a midnight tryst in the arms of a lovelorn queen. But it had everything to do with the forces that drove the first Francesco from the land where I now resided—and eventually killed him.

After months spent with my nose buried in history books, I learned what the red sash had symbolized in the Monk's youth, and what it came to symbolize by the time of his murder.

In its first incarnation, the sash was the emblem of the *picciotti,* Sicilian irregulars—most of them rural bandits, highwaymen with prices on their heads—who joined Giuseppe Garibaldi's "Thousand" in the 1860 insurgency that overthrew the Bourbon dynasty. Little more than a decade later, its meaning had been twisted out of recognition in Sicily. It had become a banner of the *sistema del potere*.

In pursuing my namesake to his death, I was to become the distant witness to that metamorphosis, to the events that breathed life into the Mafia and my own family's role in them.

AS RECENTLY AS THE 1920S, the last of Garibaldi's peasant soldiers were still marching in ceremonial village parades, turned out in white knee breeches, a blousy crimson shirt and beret, and red sashes like the one that Gaetano inherited from his murdered father. The word *"picciotti,"* literally "the boys" in Palermitan dialect, had acquired a sinister edge by the twentieth century; it was the vernacular term for *sistema* gunmen.

But in 1860, the red sash was a badge of honor, even if it was the honor of thieves, with a pedigree forged in generations of constant upheaval. It was the mark of men like Paolo Cocuzza, himself a legendary former bandit, who had been appointed overseer of the Paternella citrus estate in the mid-1850s. Francesco Viviano was one of the workmen under his direction.

I have a hazy childhood memory of Cocuzza's name. There is a long dialect poem in his honor, and a few of its lines may have cropped up in my grandmother's fables. The real Paolo Cocuzza surfaced when I turned up a dusty treatise on the *picciotti*'s outlaw origins, *Briganti in Sicilia* by the Catania poet and historian Salvatore Lo Presti, in a Palermo secondhand bookstore.

The rebellious child of a shopkeeper in Montelepre, a few miles from the birthplace of the Monk, Cocuzza had drifted into banditry as a teenager. By his twentieth year he was the leader of a band of highwaymen based in the wild mountain canyons above Terrasini. Cocuzza was celebrated for his marksmanship and uncanny ability to elude capture by Bourbon troops and police. What elevated him to a folk hero, however, was a centuries-old

Sicilian version of Robin Hood banditry. Cocuzza and his men "robbed the rich and powerful," the dialect poem declared, sharing the spoils with the Castellammare peasants who sang of their exploits.

It's tempting to think that the Vivianos were among the peasant families who benefited. More certain is that Francesco knew Cocuzza personally and was familiar with his legend. In the Sicilian manner, that legend was morally ambiguous. If Cocuzza was a Robin Hood, a primitive social revolutionary, he was also a thief and a killer.

At the age of twenty-five, the real Paolo Cocuzza barely escaped a police trap in 1836, and fled Sicily for New York. He returned when an amnesty was offered to former brigands after a failed insurgency in 1848. Eventually he came to manage the Paternella estate, which was owned by a French duke with radical political beliefs of his own. The estate's offices had been located in a vaulted eighteenth-century stone warehouse just a few hundred yards from where I was staying. A few hundred yards from the Monk's cottage.

I was closer now than I had ever been to imagining my namesake's life, and to reconstructing it.

THE EXACT NUMBER of *picciotti* who fought in the *Risorgimento,* the "uprising" that was ignited in Sicily and led to the unification of Italy, is a subject of detached speculation among historians. For Sicilians themselves, it is a matter of immense significance.

When the army that landed with Garibaldi at Marsala on May 11, 1860, completed its sweep of the island ten weeks later and prepared to invade the Italian mainland, the Thousand had swollen to twenty-three thousand. By the most authoritative estimates, between seven and eight thousand of them were Sicilian. But many more, perhaps twenty thousand in all, joined informal *squadre* that took up arms—and the emblematic red sash—against the Bourbon army. A high proportion were young men from the Castellammare towns and villages, drawn to a sixty-mile-long swath of battleground between Marsala and Palermo withTerrasini at its northeastern flank.

The Monk left no memoir, no written account of the explosion that altered his life in 1860 as thoroughly as immigration would alter his grandson's half a century later. Like almost all Sicilian peasants, he was unable to read or write. When I finally located a document with his name on it, his signature was a lopsided X hanging awkwardly over the "Vivianus, Franciscus Paulus" that a village clerk had inscribed in Latin.

The clerk was what Terrasini peasants called a *capiddu*, a "hat," a term that implied intellectual superiority and elevated social standing. On an island mired in ignorance after six centuries of paralyzing rule by Spain and her Bourbon successors in Naples, capital of the Kingdom of the Two Sicilies, the hats had emerged in the 1830s as a small but prosperous middle-class. They were the newly propertied and educated elite, ensconced between the unlettered mass and the moribund Bourbon aristocracy.

An alliterative series of couplets, *The Alphabet of the Peasant*, widely circulated at the time, suggests the contempt with which the *viddani* were regarded by the new middle class and Bourbons alike. The entry for the letter "B" in the alphabet is typical:

> *Benevolence rules him not, nor does courtesy,*
> *But only malice, deceit and coarseness.*

"Peasants are without exception crude and deformed," another couplet declares, "and should be treated brutally."

The peasants had their own response, expressed in hundreds of dialect proverbs that peppered conversation in the fields. My grandparents never lost their faith in the wisdom of these proverbs, or the worldview they reflected. They were the social punctuation marks of our family tales. "The rude man is not he who is rudely born," my grandfather liked to say, "but he who rudely behaves." In exchanges with the rich and powerful, he advised, *Senti assai, parra pica e cridi nenti:* "Listen closely, speak seldom, and believe nothing."

This was the resentment that nurtured the Monk and made a folk hero of Paolo Cocuzza. It was the bitter soil in which the *sistema* would take root.

THE HATS MONOPOLIZED public history, the written record that presents an official past. They chronicled their versions of the *Risorgimento* in minute detail, financed their publication in expensive private editions, and saw to it that the leather-bound volumes were displayed on the shelves of university and municipal libraries where I was still able to find them more than a century afterward.

The memoirs were often dedicated to Garibaldi in stiff Latin inscriptions, and invariably cleansed of references to the collaboration with the Bourbon authorities that prevailed in Sicily before the *Risorgimento.* The hats presented themselves as lifelong enemies of the *ancien régime,* ideally qualified to serve as mayors and bureaucrats in the new Italy. Even Garibaldi is transformed into a hat in these accounts, a respectable gentleman in the image of his belated supporters, his radical politics and years as a South American revolutionary lost in the polite banalities of Palermo drawing rooms.

Yet however self-serving they might be, the *capiddi* diaries were also the war's primary eyewitness records, and if their authors held the *picciotti* in contempt, they also kept remarkably close track of the peasant army and its bandit generals. Reading between the lines, ignoring the views of the diarists and concentrating on the simple recapitulation of events, I found it possible to extract and put into written words a history that its illiterate protagonists had been unable to write for themselves.

Armed with photocopies of the hats' hundred-year-old memoirs—and guided by family legends—I could visualize the peasant war with graphic, pinpoint precision, down to the actions of individual guerrilla leaders and their rough-hewn sharpshooters.

I could follow my namesake into battle.

There were two Sicilian campaigns in 1860. Indeed, there were two versions of almost every episode in the uprising that toppled the Bourbons. One lies in the official past, the other in the folk memory and its poetic reincarnation in fable. The truth is a dialogue between these accounts. It speaks to the visceral experience of history—to the last hour before dawn on April 3, 1860, when Francesco Paolo Viviano picks up his gun, slips quietly past the bed where his wife and three-year-old son lie dreaming, and into the Castellammare night.

EIGHT

The Monk

Western Sicily
April 1860

THE LEMON GROVES *are in full fruit, and as the April sun
breaks over Punta Raisi, the spring air is ripe with the odors of saltwater, lemon blossom, and wild fennel. From the trail that coils up
the face of Monte Palmeto, Francesco Viviano can see the villa of
the French duke. At first, it is no more than a colorless splash of
reflected moonlight in the dark fields; then the splash sharpens into
an amber rectangle, and the fields take on the mottled green of pasture. Even from this height—the Portella di Mircene, the pass at
the crest of Palmeto, about eighteen hundred feet into the climb—
the collar bells of the Frenchman's sheep are audible, a distant
metallic chorus.*

*If Francesco draws an imaginary line between the Torre
Paternella and the villa, then extends it toward the Bourbon road,
he can locate the cottage where his wife and son have by now awakened. It is a sunbaked brown fragment, a piece of driftwood, almost
lost in the wave of lemon trees that rolls up from the Gulf of
Castellammare. But night still clings to the face of the ridge, and
although he can sometimes hear the labored breathing and footfalls
of other men on the trail, they are invisible.*

*Far below Palmeto, Terrasini is a wedge of tile-roofed cubes
pinned to the landscape by the campanile of Maria Santissima delle*

Grazie. Beyond the wedge's base, where the port lies, a small cloud of fishing boats is wafting toward the harbor moorings. Just to the east, at the base of Monte Pecoraro, which rises a thousand feet above Palmeto, the Palermo road disappears into a smaller maze of rooftops that is Cinisi. A few miles to the west, Partinico sprawls into the Castellammare hills.

This is what my namesake saw in 1860, and what I saw from the Monte Palmeto trail one hundred thirty-six years later, the long coastal vista altered only by the trawlers and motor launches that replaced sailing dories in the 1950s, a narrow-gauge railroad line built at the end of the nineteenth century, and the autostrada and airport that were constructed in the 1970s by the Badalamenti family. It is a Badalamenti who calls Francesco Viviano to the mountain on the third day of April in 1860.

In the written history of the island, Giuseppe Badalamenti is the infamous Zu Piddu Ranturri, "Uncle Piddu the Death Rattle," an asthmatic, limping brigand chief from Cinisi who is the curse of western Sicily's landholders. One of the gentleman diarists will later dismiss him as an "unpredictable, violent mafioso." But in the unwritten history of the Risorgimento, Zu Piddu and his picciotti are among Garibaldi's key allies. They are the first insurgents, about to storm the Bourbon capital a month before Garibaldi has even decided whether to risk a landing in Sicily.

At nine, when the sun has chased the shadows from the face of Palmeto, the picciotti are beyond the ridge line and gathered in a narrow canyon where Bourbon police and troops never venture. The gathering coincides with similar assemblies in the hills behind Partinico, Alcamo, Carini, Misilmeri, Capaci, Torretta, and Sferracavallo. These are the Castellammare towns and villages that have organized squadre, irregular militia units. With or without Garibaldi, the squadre will march on Palermo tomorrow. Under the Bourbons, they are criminals. After their own fashion, which is drawn from no written ideology and has the blunt turn of a peasant sickle, they mean to become liberators.

*   *   *

FOR TWO MONTHS, *Zu Piddu Badalamenti and other Castellammare brigand chiefs have been in constant touch with a secret revolutionary committee that was established in Palermo at the beginning of 1860. A supply of weapons, most of them ancient but well-oiled pistols and hunting rifles, has been collected from the villagers. In Partinico, a political tinderbox where the Bourbon police are numerous and despised, a clandestine factory has produced two oak-barreled cannons in the home of Tommaso Giani, a cabinetmaker. There are also handmade grenades in the bandit armory, metal canisters filled with gunpowder, and a few small iron cannons that have been stolen from the Bourbons.*

By noon, the Castellammare squadre are heading east toward Palermo. Half a dozen columns file along the mountain ramparts enclosing the fertile scalloped valley of the Conca d'Oro, the "Golden Conch," where the capital shimmers in the afternoon haze. Francesco Viviano knows every switchback, every hidden cave, every nuance of weather on the mountain trails to Palermo.

The mountain slopes are a gentle green in April of 1860, washed into life by the short rainy season that floods the canyons behind Palermo. There are occasional shepherd's lean-tos, primitive stone shelters that are hardly distinguishable from the rock out-croppings. Francesco has spent many a night on the straw pallets that are their only furnishing. The French duke's flock ought to be in the mountains now, fattening on the spring grass. But the mead-ows are empty this day—Paolo Cocuzza may have seen to that, postponing the flock's departure from its lowland winter pas-tures—and the Castellammare squadre push forward, unobserved even by shepherds or sheep, to wait out the night near Monreale on Palermo's western outskirts.

The picciotti march again before dawn on April 4, and are half a mile from Palermo's city gates when the sun casts its first light on the Conca d'Oro and the signal for the insurrection breaks the still-ness: a clamor of bells pealing from the Gancia, the great Franciscan monastery at the edge of Palermo's harbor.

But the Bourbons have been forewarned and are ready, at least for the few dozen insurgents inside Palermo who respond to the Gancia bells; they are rounded up without firing a shot.

Outside the city walls, the squadre only know that the bells have ceased. A second signal from the Gancia, at which the picciotti are to enter Palermo, never sounds. The revolt suddenly takes on a different character, chaotic and unplanned.

This is the official report of the Palermo military command, couched in vulgar hysteria by an overwrought lieutenant general and delivered to the Bourbon Minister of State for Sicilian affairs in Naples on April 6:

> The insurrection having choked in Palermo in its initial vomit, it then spread to neighboring villages, and into the city's suburbs rushed a number of criminals, some armed and some unarmed, divided into small bands that harassed the forward army posts with the intention of forcing their way into Palermo.

In fact, Zu Piddu and his fellow chieftains are not thinking of Palermo anymore, not with an army many times the size of their seven-hundred-man force massing inside the city. The picciotti leaders wheel the squadre to the west. The new plan is to fall back on Monreale and seize its military post. But the Monreale garrison has also been reinforced, and what transpires next is one of Europe's first episodes of guerrilla warfare.

AT NOON ON APRIL 6, Francesco Viviano is on a wooded hillside overlooking the mountain road between Monreale and the hamlet of Pioppo. The trees are full of smoke, as the Castellammare irregulars level a murderous blanket of fire on Bourbon soldiers trying to move west toward Partinico. Telegraph wires and postal roads connecting Palermo to Partinico have been blown up by picciotti, along with the water-driven mills that supply Palermo with flour.

There is a thunderous crash from the slope above, and a shower of splinters; one of Tommaso Giani's wooden cannons has jammed and exploded. The Partinico cannoneer, Placido Vitrano, is fatally wounded.

Three more Castellammare picciotti are killed in the sniper's battle on the Monreale-Partinico road, which continues until April 13. A fourth man, Liborio Vallone of Alcamo, is captured, and he is executed with the hapless Palermo insurgents the next morning.

When an order is given to retreat, due south toward the mountain town of Piana dei Greci, the picciotti nearly mutiny. The Bourbon troops are pinned down, terrorized by the sniper fire. Francesco sees them cowering behind the rocks that line the margin of the road, hardly able to raise their guns toward the hillside before a withering picciotto volley answers back.

Why retreat? Why make the same mistake they made twelve years ago, which they have dearly paid for to this day?

Like many of the insurgents, Francesco Viviano cannot forget the spring of 1848, when Castellammare squadre brought the Bourbon regime to its knees in an earlier uprising. A year later, the revolt had sputtered into retreat and disarray, and the insurgents were forced to accept an amnesty from the Bourbon throne. It was the third humbling in thirty years. The grandfathers of the picciotti had mounted an abortive revolution in 1820. To the east, the cities of Catania and Siracusa had risen against the regime in 1837.

The terms and aftermath of the 1849 amnesty were harsh. The regional Sicilian Parliament, which had been established in 1812 to provide the island with a modest degree of reform and autonomy from Naples, was abolished. Crippling food taxes were imposed, and the Bourbon police and landowners undertook savage reprisals against the picciotti and their families. Zu Piddu's limp is a souvenir of the amnesty. The soles of his feet are laced with the scars of an especially thorough police interrogation.

Francesco Viviano and dozens of his fellow riflemen on the Monreale hillside date their criminal careers to the amnesty of 1848. Taxed beyond their means, harassed by the police, they had been left with few alternatives but banditry. Three failed revolu-

tions in less than two generations, followed by a decade in the law
less hills, have not prepared the picciotti for retreat today, not
when there is every apparent sign that the fourth revolution is
about to succeed. But Zu Piddu knows that ammunition is running
out, and his scouts have warned that a contingent of three thousand
more Bourbon soldiers, under General Cataldo himself, is headed
their way. Bravado is suicidal, he tells his men. Reluctantly, angrily,
the picciotti march behind Zu Piddu to Piana dei Greci, thirty-five
miles south of Palermo.

THEY REACH PIANA on the fifteenth, then almost immediately head west to Montelepre, an easily defended village nestled
into the rim of a mountain basin under the slope of Monte
Palmeto. The brigand captains again hold a council of war. The
decision is made to retreat to the Madonie, the towering mountain
chain in the center of the island that is Sicily's final, nearly impreg-
nable refuge. But the picciotti mutiny. They refuse to withdraw
from battle this time, and instead they rush northward, in a ragged
offensive assault on the port of Terrasini.

Francesco Viviano finds himself running, headlong, past his
own cottage, at noon on April 17. There is no one in the fields, no
one in the French duke's citrus groves, no time to learn for himself
if Maria and Gaetano have fled into the hills or are hiding under
the cottage's bed, from which he had arisen to liberate Palermo
exactly two weeks earlier.

The target of the assault, a Bourbon maritime post, proves to
be abandoned. Its guards have withdrawn to join a huge pincer
movement that soon envelops Terrasini.

The seven hundred Castellammare insurgents are trapped on a
narrow beach, just east of Favarotta, as dusk brings word that
General Cataldo is willing to offer a cease-fire. It is here, backed up
against the sea and vastly outnumbered, that the picciotti finally
accept Cataldo's offer.

The cease-fire, Zu Piddu insists, will not be the end of the revolution. They will not fail a fourth time. It is a pause, he tells his men.

Francesco Paolo Viviano starts up the hill. The dark streets of Favarotta, the Piazza Duomo, and the Bourbon road are full of trudging men when the campanile of Maria Santissima delle Grazie strike nine. They are "somber, without spirit," a bystander will later remember.

The beach at Favarotta around 1870. The Monk and his comrades were trapped here by the Bourbon army in April 1860, following their unsuccessful insurrection.

NINE

The Saint and the Beast

Terrasini, Sicily
January 1996

WINTER OPENED with a freak gale on the Gulf of Castellammare. From the rooftop at Paternella, the storm at mid-afternoon was a charcoal gray smudge under the low January sun, spilling over the wooded peninsula that led to Capo San Vito until it blotted the shore from view and roared across the gulf toward Terrasini and Palermo. By early evening, a brutal north wind was pounding the citrus grove, bending the youngest saplings almost flat against the ground and snapping off the limbs of older trees that were laden with fruit. Furious gusts tore through the upper branches, pelting me with ripe oranges as I carried the terrace chairs inside and shuttered the house.

An hour later, the wind was howling between the shutter slats with such unrelenting force that it threw the windows open, sending sheets of rain inside. The power grid of the entire western end of the island went down around midnight. The lights of Paternella flashed and then died, along with the small electric radiator that was my only source of warmth and the water heater for the bath-room and kitchen. I went to bed after four, drenched and fantasizing about a hot bath.

In the morning, after I finally managed to catch a few hours of sleep wrapped in a soggy comforter, the sky was as clear and calm as it had been twenty-four hours earlier. But the gulf was furious at the memory of the storm, tossing huge breakers at the limestone cliffs below Villa Fassini, and Monte Palmeto was blanketed in snow. At sea level the temperature hovered just above freezing. Even the ridges of the Conca d'Oro were snowcapped, Mike told me, when I drove to the store to help clean up the storm's damage. "Never been snow there before, not in my lifetime," he said.

Rosalia was pale, subdued. *"E molto strano,* Franky," she said. "Very strange . . ." She pulled Flavio to her bosom and wrapped her arms around him, as though she expected the wind to return and carry off her youngest child. He squirmed free and ran out the door past Bobby, who was tossing the shards of broken terra-cotta pots onto a pile of refuse.

MANY PEOPLE IN TERRASINI saw the storm as a malevolent omen. They were convinced that there was a connection between the unnatural snowfall on the Conca d'Oro and the events unfolding at a courthouse in the mountain city of Caltanisetta. Toto Riina, the Corleone boss, had gone on trial there with forty other suspects—including the absent Giovanni Brusca—for the autostrada bombing that had killed Judge Falcone in May 1992.

Riina had been arrested the following January in Palermo, when his car was stopped for a routine traffic violation, but Brusca was still on the run. Tanu Badalamenti, Riina's archenemy, was already behind bars in New York, convicted of heroin trafficking by an American court and sentenced to twenty-seven years in Sing Sing. He had been grabbed by Spanish police during a 1984 business trip to Madrid and extradited to the United States.

Roughly every decade since the 1870s, the Italian government has mounted extensive investigations of the Sicilian underworld. But the Caltanisetta trial was different, my neighbors believed, and the difference rested primarily on a single fact: Before his death, Judge Falcone himself had assembled and organized the evidence against Riina—and the judge was Sicilian.

"All the rest, they were outsiders," Mike said, referring to the century-long parade of mainland Italian prosecutors and magistrates who came south to confront "the Sicily problem."

The outsiders had conducted their inquests and trials, filed their weighty reports, convicted a few leaders, and decamped for the north. The best of them tried to penetrate below the surface, to unravel the code that obscured so much of Sicilian life, but the results were meager and sometimes laughable, a century's worth of mistranslated dialect words and misunderstood signals.

Giovanni Falcone had been raised speaking dialect in Palermo's crumbling medieval heart, the prime recruiting ground for the foot soldiers of organized crime. "I was born in the same district as many of them. I know the depths of the Sicilian soul," he pointed out to reporters.

Eloquent in the language of the *pentiti*—"the penitents"—the men of honor who had broken with Toto Riina and turned state's evidence, Falcone won their trust as no predecessor had been able to. They believed that his promises of leniency in return for testimony, of a new identity in another country when necessary, would be honored.

"I have faith in you, Judge Falcone," the *pentito* Tommaso Buscetta said to him. "But I have faith in no one else."

I TOOK THE TRAIN to Caltanisetta one day, hoping to attend Riina's trial. It was to convene in the Malaspina Palace of Justice, an unpainted pile of concrete blocks that local people dubbed "the bunker." The streets around it were closed to traffic. Nervous *Alpino* troops, drawn from Italy's elite mountain infantry division, patroled the area in full battle gear. The case was attracting substantial foreign coverage, and a line of reporters had formed outside the press gallery. To apply for admission, I presented my credentials to a soldier enclosed in a solid steel guard box. The muzzle of his rifle, pushed through a small aperture in the box, was aimed squarely at my chest until the transaction was completed.

We were all wasting time and anxiety. The trial was adjourned that morning, its next session postponed. No date was specified.

Outside on the bunker piazza, Gypsy children sold small statues of Falcone and Riina. The judge was depicted as a saint, with a golden plastic halo affixed behind his head. Horns poked through the brow of Riina.

For six hundred years, Sicilians have been bred on feverish Spanish-Catholic mysticism, and the tendency to frame contemporary events and characters in religious allegory is deeply ingrained. But few figures on the contemporary stage were better cast for an updated passion play than Toto Riina and Giovanni Falcone. In what Rosalia and Nanna took as an unmistakable echo of Christ before Good Friday, the judge had actually predicted his own death in 1992—during Easter week, no less—announcing to a startled group of reporters that "Falcone will die this year."

The Capaci bomb exploded a month later.

For his part, the Corleone don was a perfect embodiment of evil incarnate. Even his fellow *mafiosi* were shocked by his eagerness to kill. Before his happenstance arrest in Palermo, Riina had been a fugitive for twenty-three years, sentenced to nine life terms for murder. He was believed to have personally shot or strangled at least thirty-nine people and masterminded the liquidation of up to one thousand others. "If someone's finger hurts," he once remarked, "it's better to cut off his arm than take chances." Sicilians called him "the Beast."

With cold, relentless efficiency, Riina had eliminated any rival who stood in his way. If the intended victim managed to escape, the guns were turned on his family, targeting mothers and children, bombing their churches and burning their homes. Riina and Brusca "violated the most elementary rules of the system," Tommaso Buscetta charged, explaining his decision to testify. "And their behavior has dragged the organization to ruin."

With matching relentless efficiency, Falcone had hunted down and courted Riina's underworld enemies. If they would talk, the judge promised, the law would take care of the Beast. It was the Sicilian press, which shared the taste for religious allusion, that dubbed the turncoats *pentiti*. They were often driven by a hatred of Riina so profound that it left them without fear or remorse.

Buscetta had been one of the presiding bosses in the Castellammare hills. He was the first high-level *capo* to turn state's evidence. Since he began talking in the mid-1980s, hitmen had killed Buscetta's wife, his three sons, his parents, his brothers and sisters, his cousins, his aunts and uncles, his in-laws and their assorted children. Altogether, thirty-seven of Buscetta's relatives paid the price for his testimony. A second *pentito*, Salvatore Contorno, lost thirty-five family members to the gun.

But Buscetta and the other *pentiti* kept talking, even after the war had carried off nearly ten thousand soldiers of the *sistema*, along with Falcone, his wife, and his successor, Paolo Borsellino, and eighty other leading public officials.

By 1996, the *pentiti* testimony filled sixty thousand pages of depositions, notes, and documents, an exacting portrait of the underworld that charted its complex operations in microscopic detail and outlined its connections to respectable banks and eminent legislators. Most of it was the work of Falcone, compiled in hundreds of personal interviews of the men he had arrested, indicted, and then forgiven (Christlike, to the end) if they would bare their souls.

It seemed, at times, that he was directing his own murder trial from the grave, marshaling the evidence against his own killers.

Speaking behind a bullet-proof screen in Caltanisetta, two of the *pentiti* offered a chillingly exact description of the assassination. Their account appeared on the front pages of Italy's newspapers in minute-by-minute detail:

The Fiat carrying Judge Falcone and his fellow magistrate and wife, Judge Morvillo, was traveling at more than one hundred miles per hour, preceded and followed by two carloads of bodyguards, when it passed over the culvert where the explosives lay.

Falcone, who loved to drive, was at the wheel. He and Morvillo were returning to Palermo after what was intended to be a secret trip to the north.

Riina's men on the mainland sent word the instant the judges' plane lifted off from Ciampino Airport in Rome. Riina's men at Punta Raisi Airport, two miles from Terrasini, signaled the flight's arrival fifty-five minutes later.

The explosives had been hidden in a shipment of skateboards and trucked to Sicily from a warehouse in Tuscany.

Corleone gunman Giocchino La Barbera drove behind the judges' convoy, providing information on its progress by cellular telephone. On a hillside above Capaci, Brusca and another Riina lieutenant, Antonino Gioe, chatted on the phone with La Barbera and prepared the electronic triggering device.

They smoked Merit cigarettes as they waited.

The bomb went off at exactly 5:58 P.M.

Police chauffeur Giuseppe Constanza, who was supposed to have been behind the wheel, somehow survived in the passenger seat. Riina, the *pentiti* testified, complained that the explosives were detonated five seconds late.

THE TRIAL ENTRANCED my Terrasini neighbors. The *Giornale di Sicilia* was sold out within thirty minutes of its delivery to the village after a *pentito* testified. There was even a run on *La Repubblica* and *Corriere della Sera,* mainland Italian dailies that normally had few readers in provincial Sicily. The newsboy who hawked papers in the Piazza Duomo doubled his customary tip to two hundred lire.

Before Giovanni Falcone, before the *pentiti* who followed Buscetta's lead, Sicilian tribunals were convened in secret to mull over the Mafia's excesses, and Sicilian newspapers occupied themselves mainly with soccer and rumors; the *sistema* was present in every issue, but veiled in code, left to interpretation and suggestion.

After Falcone's murder, nothing was as it had been before. Suggestion was replaced by testimony, names, dates. It was what the judge would have wanted, everyone agreed on that. It was what he had lived and died for.

"Falcone was the only person who was able to understand and explain just why the Sicilian Mafia is a logical, rational, functional, and implacable social system," wrote Marcelle Padovani, another reporter at the trial, who had known the judge well.

Logical. Rational. Functional and implacable. Padovani was describing the Beast—and yet also Falcone himself, whose absorption in the Mafia war was the stuff of astonished wonder in the catatonic Italian bureaucracy.

The judge had a mission. And it went beyond simply putting Riina and Badalamenti behind bars. If you knew what the *sistema* was all about, Falcone insisted—if you studied it, and exposed its hidden bones—the war could be pursued in the light. It could be won.

Across the island, Sicilians digested and discussed the trial compulsively. But it was a compulsion rooted in anxiety, the profound uneasiness of a people who were disposed to darkness and communicated instinctively in code.

TEN

A Burglary at Paternella

-+->-<-+-

AS THE BRUSCA MANHUNT intensified and the Riina trial
made its stormy passage into a new year, I divided my research days
between futile morning excursions to the state archives in Palermo,
which were often closed without warning, and equally futile afternoons in the Terrasini records annex.

I felt at times that the real Sicily was as unchanging and timeless as the imagined Sicily of my childhood, but the effect was one
of suffocation. If Mike spotted me from his sidewalk table at Di
Maggio's, making my way across the Piazza Duomo toward the
annex, I could be dragged into hours of meandering conversation
over an *amaro* or coffee. When he wasn't on the road, Mike spent
half or more of each day with his friends on the piazza, one of a
dozen or so groups of men who met there with the predictability of
Maria Santissima delle Grazie's bells. The same men, forever at the
same tables. It was a fixed portrait, so nearly motionless that it
might have been an etching.

I never understood what went on at the *caffe* tables; often, fifteen or twenty minutes would pass without anyone saying a word.
When a latecomer arrived, he was greeted with huge enthusiasm—
shouts of joy, the double kiss on the cheek, a slapping handshake
that resembled a basketball player's high-five delivered at waist
level—as though he had returned that moment from decades
abroad. Yet I knew that he had been at Di Maggio's yesterday and
was all but certain to be there tomorrow.

This was another of Sicily's infinite paradoxes: extraordinary events transpired there—the phenonemal mayhem of Riina's struggle with Badalamenti, the consolidation of a global underworld empire—while it seemed that nothing ever happened at all. Sicilians were caught, always, the novelist Lampedusa maintained, between the extremes of immobilizing torpor and shattering violence.

I wondered at Mike's ability to move back and forth between the autostrada and the *caffè*, between the American restlessness that fueled his manic buying trips and the numb Sicilian patience that hung over the piazza. American or not, I couldn't begin to match his energy on the road, and I certainly lacked his Sicilian capacity for boredom. By my second month at Paternella, I took to parking the car several blocks from the piazza, simply to avoid running into Mike and his friends. Half-drowned, I struggled on with my research.

If I had learned a great deal about the Monk, it was mostly by inference: unlocking the riddle of the red sash, following the Castellammare irregulars into battle. When I woke in the Paternella morning, I looked out at the same landscape of citrus grove and pasture that another Francesco Viviano had awakened to in 1860. That meant something, to be sure, something that transcended the merely factual. But as a human being, rather than a symbolic character in a lost drama, an individual moved by his own private demons, my namesake remained elusive. I knew much about him without really knowing him, and there were many questions to answer before I could pretend to such an understanding.

When did he die? How? Where? Why? And who was Domenico Valenti, his neighbor at Paternella and his alleged killer? Apart from the reference to a Valenti farmstead on the old military map, I had come across no allusions to the man named by my grandfather as the Monk's assassin. There was no Domenico Valenti in the phone directory who might be his direct descendant. There was no Domenico Valenti among the dead registered in the municipal annex, no Domenico among the fathers of Valenti children in the village birth rolls after 1850.

MY SCHEDULE, juggling the roles of amateur historian and foreign correspondent, made it difficult to sustain focused attention on these questions. Every month, I took an Alitalia flight from the airport at Punta Raisi to the mainland, then flew onward to an assignment that left me drained on my return to Terrasini.

January was grueling. The paper had sent me to eastern Anatolia via Istanbul to report on the escalating war against Kurdish insurgents on the Iraqi frontier. The borderland was a rolling, treeless plateau, cut by the upper reaches of the Tigris River. Its low, barren hilltops were dotted with the tent camps of refugees whose villages had been bombed. Squadrons of Turkish F-16s passed overhead almost hourly, and the taxi that I hired in the rain-swamped central marketplace of Diyarbakir, the regional capital, was shadowed in the countryside by army surveillance helicopters.

It was a scene that conjured up too many others in my wanderings: blasted villages, warplanes, refugee camps, tanks patroling the streets of a tense provincial city. The signature picture of our time.

But it was also a picture of the Monk's time, I thought, save for the updated military technology. Hindsight was one of the liabilities of looking too closely at the past; it allowed little reason for optimism about the human condition.

The columns of Turkish soldiers trudging along the highways east of Diyarbakir might have been the Bourbon troops who marched toward Monreale in April 1860 as the *picciotti* took up their positions behind trees and rocks. The *picciotti* were the natural cousins of the Kurds, not simply in their guerrilla tactics, but in their violent frustration. Like the Kurds, Sicilians were an identifiable nation, a distinctive people who had always been governed by someone else's state. "For two thousand five hundred years, we've been a colony," the Prince of Salina says of Sicilians in *The Leopard;* he could well have been speaking of the Kurds. That was the heart of their mutual problem. It had led them both into the desert of endless revolution, into the murky underworld where ancient grievance shaded into modern crime.

They were partners in that underworld now. Many of the leading Sicilian dons had evolved into bankers, financing the narcotics and arms trade and laundering the profits, while others handled the actual smuggling in return for money and arms. The foot soldiers of a Kurdish *mafiya,* based in Turkey and Germany, were among the major actors in this restructuring, moving contraband across borders and enforcing contracts. They were where the Sicilian clans had been a generation ago, just as the Kurdish sharpshooters picking off Turkish infantrymen in Anatolia were where the *picciotti* had been in 1860.

Sicily, as another of its writers, Leonardo Sciascia, observed, is at once a geographical fact and a metaphor.

Sicily-as-metaphor was the murderous tribalism that had rearranged the landscape of Yugoslavia into a crazy quilt of warlord fiefdoms, financed by drug money and policed by thugs. It was the presidents of half the nations of Latin America and the Caribbean, and the opposition leaders of the other half.

It was a Paris-based newsletter that monitored the activities of the Kurdish *mafiya*—along with a Russian mafia, a Montenegran mafia, an Albanian mafia, a Nigerian mafia, a Vietnamese mafia, a Kosovar mafia, an Israeli mafia, an Armenian mafia, an Azerbaijani mafia, and a Turkish mafia. They combined in elaborate joint ventures with the Sicilians and with each other, trafficking in stolen arms, narcotics, prostitutes, and clandestine immigrants, or formed partnerships with Chinese triads and the Colombian drug cartels.

But Sicily-as-metaphor was also the wholesale corruption of the affluent world's political class at the new century's opening, announced in spiraling disclosures of money-laundering schemes, bribery scandals, and unexplained deposits to Swiss bank accounts. The money-laundering alone, according to a 1999 report by the International Monetary Fund, amounted to more than $500 billion per year, and perhaps as much as $1.5 trillion.

As the milennium turned, Sicily-as-metaphor was a worldview, embraced nowhere more fervently than in the United States, that pictured the state as enemy, taxes as oppression, and personal armories of handguns and assault rifles as an inalienable right.

I heard echoes of Sicily on every news assignment, on every battlefield. I was haunted by them.

PETRA SAID THAT a bit of haunting was exactly what I needed. She was a Cherokee Indian herbalist from San Francisco and my unlikely fellow guest at the Hotel Empress Zoe in Istanbul. Her suitcases were full of dried medicinal seeds and blossoms that could be found only in Turkey; she spent weeks scouring the bazaars for them. Over a bottle of *raki* in the hotel bar, I told her about the Monk and my lagging search. Petra, who said she also worked occasionally as a "spiritual consultant and medium," was fascinated that I was now living on the very land where my namesake was born.

"That's no accident," she announced. "The Monk is trying to communicate with you. I'm sure of it, and I am going to explain what you need to do."

She folded her arms, and smiled a Cheshire-cat grin that made me squirm. I've been a dedicated skeptic all of my life, but my eerie landing in the Paternella citrus grove—and its chance identification as the ancestral Viviano homestead on the old map—were as unsettling to me as they were illuminating for Petra.

"Here's the routine," she said. "Place a lit candle on a table next to your bed the night you return to Sicily. Under the candle, put some memento of the Monk."

I said that I had no memento of him. Petra hesitated. "Well, okay, forget the memento. It sounds as though he's really anxious to get in touch with you and will agree to overlook a few details.

Anyhow, it's the last part that's important. Just a second, I'll be right back."

She went off to her room and returned a few minutes later with a small bag of leaves.

"This is mugwort. It goes on the table, beside the candle. You might say it's the 'active ingredient' in the seance."

I thanked Petra and put the bag of mugwort in my pocket. But I had no intention of lighting a candle for the Monk when I returned to Sicily. Not so much out of doubt that her advice would work, as in fear that it might.

I TELEPHONED S. from a post office near the Blue Mosque and told her about Petra's advice. I always called S. when I was on assignment, whatever the cost. The sound of her low, throaty voice was as necessary to me as food and sleep. It was connection in a world of disconnection.

In my imagination, the calls took on a material solidity, as though I could follow S.'s words as they rose from her sitting room in a rambling Victorian house in San Francisco, bounced off the polished dish of a satellite, then wound their way eastward through a maze of trunk lines and crackling switchboards to the phone booth where I shouted her name into a plastic handset. When the calls failed, when her words were lost somewhere between satellite and trunk line, I felt myself spinning after them into space.

S. was an editor who had been helping me to shape my sentences in 1979, the year my marriage collapsed, when the sentences grew more and more intimate and the cloud of personal failure and guilt that swirled around me began to evaporate under her sun. She was half-Italian, half-Portuguese, but her face had the sculpted features of a Mayan temple relief: high cheekbones, aquiline nose, broad sensual lips.

We traveled together for a decade, when we were freelancing most of the time and travel was a roller-coaster ride between verminous hotel rooms that we paid for ourselves and luxury suites if a magazine was picking up the bill. She stuffed huge manuscripts into the single piece of carry-on luggage that she allowed herself on the road, red-penciling awkward phrases on decrepit Indian trains or through bone-shattering overnight bus trips in China, then airmailing the corrections to American publishers.

I grew to rely on S., on everything about her, as I tried to fathom opaque interviews with business magnates in Hong Kong or rebel warlords in the Philippines. She read every word that I wrote and never doubted that what I did was worth doing, or that it could be better, and would be with time and concentration. S. understood me, my possibilities and my limits, as no one else ever had. She also understood herself as few people do, and that was at once the fusion point of my attraction to her and the force that would pull us in separate directions.

In 1955, when S. was an eight-year-old living in the farmhouse that her Portuguese grandfather built on reclaimed marshland in northern California, her father suddenly collapsed on the kitchen floor as she and her sister were making sandwiches for lunch. They called a doctor, who drove to the farm and said there was nothing to worry about. "Your father just needs a little rest." A few hours later, S. watched him writhe in agony in his bed, heave into a deep shudder as his heart stopped, and then fall still.

Her mother was in the hospital that week. It was she, and not her husband, who was reckoned to be fatally ill, a tumor pressing inexorably into her brain. S.'s mother promised her and her twelve-year-old sister that she would be all right, that she wouldn't leave them. But five weeks later, she too was dead.

When I was falling in love with S., conjuring her image on the journeys that I took alone, to the first of the wars that would so preoccupy me later, I often pictured her in the years just after her parents' deaths. In my imagination, she sat pensively on a grassy knoll, staring out over the Sonoma flatland where her grandfather's dairy cows grazed. Taking the measure of pain and loss. This is not a picture that S. described. She told me just once about her father's death and her mother's promise, and she never returned to the story again. The picture was my invention, my effort to set her drama in place and time, twenty years before I tried to do the same thing with the fragments of my own family drama.

From her eighth year on, S. knew with absolute clarity that she never wanted children. She had weathered the desert and moved on.

I had not.

I LANDED AT PUNTA RAISI on January 20, retrieved the Peugeot from the airport parking lot, and headed for the *salumeria* to pick up my mail and check in with the Corteses. Alice was behind the cash register. She winced when she saw me, and mumbled a peculiar, "Hello, Franky." I could hear bad news coming.

"There's a little problem," she said. "Somebody broke into Paternella when you were in Turkey."

Bobby had driven by the house the week before to pick some oranges. He found a shattered rear window, but wasn't sure what was missing.

It was obvious, when I got home and took inventory, that the burglary was a professional job. Much too professional to be explained by the disappearance of an old portable radio, a Panasonic boom box I'd bought ten years ago in New York for sixty dollars, that appeared to be my sole loss. The burglars had cut a neat hole in the rear bedroom shutter, then just as neatly cracked open a pane of glass, unlocked the window, and climbed in. There was money in the bedroom closet, a wad of banknotes in several currencies that I kept around for unexpected assignments. There were backup cameras and a bag of lenses in plain view on the desk. There was a laptop computer on the shelf. Nothing was gone except the old Panasonic.

In Terrasini, people offered a hodgepodge of theories. The most popular was that the intruders were amorous teenagers, using what they took to be an unoccupied summer retreat. Sicilians live with their parents until they marry, Mike reminded me. "Nowhere to go except somebody's country house. You know how kids are at that age. They got no sense, just . . ."

He stroked his chin, searching for the right word.

"Appetites?" I offered.

"Yeah, that's it, appetites. They probably grabbed the radio after they had their fun, just because they had an appetite for it and it's easy to carry."

But I knew that he didn't really believe it, and as far as I could tell, the bed hadn't been disturbed. A pair of boxer shorts I'd left atop the blanket was still lying there.

A disconcerting thought occurred to me. It was the possibility that my interest in an underworld assassination, however long ago, had attracted these visitors.

THE LOGJAM IN MY RESEARCH broke quite suddenly, three days after I returned from Turkey. I had been rooting around in the annex, with no particular success and modest expectations. There were still details of interest to me in the municipal records, more in the way of capturing a sense of the past than a sense of the Monk himself. The archives were the coded script for other dramas, as well as mine.

Leafing through the mortality ledger for 1919, in the faint hope of locating a Domenico Valenti, I had come across page after page of German names. The entries were for Austrian soldiers, the annex clerk told me, World War I military prisoners who had been shipped to Sicily in 1917 and cooped up in a Terrasini warehouse.

Notwithstanding his absorption in the *Gazzetta dello Sport,* the clerk knew the village records better than anyone else. He had been consulting them for twenty years, mostly on behalf of fellow clerks in Germany, Switzerland, or America who were updating their own municipal records of Sicilian immigrants. It was my bad luck that he had no recollection of the Viviano and Valenti files I was hunting; they were too remote, half a century or so older than the Austrian entries, to have come to the clerk's professional attention.

"It seems that the Allied generals forgot completely about these prisoners," he continued. "In all of the confusion, our officials here couldn't get anybody in Rome to take responsibility for the matter, to decide what to do with them, after the armistice was signed."

Then abruptly, it was too late. The Austrians had died by the drove in the warehouse when the catastrophic Spanish influenza swept the island and the world. They were just boys, adolescents of sixteen or seventeen who had been drafted during the war's final offensive on the northern Italian front, then captured and carried off by an epidemic that killed more than twenty million Europeans between 1918 and 1920.

While we were talking about the Austrians, I noticed the worn spine of a ledger, buried under the pile of newspapers on the useless photocopy machine. *"Ma, che cosa?"* I said, pointing at the ledger.

The clerk shrugged and answered that he didn't know what it was. "Let's just see," he said, and pulled it out, sending a mountain of *Gazzeta* issues tumbling to the floor. He stared down at the mess, puffing thoughtfully on a Marlboro, and handed me the ledger.

It was a marriage register for the year 1855, more than thirty years older than the next volume in the series on the annex shelves. It should have been with the other inaccessible ledgers, locked up in the storeroom. The index was intact, and under the name "Viviano, F.," it referred the reader to the entry for May 14.

The entry recorded the marriage of Francesco Paulo Viviano, age thirty, to his cousin Maria Bommarito, age thirty-five. In a single stroke, it provided many of the facts I lacked, including the Monk's exact year of birth, 1825, and the names of his own parents, Gaetano Viviano and Vincenza Bommarito. It was signed with the awkwardly penned "X" of an illiterate.

A small note had been written in the right margin by the village clerk. Under the heading "additional documents," it read: "Medical certificate presented by the groom, attesting to the death of his first wife, Antonina Randazzo."

Her name, as much as Domenico Valenti's, was a cypher. The Monk's first marriage had been forgotten by the family he raised with Maria Bommarito. Weeks would pass before I knew any more.

THAT NIGHT, another storm boiled across the Gulf of Castellammare. I woke with a start, to the shriek of a fierce wind howling through the lemon trees. To the left of my bed, at the window, a figure in dark, flowing robes swayed back and forth.

I sat up and tried to scream. My throat was so dry with fear that no sound was produced. "Who are you?" I eventually croaked. "Who are you?"

But I knew that it could only be the Monk.

Somehow, I fell back into an agitated sleep. When morning finally arrived, and the sun broke through the retreating clouds, my brown bathrobe dangled from the window shutter where I had hung it the night before, swaying back and forth with occasional gusts that still rattled the house. The window was half open, blown ajar by the storm. A pool of rainwater covered the ledge and dripped onto the floor, soaking a pair of socks I'd

Monacu the cat on the terrace at Paternella. Photo by Chiew Terriere.

tossed there. I walked out to the terrace to hang them on the clothesline.

A small, wiry black cat, with a splash of white across his chest and face, was cowering under the window. I'd noticed him before, scavenging in the garbage containers at the entrance to the Paternella lane. He sidled up to my legs, purring. The storm had been hard on the cat, too. I went inside and opened a can of tuna fish for him.

The cat seldom wandered far from the house after the storm, and soon took to sleeping in the bedroom. I named him Monacu.

ELEVEN

Dark Franky

➤ ➤ ⟨ ⟨

Vukovar, Croatia
August 1992

NOT LONG BEFORE MY GRANDFATHER'S DEATH, a chronic childhood dream had returned to plague me. It was set in my grandparents' house in Detroit. Lost in a book, or in a dream within the dream, I looked across their living room and saw a stairway that had never been there before. It was at once ominous and irresistible.

I turned around, wondering if anyone else in the family had noticed; the house was always full of aunts and uncles and cousins, somebody at the piano, a song threading its way through the shouts and wails of the younger kids. But only Grandma Angelina paid attention as I walked toward the staircase.

She smiled and embraced me once very tightly, and said, "Franky, don't forget us!"

At the top of the stairs I found an immense room, much older than the rest of the house, its stained wooden floors piled high with tattered furniture, crates, and moldy paintings. A little boy sat against the wall, opening one of the crates. Four decades after the dream first came to me, he was still the same boy, a friend who had suddenly vanished—from the neighborhood, from my life—when we were around six or seven. Had he died? Had his family moved away? I couldn't muster the courage to ask my parents what had happened until years later. When I finally brought the subject up with my mother, she had no memory of my friend.

He beckoned me over, and the two of us set to opening more crates. Like the room, everything in them was old and worn. There were moth eaten clothes, tarnished medals and coins, faded pictures of people I didn't know but who were strangely familiar. Then, as suddenly as in life, my friend was gone and I was alone, and yet another staircase loomed at the far end of the attic. I walked to the foot of it, and looked up into an even larger room, vaulted with blackened, exposed beams.

A dim light shone from it, and although I was frightened this time, I was driven up the staircase by a compulsion that made it impossible to turn back. From the uppermost step I could see piles of trunks, and beyond them a door, cracked slightly open.

The dream always ended there, as I climbed into the shadows of the second attic.

Sicily lay beyond the door, I believe, or at least the cathartic Sicily I now sought, where a murder had ocurred at the end of an unmapped road.

It was only one itinerary among many that could have been read into the staircase and the attic; the fate of my childhood friend no doubt offered another. Even dreams and their crusty symbols offer choices. But Sicily was the door that I chose to enter when the attic dream returned, the setting in which I would frame my search, my reporter's narrative, with its three principal characters linked across five generations. The Francesco who became the Monk. My grandfather. And Franky, me. Their heir and their pursuer.

IN MY MID-FORTIES, alone on the razor's edge, I realized that I wanted my grandfather's life. The life Paolinu Viviano chose, deliberately, in the back room of a St. Louis gambling house, then methodically built in Michigan over the next fifty years. The basket of fish in Harlem. The Detroit pushcart. The horse and wagon and the Republic truck. The family that grew with the business, six children between 1918 and 1928. First Giuseppe, named after the Monk's son, then in quick order, my father Gaetano, Grazia, Pietro, Salvatore, and Angelina—Joe and Tommy, Grace and Pete, Sal and Babe. The American family of Angelina Tocco and Frank P. Viviano.

I wanted to be *him,* the gentle patriarch I remember from the early sixties, seated in a wing chair in the living room at Christmas.

My grandmother is at the piano and my cousins Little Joanne and Anthony from Brooklyn, Aunt Babe and Uncle Vince's kids, are halfway through their annual song-and-dance act. This year, the act is Steve Lawrence and Eydie Gorme. Anthony flubs a step, pirouettes in the wrong direction; without missing a beat, Little Joanne reverses her own turn to cover for him. The Brooklyn cousins are our Broadway, permanently installed at the top of the bill, ahead of my brother Sam's comedy routine with a ventriloquist's dummy and cousin Angela's guitar solo. I stand off in a corner with Big Joanne, trying not to admire them. We are in our self-conscious teens and haven't performed for the past two Christmases.

I'm "Dark Franky" now, to distinguish me from "Red Franky," the carrot-topped son of Uncle Sal and Aunt Santina. There are eighteen grandchildren in the living room, my father and ten aunts and uncles, Grandpa and Grandma. Thirty-one of us.

My mother isn't there, an absence that became more and more common in the late fifties and was permanent by 1962. Things are not right between my parents, and haven't been for as long as I can remember, which is why Sam and I have spent many months in the care of our grandparents. It's better that Mom isn't there, I think, without daring to say it aloud. This way there will be no screaming matches between my mother and father in front of everyone else, or between my mother and Grandma Angelina over my father.

My grandfather has rough, beard-stubbled cheeks by the end of

Christmas day, and his kisses smell of cigars and brandy mixed with the fading scent of Old Spice cologne.

When the music ends, the kids line up before him according to age, Baby Sal and Betsy first, held in their mothers' arms. Grandpa has a wad of five-dollar bills in his left hand and one by one, he peels them off and pushes them into the boys' pockets and the girls' purses.

"Okay, I'm broke, everybody go home," he says when the line reaches Big Joanne and me.

"Franky, talk to Grandma, she's lonely," he whispers in my ear. Which means that he knows I am too old to feel comfortable with this ritual, even if I love it too much—I love him too much—to let it go.

The thirty-one people in that living room were the measure of my populous childhood, the measure of a fierce embrace. I longed for that embrace when I was in my forties, alone on the road. That was the operative number now, as I saw it: one. In my friends' estimation, my life was a resounding success, charted in books and Pulitzer Prize nominations and a foreign correspondent's dog-eared passport. But the measurement that counted for me was the heart-wrenching decline from thirty-one to one. Privately, I regarded myself as a kind of lab specimen in this regard, an experiment whose object was to play out the richest fantasies of my generation in America—the baby-boom generation, the sixties generation—and see where they led. I knew very well that my life was a fantasy made real for most people my age, an extraordinary adventure. How could I explain that it seemed empty to me? An accident. It was a career that grew out of wanderlust and false starts—as a law school dropout, a would-be academic, a bored magazine editor—to produce a failed marriage and a recklessly unmoored existence.

Between 1989 and 1995, I had lived in eleven apartments. They were usually sublets, short-term arrangements with owners who were trying to sell their flats or who were spending a few months abroad and needed someone to water the plants. Over the same six years, I spent more than a thousand nights on the road in hotel rooms. There had never been a reason for a normal lease, or furniture, because I was always on the move.

Motion had become my life, my career. I specialized in a reporter's version of the road saga, in which the journey itself was the story: frontier crossings, chance encounters with strangers, unexpected developments. The articles succeeded, when I was at my best, in representing the ground-level experience of events. It was the immediate shock, the "feel" of history, that I was after. The road taught me to look elsewhere than official interviews for the truth.

But I recognized, as I grew older, that the road was no place to live. Having achieved the great fantasy of my generation, I found myself living nowhere.

BEFORE THE LATE AUTUMN OF 1990, I had never thought about children. It was not a matter of indecision, an inability to make up my mind about whether or not I wanted a home and a family. It was something much worse: to have reached the age of forty-three without thinking about a family. Not in a ten-year marriage that failed, in large part because of my wandering. Not in the long, passionate relationship with S. that followed it. I never thought about children until the second week of October in 1990.

I know the date, because it was then that I met L., a professor who sat in on a talk that I gave at her New England university. The subject was the Chinese democracy movement, which I had covered from its hopeful first days to the terrible debacle at Tiananmen Square. The university had organized a colloquium on "China in turmoil" and asked me to speak. Professor L. wasn't especially interested in China, but she was free that evening—the kids were at their father's—and the mutual friend on the faculty who arranged my speaking engagement invited her to join us for dinner. I saw L. again the next evening and several after it.

She was divorced and had an eleven-year-old son and a seven-year-old daughter. They lived in a red-brick house with a baby grand piano in the living room. The piano was covered with framed snapshots: the boy in a hockey uniform, the girl hanging a tin Santa on a Christmas tree.

I made two more trips to New England to visit them. The routines of their day rolled before me, vignettes of a life I had forgone without ever acknowledging that I had made a choice. The children's laughter and wails over breakfast. The professor waiting in her car outside an elementary school, in the waning light of a February afternoon. Reheated macaroni-and-cheese in the kitchen. An evening at a hockey tournament, L. gasping when her son lost his balance on a rush at goal and fell headfirst into the net, the daughter squirming on the bleacher seat next to me.

Just an ordinary life, L. said, and by comparison with mine, it was. But the fundamental beauty of that life, its breathtaking ordinary grace, unhinged me.

The morning after the hockey tournament, I took the bus to Boston and caught a Swissair flight to Zurich, then another across the Mediterranean to Jordan. The Gulf War was winding down. The Yugoslav war was about to begin. I never went back to New England after that.

But I carried its images of an ordinary life everywhere: to the empty wastes between Amman and Baghdad. To a distant river bank in the Balkans.

THERE WERE TWO OF US in a rented Toyota, an American reporter and a Dutch photographer. Eighty miles north of Sarajevo on a sweltering August morning in 1992, we parked the car in a city without a single building left whole. Every home, every school, every church was flattened, pitted with shrapnel, or burned to the ground.

The Yugoslav army had opened up with heavy artillery from across the River Danube, when Croat nationalists overran Serb neighborhoods in a seesaw battle between rival militias. The guns fired day and night, over a four-month siege, until there were no more Croats left alive in the city. A shoe factory on the bluff above the river had been hit squarely by a round of 155-mm shells. The streets were littered with sandals and loafers.

This was Vukovar, Croatia, three months before my last day with my grandfather.

A Serb policeman agreed to walk us through the remains of his beat. He showed us the cellar where he had hidden during the Croat assault and the shelling, dodging out once or twice a week to forage for something to eat. Half a dozen of his neighbors were still living on the sites of their former homes, burrowed into collapsed apartment blocks. One of them was a gaunt man, probably in his late forties, who stared out at us from a crater. A plate of canned tomatoes and dry bread sat on the ground before him. The woman in the ruin next door told us she had put the plate there, "but he won't touch it. He prefers to die." The man's family was under the rubble, she said. A wife and two daughters.

Just down the street, a contraband dealer had set up shop. Militias from both sides were blocking relief shipments from entering the battle zone, and there was nowhere else to buy food. He complained, in English, that his inventory was down to "three cases of fucking Coca Cola and ten kilos of beans."

On a hill that rose over the city center, the rubble gave way to a raw landscape of half-filled trenches; pieces of clothing jutted out from the dirt. Hundreds of bodies lay in the trenches, thrown into a common grave and hastily covered. "No one knows which of the bodies are Serb and which are Croat," the policeman said. I wondered if it mattered to him, but didn't have the courage to ask. Jeremy, the photographer, shot several rolls of film, while I spoke to anyone who was willing to talk about what had happened. The policeman translated.

As dusk neared, he told us we'd better leave, that "Vukovar is very dangerous at night." Amid the utter destruction around us, his warning sounded hollow. But he repeated it for emphasis, and refused to leave us until we got into the car and headed toward the frontier, where we expected to check in at a UN observation post before midnight.

A militia company swept down from the bluffs just as we reached the crossing. They were from a renegade Serb detachment, men who had lost their own families in the war and gone on a blind rampage that left gutted homes and mutilated corpses everywhere along the west bank of the Danube. There wasn't much doubt what they meant to do with us. From the wheel of the Toyota, I remember gazing out at the broad, fertile plain beyond the river's far shore, where the war had yet to arrive. A tractor moved dozily across the horizon, a small black silhouette inching forward under the crimson sunset sky.

Three of the Serbs climbed onto the rear of a Jeep, trained their Kalashnikovs on the Toyota, and ordered us to follow them. A second Jeep brought up the rear, penning us in. I drove to what I expected to be our execution site: a wrecked Orthodox church, its steeple toppled over the road. Tovarnik, the village that surrounded the church, was Serb. The Croats had shelled it a year ago, hammering it into a pile of shattered brick and burned timber. Nothing had been rebuilt.

We were seated in a cinder-block shed behind the fallen steeple, under the guard of a grotesquely fat, bare-chested psychopath in jeans who compulsively loaded and unloaded his revolver, pointing it at our heads or at the wall behind us and fiddling with the trigger. When we tried to speak with him, in the pidgin German that was our common tongue, he only laughed. The calm of absolute powerlessness overcame us.

A STRANGE, DISCONNECTED NARRATIVE passed through my mind in those hours, not the unreeling of a whole life, but a sequence of random memories and thoughts that didn't seem to add up to anything. I was conscious of that: the randomness, the abrupt shifts between the deeply reflective and the banal.

I worried about the rental car. Would it be returned? I worried about Jeremy, about how terrible the next few minutes would be if they shot me first. I planned a lead paragraph for the story I'd file if I lived to write it. I imagined the obituary if I didn't: "CHRONICLE REPORTER KILLED IN YUGOSLAVIA," probably with a picture, in the lower right corner of the front page. I hoped S. would hear about it before she saw the paper. I wanted her to remember me. I wanted her to forget me. Images of that living room in New England flooded in, until I was distracted by a jagged purple birthmark on the gunman's neck and couldn't take my eyes off it.

I thought again about the story I would have written, the rational balance sheet of political disputes and cultural hostilities that was supposed to make sense of the inexplicable in a thousand-word newspaper dispatch. It was an exercise in illusion. There was no explaining the fratricidal madness of Yugoslavia. There was no explaining what compelled me to witness it. There were only questions.

How had Serbs and Croats and Bosnian Muslims been reduced to leveling each other's homes, slaughtering each other's children? Why was I seated in a ruined church with a gun aimed at my head when I might have been selling oranges in the midwest, with a gaggle of my own children in a big, raucous home?

The questions pursued me through the rescue that was engineered by a Russian colonel, whose U. N. troops had seen our capture and surrounded the church. In the months and years that followed, the questions that seized me in Tovarnik, waiting for a bullet, cycled like a looped tape through my head.

In December, 1994, I signed a lease on an apartment near the Place St. Michel in Paris, with a terrace that looked out on the Cathedral of Notre Dame. I acquired two marble bistro tables and four chairs, two halogen floor lamps, a couch, and a bed. I even bought a washing machine, along with a four-burner stove and oven, an electric espresso maker, and a compact disc player.

At heart, I wanted my grandfather's life, sixty-eight years with one woman, a house where children tap-danced and sang show tunes, and I knew that a washing machine and a view of Notre Dame couldn't make that happen.

Less than a year later, I gave up the apartment and put the furniture in storage. I had hardly used any of it. I continued living in sublet apartments and hotel rooms, with my unused furniture piled up in a warehouse. Not in a bachelor's defiant independence, but in a middle-aged loner's despair at unanswered questions.

The questions drove me to Sicily. In search of a namesake. In search of an elemental tale, a drama that I shared with a murdered highwayman in the robes of a Monk. Not because the violence of his life was reenacted in mine. I was too much the rationalist to accept that. My history, as much as his, was dictated by a conjunction of public events and private choices, my own conscious and deliberate choices, as muddled as they proved to be. The link between us was not fate, I told myself. It was a frame, embracing a portrait of one Francesco Viviano that drew on another. This is what I needed to believe. And up to a point, it was true.

TWELVE

The Frenchman's Palace

Western Sicily
January 1996

ON A SUNDAY MORNING in the last week of January, Mike swung by Paternella in his Lancia and honked the horn outside the iron fence that surrounded the citrus grove. He had a key to the padlocked chain on the gate, but never carried it. There was some principle at stake that I couldn't quite grasp, because he also refused to carry a key to his house in the village. Whenever we arrived there together, Mike rang the bell and waited impatiently for Rosalia or Nanna to open the door, shuffling from foot to foot as though he were a postman on a tight schedule. If nobody answered, we'd leave and return later.

It was after seven when he pulled up at the villa, late by Mike's standards. He was usually out of bed at dawn, puttering around in the *salumeria* or bullying his car down the autostrada toward some rumored fire sale in Marsala or Castelvetrano. Yet he seldom turned in before midnight.

"My dad doesn't believe in house keys or sleep," Alice said, when I brought up the subject of her father's habits. "He doesn't believe in credit cards or checking accounts, either," she added.

I'd noticed that, too. Everything Michele Cortese bought, including the discounted products for the store, was purchased in cash. All the family's calls were made from a payphone on the wall behind Alice's cash register; she maintained a large supply of two-hundred lire pieces to feed it.

The *salumeria* was in a state of chaotic transition, as usual, this time from grocery store—delicatessen—nursery to beer-garden-and-sandwich-shop. Wooden picnic tables were piled up in a corner of the parking lot, ready for arrangement under *caffè* parasols when spring arrived. Inside, Bobby was hard at work on the business plan for a hardware store, an idea he'd picked up from *Millionaire* magazine. In slow hours behind the *salumeria* counter, he read every word of *Millionaire,* an Italian monthly that profiled successful entrepreneurs and offered shortcut tips to a quick fortune.

I sometimes helped him draft letters to international franchisers—hamburger chains, computer outlets, discount hardware retailers—who advertised in *Millionaire.* They never responded. For reasons Bobby understood all too well, there were virtually no chain stores in Sicily; the multinationals had heard of Tanu Badalamenti and Toto Riina.

But the hardware idea had merit, I thought. Although half the houses on the Castellammare coast seemed to be under permanent construction, the closest shop offering more than a rudimentary selection of tools and supplies was in Palermo.

There were other brainstorms in the wind. The storeroom next to the Cortese home was no longer a storeroom. It had suddenly been cleaned up. Mike's collection of abandoned refrigerators and Nanna's old pant-suits had been removed and an office installed in their place, complete with a large executive desk and bookshelves. Pietro Serra, Alice's fiancé, sat behind the desk, doodling in a notebook. A sign over the door to the street read "Management Services and Consulting." I was fairly certain that this idea, too, had come from *Millionaire* magazine.

"What's up?" I asked Mike, trying to sound nonchalant as I fumbled with the padlock.

The Lancia shook and shuddered in neutral at the gate, sending waves of black smoke into the lemony air of Paternella. It was clearly in its death throes, and I'd developed severe misgivings about our long morning rides. The last time I'd accompanied Mike to Castelvetrano, where we loaded three hundred kilos of half-priced prosciutto into the trunk, the backseat and the space around my legs, the frame of the car had scraped against the tires all the way home. The trip left us both sick from the mixed odors of cured ham and burnt rubber.

Mike's restlessness always had troubled Rosalia, and the Lancia's condition provided her with a weapon to brandish in the name of Sicilian immobility. Personally, she refused to get into the car at all, on the grounds that it was *"una bara fitusa di diaulu,"* as she put it one evening. A dirty coffin, fit for the devil. Her choice of words gave me pause—and infuriated Mike. He stomped away and made a point of not showing up for dinner the next three nights.

"I work like hell all the time, Frank. But my family, they don't know how to be grateful," he said, when I sat down next to him at Di Maggio's and tried to nudge him into joining me for a bowl of Nanna's pasta at his own home.

After Mike resumed his dinner appearances, an uncomfortable chill reigned at the table for many days, broken only by Nanna's monologues on recent visitors from outer space, the latest marriage woes of Monaco's royal family, or the treachery of Prince Charles. Thanks to the Italian tabloids, she could hold forth for hours on extraterrestrials, as well as on the busy lives of the Prince of Wales and the daughters of Prince Rainier. Mike had ignored her and ate his pasta without speaking.

But he was in a buoyant mood this morning. "What's up, huh!" he parroted me. Mike loved it when his kids or I used American slang. "I'm gonna show you something very special you never seen before. That's what's up," he said.

It was as close as I ever arrived at the specifics of our destinations. I'd learned not to press for more information. When Mike said something was interesting or, even better, "special," it invariably proved to be so. I did win a minor victory, however, or a major one if Rosalia's characterization of the Lancia was taken at face value. He agreed to leave his car at Paternella and let me drive. I put a dish of cat food on the terrace for Monacu, who had run off into the citrus grove when the Lancia belched and shuddered up to the gate, and we headed west.

THE SUN WAS ALREADY WARMING the pastures, a great crimson globe shimmering over Punta Raisi, when we reached the junction with the road to Montelepre. Mike gestured for me to turn left, into the hills. It was hard to believe that a blizzard had swept through not long ago. The snow was gone from all but the highest ridges behind Palmeto, and the shepherd boys goading their flocks along the roadside were in T shirts.

There are few places on earth more radiant in winter than Sicily. The mandarin and orange groves of Castellammare ripen in the same weeks, just after Christmas, when the lemon trees burst into extravagant flower. From the road that climbs toward Montelepre, the coastal plain is a dazzling patchwork of white blossom and orange fruit, spread out against the turquoise gulf. The upland valleys are blanketed in gold, their wild grasses swollen from the February rains and abloom with mustard and buttercups.

The ancient Greeks had set their allegory of winter death and spring resurrection in the interior of Sicily. The small lake of Pergusa, south of Caltanisetta, was the site of the mythic abduction of Persephone. Hades, lord of the underworld, had fallen in love with the girl and carried her off to his infernal realm of smoke and fire. Her grief-stricken mother, Demeter, goddess of grain and fertility, brought all procreation to a halt in the world above. Eventually, mother and lover reached an agreement to prevent the Earth from becoming a lifeless desert, with Persephone spending six months annually in each of their kingdoms. The onset of winter marked her yearly descent into hell, the Greeks believed, and spring her fecund return.

Twenty-seven centuries after Greek settlers first established colonies on the island, Sicilians remained transfixed by the metaphysical interplay of death and resurrection. The passion-play

resonance of Giovanni Falcone's murder was of a piece with that
ancient Greek allegory, as were the tortured Holy Week processions that wound through Sicilian towns.

But unless the climate had undergone radical changes in the
past three millennia, the myth simply didn't jibe with the profound
fertility of winter in Sicily, the riot of color that lit its sunstruck pastures. It was summer, with its windless nights, oppressive heat, and
scorched fields, that made me think of death.

ABOUT TWO MILES up the Montelepre road, Mike told me to
stop. *"Ghistu ca, a sinistra,"* he said, lapsing into dialect. To the left,
where he pointed, a broad avenue lined with carob trees mounted
the slope of a vineyard. It was the formal entrance to an estate,
intersected at precise right angles by the vineyard's harvesting
lanes. A mile up the slope the avenue of carobs forked in two and
circled a cluster of buildings set amid palms and flower beds.

I knew what I was looking at. This was "Lo Zucco," the principal residence of the French duke whose stables were at the seaside

*The abandoned villa at
Paternella, where the
Monk worked in the
stables of the Duc
d'Aumale, son of King
Louis-Philippe of France.
Photo by Guido
Orlando.*

end of the Paternella citrus grove. The man who'd made Paolo Cocuzza his overseer in 1851. The estate was so large that it filled a quarter of the architect's map. "The Frenchman's palace," I said. "It must have really been something in the old days . . ."

Mike was always showing me the local sights. I assumed we would discuss the glories of the estate for a few minutes, and then press on toward whatever destination he had in mind.

"Let's get going," he abruptly said. "It won't look good if you park down here too long."

He meant for me to turn into the carob avenue. I did, very slowly. Every hundred yards so, one of the estate workers peered out from the vines as we passed. They had rifles slung over their shoulders.

At the top of the slope, Mike motioned toward the right curve of the circle, and I parked in front of a limestone palazzo trimmed with elaborate Moorish floral designs. Or what was left of it. The roof of the main building had caved in, and through the open windows I could see the morning sky where the ceiling ought to have been. Shafts of sunlight broke through gaps in the heavy damask curtains that still hung over several of the gaping windows. One wing of the palace had been kept up. There was glass in the windows, as heavily curtained as the ruined structure next door had been, and the original roofing had been replaced.

A muscular young man in a tight yellow polo shirt watched us from the terrace. He had steel blue eyes and wavy blond hair, souvenirs of those Norman crusaders who conquered Arab Sicily in the eleventh century.

"Michele, *bon giu,*" he said. *"Ghe si dici?"* It was the Sicilian version of "What's up?" I was asking myself the same question.

The proprietor, who was the young man's father, stepped out through the door and joined us on the terrace. He was in his seventies or early eighties, I guessed, and his stomach hung well out over his belt. But he had the same powerful shoulders as his son. They were draped by a florid, loose Hawaiian shirt decorated with outrigger canoes and ukulele-strumming wahines.

Mike introduced me. *"Salve,* Mister Viviano," the lord of Lo
Zucco said, using the archaic Latin greeting. Later, he would
acknowledge that he knew me to be a writer, not with any direct
reference to my work, but through discreet yet unmistakable allusions to the purpose of my stay in Terrasini. Just as discreetly, he
made it clear that his own name was not to be mentioned in print.
Even in conversations with my Terrasini friends, I took to calling
him "Signore Zucco." Everyone knew who I meant.

"Beautiful, isn't it?" Signore Zucco said in English. He nodded
toward the landscape that stretched out below us, verdant with the
citrus groves and vineyards that the French duke had planted more
than a century ago.

We stood on the terrace, talking. I asked about the ruins. The
Moorish palace had passed into the hands of the Princess of Gangi,
a Bourbon heiress, after the Frenchman's death, Signore Zucco
explained. But the Princess did nothing to keep it up, and an earth-
quake in 1968 had put paid to the roof. Signore Zucco had
acquired the compound ten years later and rehabilitated the north
wing. He was pessimistic about the main building ever recovering
its lost grandeur. It was *esaurita,* he said in Italian, "exhausted."
Like most of the people around Terrasini, he and his son moved
effortlessly back and forth between dialect and grammatical modern Italian, with the odd English phrase thrown in. Each language
had its uses and its place.

There was a distant pensiveness to the old man as he gazed over
the vineyards, something beyond the normal Sicilian melancholy, a
suggestion that he was also *esaurito.* "My wife loved this view," he said.
"We spent hours, just staring out at the sea, before the end came."

She had died three months earlier. Cancer. "We were together
forty-five years. Not so long as your grandma and grandpa, Mister
Viviano, but a long time, a long time."

It was a deliberate allusion. He knew more about me than the
fact that I was a writer.

"Okay, *andiamo,"* Signore Zucco suddenly announced. Mike
walked over and opened the passenger door of my car. The old man

folded himself into the front seat of the Peugeot, and Mike slid into the back. I drove down the carob avenue, the vineyard foreman raising his rifle in salute as we passed.

AT SIGNORE ZUCCO'S DIRECTION, I turned into a graveled road that skirted the estate. After a mile or so, the gravel disappeared and the Peugeot bumped forward on a dirt farm track, heavily rutted by the wheels of tractors that had churned up the winter mud. The road was dry and sun-hardened for the most part this morning, but it was dizzyingly steep, with no more than half a dozen sharp switchbacks to ease the climb.

We inched our way along a ledge above a creek bed that ran down the western slope of Monte Palmeto. Once, I briefly lost control of the wheel in an unexpected mud hole and we fishtailed sideways to the verge of a sudden precipice. A thousand feet below, I could look down into the gaping shell of the Moorish palazzo. Mike and Signore Zucco appeared not to notice. They were deeply engaged in conversation; the word "Paternella" came up often, in a flood of mumbled dialect so thick that I could barely follow it.

The valley narrowed to a shallow canyon, with the path clinging to its southern wall. Across the creek bed, the weed-choked remains of a stone hut sat on a patch of flat ground. All that was left of it, after a century of winter rains, was a single crumbling wall; the roof had been carried off by the mountain winds long ago.

Signore Zucco tapped me on the arm. "Your ancestor," he said. "That house belonged to him. The one who was killed."

He used the verb *ammazzare*. It had a specific meaning in Sicily, suggesting an especially violent death. An assassination.

We drove on another twenty minutes, almost to the Portella di Mircene, the pass at the summit of Palmeto directly above Terrasini. Cows grazed on a pasture that opened to the south. There was a wooden shed on the pasture's edge, surrounded by piles of straw. Inside the shed, two enormous copper cauldrons gurgled over a log fire. The smoke made it difficult to see clearly, but I could make out a pair of swarthy young men, sitting on raised brick platforms above the cauldrons. They stirred the contents in slow rhythmic sweeps, wielding flat wooden paddles the length and breadth of rowboat oars. Rivulets of sweat ran down their necks.

"The *tuma* is ready," Mike said, referring in dialect to the whey from the local cheese, *cacciocavallo*. He grabbed a spoon from a table next to the cauldrons, dipped it into a bucket that sat between the two stirring men, and filled three ceramic bowls with mounds of the soft, sweet, yellow whey. We ate in silence, watching the steam rise from the cauldrons. A boy came into the shed with two large plastic containers and filled them with *tuma*. When we were done eating, Mike carried the containers out to the Peugeot and put them on the floor of the backseat, along with a two-kilo round of *cacciocavallo* for each of us. The *tuma* was for Signore Zucco.

It took nearly an hour to bump back down the mountain track. No one spoke. When we arrived at the palazzo, the old man walked around to the driver's side of the car and gravely shook my hand, as Mike climbed into the front seat

"*Auguri,* Mister Viviano," he said. "I hope you find what you are looking for."

Signore Zucco paused, and trained his eyes intently on mine. Then Mike spoke: "A lot of people want you to know they're unhappy about that robbery out in the country," he said. "A lot of people want to find out who did it."

He meant the burglary at Paternella, while I was in Turkey. The old man nodded to Mike, and walked back into the Moorish palazzo. His message was as clear as the bells that struck the hour at Maria Santissima delle Grazie.

I knew now who was *not* responsible for the break-in.

THE ENCOUNTER WITH SIGNORE ZUCCO renewed my interest in the architect Orlando's old map. I pored over every square inch of it, trying to place its landmarks in their twentieth-century setting, exploring its roads and lanes with the *Risorgimento* diaries and hundred-year-old travel memoirs as my guidebooks.

With Monacu the cat curled up at my feet in the chilly evenings, both of us nudging a kerosene space heater that Rosalia had loaned me, I also set out to learn as much as I could about the French aristocrat who once owned the estate. The Monk, indeed all of the Vivianos up to the birth of Paolinu, had effectively been this exiled duke's vassals.

Like Signore Zucco, Grandpa always referred to him simply as *lu Francese,* "the Frenchman." More formally, he was Henri d'Orleans, Duc d'Aumale, whose vast properties had once embraced the entire Contrada Paternella. He was the fourth son of King Louis-Philippe of France and Queen Maria-Amelia of the Two Sicilies.

In 1853, Aumale purchased his Castellammare estate—the *Tenuta dello Zucco,* "Domain of the Vine"—from a Bourbon grandee fallen on hard times. When other noble domains were placed in the care of leaseholders or sold off piece by piece to wealthy commoners after the *Risorgimento,* the French duke refused to part with a single hectare. Lo Zucco remained whole until his death there in 1897, its nearly seven square miles of vineyards, almond, pistachio, and citrus groves presided over by the grand Moorish palazzo six hundred feet above the sea on the flank of Monte Palmeto.

From its tiled semicircular terrace, Aumale could see as far as *Capo* San Vito, fifty miles across the gulf, and nearly as far as the North African coast where he had passed an exceptionally eventful youth. In 1840, at the age of eighteen, he had been sent to Algeria as ordnance officer in the army of his older brother, the crown prince. By 1843, he was the army's commander in North Africa and led a surprise assault that overwhelmed the Algerian resistance to French rule. In 1847, when he was still only twenty-five, he was appointed Algeria's governor general.

A few months later, the revolution of 1848 descended on Europe, toppling Louis-Philippe from the French throne and nearly bringing down the Bourbons in Sicily. Yet when the news reached Aumale in Algiers, he immediately handed over his command to an officer who sided with the revolution. At heart, the French duke was a liberal.

He was a liberal of immense wealth, however—arguably the greatest private fortune in Europe—and infinitely too distant in class and temperment from his *viddani* tenants to earn more than their grudging respect. Terrasini's Frenchman was the son of a king, with the chill intellectual bearing and hawkish aristocratic face of the Orleans line, punctuated by a Vandyke beard that was always in military trim. In addition to Lo Zucco, he owned a palace in the city of Palermo surrounded by a 175-acre private park, five thousand acres of sugar cane in Brazil, and an art collection that included celebrated works by Raphael, Delacroix, Ingres, and Watteau. They hung on the walls of his most imposing property, the grand Chateau de Chantilly north of Paris, with its miles of landscaped gardens and a stable that accommodated 240 horses and 150 hounds for the hunt.

But it was Aumale's distinctly modern mentality, and not aristocratic pride, that accounted for his refusal to sell his Sicilian lands. Even in exile in the most backward countryside in Europe, the French duke had been determined to bring contemporary technology to bear on the cultivation of his adopted soil. He refashioned Lo Zucco into an enormous agricultural experiment, a model farm. On the village waterfront, he constructed an imposing stone warehouse that still commands the port. It was connected by rail, from 1880 on, to a freight station in the center of Lo Zucco's vineyards. (The doomed Austrian boys had been imprisoned in Aumale's warehouse when the influenza struck in 1918.)

The result of his efforts, to the amazement of his sluggish fellow landlords, was that Aumale created an export industry in Terrasini. For a generation or two, his "Zucco" wines commanded a hugely profitable market in northern Europe.

Aumale was a dissident. A modern man in an antique land. An aristocrat who transformed himself into an entrepreneur. He was a liberal in a corner of Europe that never shook off the feudal mentality, even when it cultivated the appearances of democracy after the *Risorgimento*.

NOWHERE WAS THIS CONTRADICTION more apparent than in the distribution of land. After the unification of Sicily and Italy in 1861, fertile estates were steadily acquired by men who were seldom interested in the new methods that the proprietor of Lo Zucco championed. Their interests, their profit margins, were served by keeping Sicily in the darkness, not in forcing it into the light.

The Duc d'Aumale couldn't be expected to understand local realities. He would always be "the Frenchman," in a countryside where natives of Terrasini regarded visitors from the neighboring province of Trapani as *straneddi*, "foreigners," and Italians as another race altogether. He would always be the odd man out, who refused to part with any of his land, surrounded by neighbors who retained only what was valuable and did nothing to exploit it.

What was left for the *viddani*, and often sold to them in exchange for labor since they had no capital, were postage-stamp plots on barren hillsides that supported a few emaciated sheep. In Montelepre, the rocky hill town that gave birth to Paolo Cocuzza and the celebated twentieth-century bandit Salvatore Giuliano, two thousand acres of arid mountain pasturage was divided up among eight thousand peasants in 1890.

It was the same distorted picture that materialized in the architect Orlando's old military map, with its tiny farmsteads bearing the names of the Viviano, Valenti, and other Terrasini *viddani* families.

Nobody could survive on the output of farms this size, which is why my namesake cleaned the stables of the Duc d'Aumale, when he wasn't in the mountains, robbing government supply transports or wealthy travelers—a pursuit that had no shame attached to it in the resentful countryside.

The Italian government could not begin to confront the problem of crime in Sicily, an 1874 parliamentary report warned, unless it recognized how thoroughly the state was despised there. The warning went unheeded. By twenty years later, the cancerous relations between Sicily and Rome had fatally undermined whatever influence the central government still bore in the island's affairs, and metastasized into the *sistema.*

Of the seventeen peasant families named on architect Orlando's map of Terrasini, nine would later figure in criminal investigations in Italy or the United States. By then, banditry had given way to large-scale crime, to the fully matured *sistema del potere,* and to a large-scale taste for land.

The same family names appear among major purchasers of the fragmented Aumale estate in the twentieth century, a few years after the French duke died and his heirs had traded off their shares of Lo Zucco for apartments on the banks of the Seine and yachts in the harbors of Porto Fino and St. Tropez.

THERE WAS SOMETHING ELSE that caught my eye on the architect's map, something that I'd like to think was a nod from my grandmother.

In the nineteenth century, a house labeled "Villa Carolina" stood directly adjacent to the stables where the Monk had worked. It was an outlying dependency of Lo Zucco, named for his wife Maria-Carolina Augusta, Princess of Salerno, and used by the ducal household when winter temperatures in the highlands made the Moorish palace uncomfortable. Constructed of amber Palmeto limestone, Villa Carolina was a handsome, well-proportioned building according to contemporary accounts, a prominent local landmark until the Baronessa Fassini tore it down and replaced it with her Art Nouveau mansion.

The Duc d'Aumale hosted a glittering cast of royal cousins and acquaintances at Villa Carolina, in gatherings of the European nobility that brought German and Russian counts, deposed Bourbon princes, and even the Empress Eugenie of France to Terrasini. One of the villa's frequent guests, bedded in silk sheets just a few hundred yards away from the cottage of Francesco Viviano and his sons Giuseppe and Gaetano—the Uncle Gaetano my grandfather knew as "The Falcon," the red-sashed lover of a queen in Grandma Angelina's fable—was the former Princess of the Kingdom of the Two Sicilies.

Not the Queen of Naples, but tantalizingly close.

She is a seductive smile, a glance across the village marketplace, on May 11, 1860, as Giuseppe Garibaldi lands at Marsala with his thousand volunteers

THIRTEEN

Risorgimento

+>=<+

IN HIS MUD-WALLED COTTAGE at Paternella, Francesco Paolo Viviano listens to the runner from Cinisi, then tells the news to Maria. He picks up his gun, which has lain hidden in the cottage since April 17. Their three-year-old first son, Gaetano, who will carry many guns of his own, watches. Francesco kisses Gaetano twice on each cheek, and wraps the red sash around his waist. He looks at Maria. She turns the other way.

Paolo Cocuzza watches from the grounds of Villa Carolina as his stablehand crosses the Bourbon road. Cocuzza is the French duke's overseer, a brigand made respectable. But to the men who work for him, he remains the Robin Hood of Montelepre, and he has been discreetly informed that Giuseppe Garibaldi's army is en route to Sicily. Cocuzza is too old to return to the mountains himself. He can only watch.

The Duc d'Aumale is traveling south toward Sicily from a business engagement in Brussels when a message from Cocuzza reaches him and the trip is canceled. It has been twelve years since the collapse of his father's monarchy sent Aumale into exile; he knows that another dynasty is about to fall. The duke is sorry for his wife and mother, who are Bourbon princesses, and realizes that his connections to the old regime make a return to Sicily impossible. Nine *years will pass before he sees the island again. But he has also let it be known, in conversations with Garibaldi's northern allies, that he supports the establishment of an Italian republic.*

Aumale believes in the logic of evolution, in the inevitability of change. He wonders if Lo Zucco, his great experiment, will survive the next weeks.

Above the coastal flats in a Palmeto canyon, Zu Piddu Badalamenti waits. One of Garibaldi's Sicilian lieutenants is at his side, with detailed plans for the coming invasion. The old, half-lame capo has made good on his word. The cease-fire of April 17 was a pause, not the end of the uprising. The men who walked disconsolately home from the beaches of Favarotta that day, surrounded by Bourbon troops, are again to form squadre. They are not the same men who met here five weeks ago. The Battle of Monreale is behind them.

The king's soldiers also remember Monreale and hurry west to face Garibaldi in terror of every lemon grove, every large rock on the Castellammare plain. The picciotti could be hiding anywhere, waiting to disable them with a gunshot, followed by a knife to the throat. This fear will prove a decisive element in the lightning war that ends nearly six centuries of Spanish and Bourbon rule in Sicily. It will be prophetic.

Giuseppe Garibaldi is fifty-three years old in the spring of 1860, an itinerant soldier of fortune who has spent most of his adult life abroad, lending his hand to Latin revolutions or biding time as an immigrant factory worker in New York. He recognizes that the invasion of Sicily is his greatest, and probably final, opportunity to shape history, to be something more than its flamboyant servant.

Garibaldi is profoundly unrealistic, even naïve, in his political sensibilities. "His educational acquirements are not great, and his views, although broad and honest, hardly ever rise above the level of trite and popular generalities," a British military attaché in Italy reports to Lord John Russell, her majesty's minister for foreign affairs. But Garibaldi is also the son of a fisherman and a poor man himself, a former deckhand and cattleherd who raised his family among tenant-farmers in Brazil, Uruguay, and Argentina. He is closely attuned to the peasant mind, and unlike his middle-class supporters in the north, he recognizes that there will be no revolution without the viddani.

His first official proclamation is comprised of just two orders, to be imposed after the Bourbons are conquered:

> Article One: No one shall be further required to address a landlord as "Your Excellency."
> Article Two: The bacciamano [a custom obliging peasants to kiss the hand of a landlord] is declared illegal.

Garibaldi understands that an insurgent peasantry is the sea in which a revolutionary army must swim. He does not fully understand the consequences of such an insurgency in Sicily.

THE LANDING AT MARSALA is unexpectedly, even comically, bloodless. The Thousand steam into the harbor just after noon on a pair of stolen paddle wheelers, the Piemonte and the Lombardo, the latter of which promptly runs aground one hundred yards from the jetty. As the Piemonte's men disembark and fishing boats begin ferrying passengers and artillery pieces ashore from the crippled Lombardo, a sixty-gun Bourbon frigate and two armed steam sloops arrive from the south and take up firing positions just outside the harbor. A well-aimed broadside of grapeshot at this point, raking the Lombardo from stem to stern and leveling the jetty, would have decimated Garibaldi's ranks, almost certainly ending the invasion.

But the Bourbons hold fire for a fatal hour, paralyzed by the sight of H.M.S. Intrepid and H.M.S. Argus, two British warships anchored a mile offshore. They represent the most powerful navy on the seas, and the Bourbons are convinced that it is about to intervene on behalf of the rebellion; the British government has made no secret of its hostility toward the regime in Naples, which London regards as a dangerous feudal anachronism. The Bourbon commander appears "excessively nervous and agitated," when the captains of the Intrepid and Argus are rowed out to assure him of their neutrality, so long as British commercial interests are respected. They refer to the exporters of Marsala's celebrated wines, English businessmen who own the portside warehouses and a fleet of merchant vessels moored in the harbor.

Not entirely reassured, the Bourbon ships finally open fire, too late and far too carefully. Most of their shots slash harmlessly in the open sea. Garibaldi's men have by now occupied Marsala and are protected by the city's walls. The Thousand's entire casualty list, on a day that will alter the political geography of Europe, is one man wounded in the shoulder and a guard dog wounded in the leg.

BY MAY 15, word of the landing has reached the most isolated villages. The Castellammare roads are jammed with peasants heading toward the front. The squadre have leaders and orders, but the fever to overthrow the old regime, inflamed by Bourbon provocations since the amnesty, has outgrown Garibaldi's efforts at organization.

For weeks, the police have been ransacking peasant huts in search of arms. The royal army has occupied the market towns, billeting thousands of troops in their homes and piazzas. Twenty-five Bourbon infantry battalions, supported by two artillery and cavalry divisions, await Garibaldi's tiny band in the provinces of Trapani and Palermo. The cavalrymen, sons of the nobility and great landowners who scarcely regard the viddani as human, feed their horses on the wheat fields of peasant farmers between Alcamo and Partinico.

As Francesco Viviano and his comrades march behind Zu Piddu, they are engulfed by furious mobs of villagers, pouring across the landscape, determined to be part of the reckoning. Guns are scarce. The largest of the squadre columns is a combined force of several hundred men from Partinico, Corleone, San Giuseppe Jato, Montelepre, Piana dei Greci, and Campofelice. They have *eighty pistols and rifles at their disposal. Most of the* picciotti, *like the people who rush past them, carry knives, pickaxes, scythes, shovels, rakes, and staves with nails driven through their ends.*

Thirty-five miles west of Terrasini, outside the village of Calatafimi, the critical battle is about to be joined. The Bourbons have been encamped on a hill facing the village since May 13. On the morning of May 15, their scouts report an enormous rebel force approaching from the town of Salemi, fifteen miles to the south.

It is an illusion, the fruit of Garibaldi's genius for the strategic bluff. He leads fewer than nine hundred trained volunteers to Calatafimi. But they are quick-marched and constantly doubled back, the same small detachments sighted on dozens of nearby ridges, to produce the semblance of an army of several thousand.

The Bourbon commander, General Landi, draws his men up in formal battle lines, then slowly advances on the nearby plain. Behind them, in reserve, is an islandwide royal military force totaling more than ninety thousand troops.

At noon, Garibaldi nods to his chief aide, Antonio Bixio, and the rebels fall on the Bourbons from half a dozen directions. "Nino," Garibaldi calmly says, "we will make Italy here, or we will die."

By late afternoon, the Bourbons have been routed and are fleeing east in confused disarray. Into the guns of the squadre. *Into the furious peasant sea.*

SIX CENTURIES OF HUMILIATION *roil up in that sea, six centuries of waiting, made unbearable since 1820 by three generations of failed revolts. There is blind rage in the Castellammare air when a warm, clear day dawns over Monte Palmeto. Decades later, people will recall everything about May 16, 1860, with the sharp, sensual intensity of madness. The lush green pastures of the Castellammare spring, the golden wildflowers on the valley slopes, are almost painful to the eye.*

Rumors swirl through the mob, which has passed the night

under the stars. Francesco Viviano hears that Garibaldi is invulner-
able, that he carries a magic shield with which he swats away
Bourbon gunshots as though they were no more than irritating
swarms of gnats. He hears that Garibaldi, who detests the Roman
Catholic Church, is the living reincarnation of Jesus Christ. He
hears, from Zu Piddu, of the victory yesterday at Calatafimi.

The squadre break camp before dawn, climbing back into the
mountains to join Garibaldi's advance on Palermo.

Exhausted, demoralized, hardly more than an irrational mob
themselves by now, a column of twenty-six hundred fleeing
Bourbon soldiers crosses the river Jato as morning breaks and halts
for a rest in the hamlet of Valguarnera, two miles from Partinico.
Bullets suddenly rain down on them from hidden Castellammare
sharpshooters.

General Landi sends a contingent of one hundred cavalrymen
at full gallop into Partinico, in a futile effort to secure the royal
ammunition stores, while his infantrymen lay waste to Valguarnera
under artillery cover. When they move out, the hamlet and its
small church are burning. The Castellammare sharpshooters never
let up, and the two-mile march into Partinico is a nightmare. But
nothing like the nightmare to come.

The Bourbon artillery obliterate several blocks of houses on the
outskirts of Partinico. The royal infantrymen enter the town, wildly
firing in every direction, breaking down doors and sacking homes.
Soldiers run down the streets with their arms full of stolen linens
and silverware, shooting mothers in front of their children and robbing churches. Landi has lost all control over his men. He is a professional and knows that the survival of the regime hangs on an
orderly retreat. He knows that the battle is lost.

Scattered across the ancient town as they pillage, small groups
of Bourbon foot soldiers soon find themselves out of ammunition
and trapped in medieval alleys and courtyards. It is not the sharpshooters who confront them now; it is the women of Partinico, with
butcher knives and cleavers.

*   *   *

WHEN GARIBALDI AND HIS VOLUNTEERS *march into Partinico at 10:00 A.M. on May 18, led by Castellammare picciotti, they are dumbstruck with horror. This is the word that recurs, over and over, in the private diaries of Garibaldi and his officers: "horror." They cannot believe, they do not want to believe, what they see.*

The impression is so powerful that it imparts a remarkable consistency to their descriptions, as though the diaries speak with a single voice. One of the diarists is Giuseppe Cesare Abba. "On the doorsteps of the little city," he writes, there are

> *piles of the dead, burned, swollen, tortured in a hundred ways. Linking hands in a chain and singing, young girls dance around the corpses, their hair as wild as the Furies, against the background of a main street black from fires that have not yet been extinguished. The church bells peel in storms. Priests, friars, people of every class scream at the militiamen running behind Garibaldi, who rapidly crosses the city with his cap pulled down to his eyes.*

Along the roads leading from the town, Abba writes, "there is an unbearable stench, rising from the corpses of soldiers and peasants, of dead and dismembered dogs and horses."

Garibaldi camps in a nearby olive grove for the next two days, as the town gradually regains its reason. Decades will pass before he gives words to what he witnessed in Partinico. Looking back, Garibaldi will remember the town as a charnel house, its streets laden with "men who had been tortured and torn to pieces by their own brothers, with a madness that would horrify the Devil."

On May 18, 1860, Giuseppe Garibaldi is badly shaken. But he cannot show it, not now. It is the revolution that matters. Palermo is ripe for the taking. Garibaldi needs the viddani. He needs this town. From the balcony of a small house where the road branches off toward Terrasini, he addresses the mob.

"Partinico," he tells them, *"will occupy the best page in the history of the Italian* Risorgimento."

On May 27, Palermo falls, as the Castellammare squadre overcome stiff Bourbon resistance in a vicious battle at the Ponte dell'Ammiraglio, the stone bridge that guards the eastern gates of the city.

On July 20, 1860, Sicily is no longer in Bourbon hands.

FOURTEEN

A Parable

Terrasini, Sicily
February 1996

BY RIGHTS, PADRE VINCENZO CONSTANTINO ought to have been one of Terrasini's leading citizens in 1996. He was the pastor of Maria Santissima delle Grazie, the village's principal church, a French speaker, and an expert on the Latin and Greek classics.

But he was also a native of Partinico, where the Constantinos were an influential family, and not of Terrasini, where the Constantino name was nearly as foreign as Aumale. All of his predecessors, since Maria Santissima delle Grazie was founded in 1684, had been born within five hundred meters of the Piazza Duomo.

"Don Constantino doesn't understand us, and we don't understand him," Rosalia flatly said.

She was referring to everything about the sixty-three-year-old priest, and not just his stubbornly *partinicosu* dialect. His quick temper. His slightly rough hill town edges. These were regarded as Partinico traits, at irreparable odds with the Terrasini norm.

"They should have let him stay with his own people, where he could be useful," Mike agreed, as though Partinico were in another hemisphere, rather than a few miles to the west overlooking the Castellammare plain.

Whether the fault was Padre Constantino's own refusal to aban-

138

don his Partinico inflections and habits, or Terrasini's pronounced inwardness, the relationship between pastor and flock was one of overt mutual suspicion. The village faithful deserted the grandiose baroque church on the Piazza Duomo by the score during his tenure; most switched allegiance to the modern, poured-concrete Maria Santissima del Rosario (which was located, ironically, on the Via Partinico).

Vincenzo Constantino had been pastor of Maria Santissima delle Grazie for thirty-one years.

A short, wiry man in Coke-bottle bifocals, Padre Constantino did not take slights with aplomb. He seemed permanently angry with everyone except his office assistant, Signora Notaro, a woman of saintly patience whom he had imported from Partinico, and his elder sister, who also lived in the rectory and cleaned the church. The anger was expressed in imperious outbursts, shrill priestly commands to support renovations or property improvements that were meant to reinforce his authority as the village's senior spiritual counselor, but often had the opposite effect.

Early in my research, I had made several failed attempts to gain access to the parish records, although there was no consensus in the village that a complete set of such records existed. Each time I rang the intercom-doorbell of the rectory and announced the purpose of my visit, the disembodied voice of Padre Constantino's sister squawked out—her Partinico dialect a slur of mutilated consonants—informing me that the pastor was on some unspecified mission.

"You again, Viviano? Come back another time," the sister's voice sputtered through a blizzard of static. She never said when.

I tried to take my request directly to Padre Constantino, as he marched down the aisle of Maria Santissima delle Grazie following an early morning Mass and communion. "Padre, can I have a word with you?" I whispered, trying to muster up the obeisance of my altar boy days in the 1950s.

"Not now!" he hissed back. "I have the body and blood of our Lord in me!"

According to Giovanni Orlando, the village architect and historian whose pamphlet supplied me with the old military map, "important church papers" had been shipped off to the state archive in Palermo during World War II. He was evasive about details. "It is my recollection that your fellow Americans destroyed them," he said at one point, when I asked about the parish's nine-teenth-century baptismal registers.

Palermo was bombed by the Allies in 1943, and I had heard from others that many documents had gone up in flames.

In the beginning, Orlando was helpful, providing the names of scholars and librarians who might aim me in a productive direction. But I sensed that he thought of me increasingly as an unwelcome rival, plowing historical ground that he regarded as his own. I was paranoid enough, after the mayor's inexplicable stonewalling and several months of research setbacks and dead ends, to believe that the bombing story wasn't the last word on the church records. My suspicions were fanned by Giuseppe Viviano, the reclusive distant relative I'd met on the bus to Palermo the previous spring, who had advised me to forget about the archives. I had given up leaving notes for him at Di Maggio's *Caffe* and behind the statue of the Virgin on the Via Cataldi; there was still no response. He too was said to be working on a history of the village.

Mike was reassuring. "Don't worry," he said, when I mentioned the rumor. "Giuseppe been writing that book, whatever it is, for thirty or forty years. He's never gonna finish."

But it wasn't a competitor's book that troubled me. It was the snail's pace of my pursuit of the Monk and his murderer. It was the recognition that I was out of my depth as a detective, and would remain there without the help of someone like Padre Constantino.

MY SORTIES up and down the waterfront and in step with the evening *passeggiatta* produced little in the way of unambiguous clues to the mystery. But in their own peculiar way, these walks were more productive than my work as a detective and reporter.

They carried my narrative deeper into the village's shadow life, into the realm where unspoken yet immensely powerful understandings were lodged. They provided insights into the Monk's life and death that would never emerge from the municipal archives.

As I stopped to introduce myself to people, to nudge conversation, my notebooks began to fill up with parables. I don't know how else to describe the stories that I jotted down, spelling out the dialect words as best I could and hoping I'd correctly grasped their nuances. When the villagers responded to my questions, it was very often in parables, morality tales that couched the ferocious violence of the Monk's world—their world—in an equally ferocious conception of justice.

I heard again and again, so often that it clearly had a talismanic significance, the saga of a former shepherd who was more commonly referred to as *Adannatu*, "The Damned." He had died in Terrasini at the age of ninety-seven, a year before I began my search for the Monk. His long life overlapped that of my grandfather's for eight decades.

In the town of their shared childhood, he had carefully and with great deliberation murdered thirty of his neighbors, one by one.

Adannatu's baptismal name was Pietro Palazzolo, "Petrinu" in dialect. His family was related to that of my maternal grandmother and was one of the largest of the village's peasant clans. He was not an executioner for the *sistema*. His violence was of an earlier order. More redeemable, in the Sicilian scheme of things.

This was the unanimous opinion in Terrasini, even among the *carabinieri*, the police. *Brigadiere* Palmi, a gentle old codger who manned the village *carabinieri* post's reception desk, told me it was "a pity, an unfortunate pity," that I had not been able to meet Adannatu. "Nobody could have helped you like he could have, Signore. Don Petrinu was the same age as your grandpa. They grew up together. He knew the story, that's certain."

Palmi himself spoke of Adannatu with reverence, using his baptismal name and preceding it with the honorific "Don" that was generally reserved for priests, municipal officials, and *sistema* bosses. Like most policemen on the Castellammare coast, the *brigadiere* was from somewhere else, in his case a hamlet in the mountains of Calabria. After forty years in Terrasini, he was still a "continental" in the village parlance. But Palmi was also something more than an outsider by now, and he had absorbed many of the beliefs of the people he policed.

He was genuinely apologetic about the fact that he could be of no help to me. I had come to the police looking for arrest records, a paper trail of any sort that might lead to the Monk. Palmi pulled a couple of mildewed ledgers out of a filing cabinet. They held brief sketches of "malefactors" erratically compiled by the *carabinieri* three or four generations earlier. The first entry was for 1929. The next skipped ahead to 1932. The police archives were even more haphazard than the municipality's. Palmi was embarrassed: "Our records in those days were not well organized . . ."

He sighed, then put the ledgers down on his desk, and told me how Petrinu Palazzolo became "Adannatu." The tale began, as such tales often do in Sicily, with a foolish mistake that is interpreted as an unforgivable insult.

AT DAWN ON A SPRING MORNING in 1925, my grandfather's childhood friend Petrinu rises from his cot to lead the Palazzolo sheep to pasture. He counts: two animals are missing. They are pascal lambs, which will bring a very good price in Holy Week.

The following morning, another lamb has vanished.

The flock is not yet in the mountains, where a lamb might be carried off by a wild animal. Petrinu knows that the predator must be human. His suspicions focus on a brother-in-law, a dubious man with no sheep of his own and a fondness for card games; he has been pressed into service, occasionally, to work the pastures for the Palazzolo family.

There is a Castellammare proverb that fits this situation: *Raccumannari la pecura a lu lupu.* "To entrust the sheep to a wolf."

The proof is simple to establish. Three freshly gutted lambs hang in the butcher shop of a neighboring village. Petrinu mentions his brother-in-law's name, in passing, with no reference to the lambs. The question is not directly put, but it is understood.

The butcher nods.

At twenty-five, Petrinu has spent a dozen summers in the steep Castellammare mountains, sometimes carrying sick ewes on his shoulders for miles. He is a powerful man, and he beats his brother-in-law mercilessly, in the full light of day at the center of the Piazza Duomo. The Palazzolos have been insulted.

But so, too, has the brother-in-law. He lies bruised and humiliated on the cobblestones of the piazza, weeping before the men who sip *amaro* at the Circolo Contadino, when his father arrives to carry him home on his shoulders. Like one of the sick Palazzolo ewes.

The brother-in-law has long nursed a profound hatred of the Palazzolos, who opposed the marriage that brought him into their family and have never disguised their contempt for him. Now he is entirely lost to reason.

On Good Friday, Petrinu Palazzolo's mother is found dead on a country path, a thin knife line across her throat.

No one in Terrasini is surprised when the brother-in-law also turns up dead three days later. No one is surprised when Petrinu Palazzolo is arrested, convicted of murder, and sent to Ucciardone Prison in Palermo. Some people remember the brother-in-law's end as a knifing, others as an *incaprettamento,* a "goat-throttling," in which the victim's legs are bound at an excruciating angle and attached by a taut line to a noose at his throat. The more frantic his terror and efforts to relieve the pressure at his knees, the tighter the noose is drawn.

Eventually, he strangles himself.

SEVERAL YEARS PASS. Petrinu Palazzolo is a model prisoner, the Ucciardone guards say. A humble man, who makes no trouble. They pity him: "For a mother to die like that, without a priest to oil her brow for heaven, or her children to weep over her . . ."

In 1929, Palazzolo is already Adannatu in his heart. But the prison officials don't recognize it.

He is furloughed at Easter that year, permitted a twenty-four-hour leave to spend the solemn holiday with his family. He goes first to the Palazzolo farm, where he kisses his widowed father once on each cheek. Then he heads straight for the family home of his late brother-in-law. The dead man's father is at the table, about to carve the pascal lamb, when the door is kicked open and shots are fired from a stolen revolver.

For two years, Palazzolo is on the run, and the brothers and uncles and nephews and male cousins of his former brother-in-law are in hiding. But none of them escapes Adannatu. In mountain huts, in village cellars, in Palermo back streets, he finds them. Some are knifed. Some are shot. Others are strangled.

When there are no men left in the brother-in-law's family, Petrinu Palazzolo surrenders to the police and goes back to Ucciardone without a struggle.

"Blood washes blood," Brigadiere Palmi said. He told me that he had work to do, and said he hoped I'd come back and say hello before I left Terrasini.

MIKE TOLD ME the rest of Adannatu's story during a long drive back from Trapani, where we picked up several crates of salted anchovies for the *salumeria*. I had insisted, again, on taking the Peugeot.

"He was in prison for more than thirty years," Mike said. "After he was released, he had a bit of money. People still felt sorry for him, even with all that killing, and they sent him a few hundred lire now and then."

Adannatu had worked in the fuel yard of the prison, and he used his savings to build a small gas station on the Bourbon road. Before it opened, the only gasoline in the area was sold by the Badalamenti family. One night, as Mike put it, the gas tanks at the new station "mysteriously blew up."

The day after the explosion at the gas station, the old shepherd had suddenly burst into a room where Tanu Badalamenti was meeting with his colleagues.

"Nobody could figure out how Addanatu learned about the meeting, or got past the bodyguards. But there he was. He didn't do anything. He just stared at Badalamenti a long time, then he says, 'I been in prison thirty-two years. And I done things that guarantee I'm going to hell. So if you want me to die, you kill me right here, Signore. Shoot me through the heart. But don't ask me to die a poor man, with nothing.'"

According to Mike, Addanatu had ripped his shirt open and stood bare-chested in front of the astonished Badalamenti, until the meeting broke up in confusion.

When Addanatu's gas station was rebuilt a month later, his talismanic legend was complete. The man who killed thirty of his neighbors became the principal village sage in his eighties and nineties, dispensing advice from his small office behind the fuel pumps.

"People took their problems to him, all kinds of problems," Mike said. "When your life is as terrible as his, you learn things, and those things are valuable. He was better than any judge."

But like everyone in the village, like Addanatu himself, Mike was sure that Petrinu Palazzolo had gone to hell.

I EXITED FROM THE AUTOSTRADA as Mike spoke, and onto the Bourbon road. We were at the turnoff to Montelpre, about halfway between Lo Zucco and Terrasini, when a group of five or six men waved their arms at me and stepped in front of the car. I pulled over and Mike rolled down the passenger window.

The men stared at the Peugeot's French license plates and talked among themselves without addressing a word toward us. Then one of them came to the window and said something softly to Mike. He answered, just as softly, and we were motioned through.

The road beyond the curve was full of milling men, hundreds of them. Several carried thick wads of cash in their hands. The crowd parted to let us pass. I crept along, at ten miles per hour, into a second curve, and braked to a sudden halt as a horse danced across the road. He was a jet-black stallion, a thorough-bred by his sleek and pampered looks. A boy in red silks led him by the reins. I saw five more riders and horses off to the left, lined up along a high fence. A kilometer ahead, a cluster of men like the one that had confronted us at the first curve was stopping another car.

I turned to Mike. "It's a horse race, that's all," he said, before I could ask a question. "A private horse race."

In the days that followed, I thought often of that private horse race, that ostensibly secret gathering at high noon on a country road. Of course, it was not "secret" in any absolute sense. It couldn't be, a twenty-minute drive from Partinico and Terrasini, with their *carabinieri* posts and the visible public authority that they represented. The police must have known that hundreds of men had crowded into a field below Lo Zucco, to place cash bets on six thoroughbreds taking the circuit of a two-kilometer turf racetrack.

The cynical explanation was obvious enough. But the corrupt logistics of the secret race, the police bribes that must have made them possible, were not what compelled my interest.

The longer I was in Sicily, the more I understood that the *sistema del potere*—the clandestine power structure behind the visible institutions of government—was itself but one feature of a much larger clandestine universe, the same shadowy universe that transformed Adannatu into a Solomonic judge and cloaked my grandparents' fables in hidden meaning. Sicilians inhabited opposing, simultaneous realities.

These were not merely parallel worlds but parallel universes, complete to the language they used to describe their lives and the very names by which they knew each other: Adannatu, the Falcon, the Monk. None of these names appeared in the archives. They were drawn from the real history of Sicily, the history in villagers' parables, the history that was not written in books.

Apart from the architect Giovanni Orlando's pamphlets, the chief reference work on Terrasini was a formal history of the parish of Maria Santissima delle Grazie written in 1949 by Monsignor Francesco Evola, a predecessor of Padre Constantino. Evola was born in the village in 1866 and died there ninety-six years later, after a distinguished career as a prelate and scholar. Few observers over the centuries knew Terrasini more intimately, or were better equipped to shed light on its secrets.

The striking thing about his work is that it makes no mention of the hidden universe, its coded vocabulary and customs. There is no allusion to the *sistema del potere,* which evolved from anarchistic local brigandage to highly organized crime in the years when Evola was a young priest. There is no mention of the men who presided over the *sistema,* although they were among the most influential parishioners of Maria Santissima delle Grazie. No mention of Adannatu, who had been in prison for mass murder a quarter century when the monsignor wrote his history.

Terrasini, the author writes at several junctures, "is a peaceful town." He leaves it at that.

Had Evola accompanied us that Sunday morning on the Montelepre road, he was the kind of historian who would have recorded the precise temperature and offered his readers a detailed genealogy of Lo Zucco's duke. But he would have taken no note whatsoever of the horse race. The monsignor, along with the vast majority of Sicily's historians, refused to acknowledge the parallel universe. He preferred that it remain invisible. His book is a catalog of aristocratic successions, mayoral decrees, and complex intellectual disputes over episcopal jurisdiction.

Yet the villagers who spoke to me about the past, among them Evola's own relatives, seemed to have forgotten these matters completely or never heard of them. Their attention, their obsession, was riveted on the coded landmarks of the hidden Sicily, of the parallel

universe, rather than the world of visible appearances that commanded the written word.

It was only in the parallel universe, I now understood, that I
would unlock the mystery of the Monk's death.

THAT SINGLE EVENT, the killing of the Monk, weighed ever
more heavily on my research. After months of hunting, I was no
closer to the date and details of his murder than I had been a year
earlier. I had turned every page of the available ledgers in the
municipal records annex without finding his death certificate. I had
read every tombstone in the Terrasini cemetery, and combed the
archives of the Gancia in Palermo.

There were plenty of Francesco Paolo Vivianos in the cemetery, but they had been born long after 1825. In a spate of morbid
tidying up six decades ago, Benito Mussolini's local officials had
torn out the old tombstones and disinterred all pre-Fascist remains
in Sicily, piling them into common graves. If the bones of the
Monk were in his native village, they lay under the marble floor of
Maria Santissima delle Grazie, thrown together with countless others in an unmarked tomb that had been dug and filled in the 1930s.

Domenico Valenti's bones might be there as well, but there was
no way to know. In their zeal to launch the new millennium, the
fascisti hadn't bothered to keep lists of the disinterred. The old
tombstones were dumped into the sea, next to the limestone blocks
that the fishermen referred to as "Atlantis."

PADRE CONSTANTINO was my last chance. I had to get
beyond that squawked "come back another time" over the intercom. For the next several days, I camped out at Maria Santissima
delle Grazie. It would be impossible for Vincenzo Constantino to
avoid me if I hung around the church and rectory from dawn to
dusk.

Mike had explained the situation to the regulars at Di Maggio's *Caffe* and the Circolo Contadino. They watched me lay siege to Maria Santissima delle Grazie from their chairs on the piazza, discussing the fine points of my strategy. My search for the Monk was a village cause by now, with its supporters and its detractors. Both camps referred to me as "the author of our book," although I had yet to write a word. They followed my efforts with the partisan enthusiasm and close attention that they accorded to the local soccer team.

"Everybody is real interested in what you're doing," Mike said. But they kept their distance, just the same.

One morning, as I strolled past the rectory just after the 8:00 A.M. Mass, the door was open. I hesitated for a minute, then walked into the foyer. At the left, there was a closed inner door, to which a small plaque was affixed: " Don V. Constantino." It was the pastoral office. He was inside, barking into the telephone, angry as usual.

Enormous paintings of Padre Constantino's predecessors glared down from the foyer walls, next to a framed print from the Vatican that pictured all of the popes, from Saint Peter to John Paul II, in 321 tiny portraits. I studied it for half an hour, while the pastor continued chewing someone out on the phone. There were brief biographies under each portrait. The artist had been unimaginative in his depictions of the early pontiffs. The long, esoteric Vatican succession in the Dark Ages—Damasus I, Hormisdas, Simplicius, Felix IV, Adeodatus, and so on—was essentially rendered as the same thin, white bearded man, his nose slightly enlarged if he was Roman, his hair slightly curled if he was Greek or North African.

"Are you looking for an ancestor there, too?"

It was Padre Constantino, peering out from the doorway of his office. Like almost everyone in Terrasini, he knew who I was, even though we had never formally met.

I restrained the urge to throw myself to my knees. "Don Constantino," I stuttered, "I'm need you help very muchly." My Italian grammar had deserted me in panic.

He had heard that I'd lived in Paris, and answered in French.

"*A votre service, mon fils.*" But he was in a hurry, he added, and could only give me a minute. I followed him into the office, and instantly recognized that my prayers before the 321 popes had been answered.

Along the right-hand wall, in a glass-fronted case, were six shelves of ledgers. They were leather-bound, like their counterparts at the municipal annex, but smaller in format—about the size of a deluxe American paperback—and in far better shape. The parish archive not only existed, it had been carefully maintained, the volumes regularly aired and dusted by Padre Constantino's sister.

She sat on a bench in the office, next to Signora Notaro and her son, whom I recognized as one of the village's junior *carabinieri.* Had they all sat there, quietly doing nothing, while the priest was screaming into the phone? In any case, after four months of "come back another time," the staff of Maria Santissima delle Grazie was suddenly genial.

"*Buongiorno, Signore,*" the two women and policeman said in unison. I *buongiorno*-ed back and made small talk, my Italian recovering its grammar and my eyes glued to the bookcase.

The question now wasn't *whether* I would find the date of the Monk's death. It was *when.*

FIFTEEN

Death on a Country Lane

MY FIRST ENCOUNTER with the archives of Maria Santissima delle Grazie lasted no more than ten minutes, but it was enough to take a rough inventory of their contents. I could see that the shelves held three registries: the *Battezzati*, the *Coniugale*, and the *Defunti*. The "Baptized," the "Joined," and the "Deceased." They were the church equivalents of the municipal ledgers, recording the births, marriages, and deaths of Terrasini residents for twenty generations. Dates were embossed on the spine of each volume; the collection stretched back to the seventeenth century.

It was excruciating, peering through the glass of the bookcase but not daring to open it without an express invitation from Padre Constantino. I chatted mindlessly with Signora Notaro's son, reviewing the latest soccer results, while the priest went over the Lenten schedule with his assistant and sister. There was no choice but to bide my time. If I made the wrong impression now—too much haste, too little respect for Padre Constantino's sensitivities—the parish registry might be closed to me forever.

I edged toward the desk, softly clearing my throat to attract attention. Then I played what I hoped would be a trump card: "*Allora*, Don Constantino, I understand we're both *partinicosi.*"

He looked up. "*Comu?*"

"My mother's father, Salvatore DiGiuseppe, was born in your hometown," I said, neglecting to add that his family had moved from Partinico to Terrasini when he was an infant.

"Fine, wonderful," the priest answered. "Then you won't mind loaning your services to a fellow townsman for a few hours."

With that, he stood up, took me by the arm, and led us out the rectory door and straight to my Peugeot on the Piazza Duomo.

We spent the remainder of the day on parish errands: checking progress on cleanup work at an outlying chapel; dickering with the owner of a local forge on the price of an iron grill for the front gate of the church; trying to find out why transmission repairs on the priest's own car, a black Fiat, had not been completed as promised. It hadn't occurred to me that a country pastor was saddled with so many unecclesiastical responsibilities—that he had to be an adroit businessman and personnel manager, as well as a confessor and priest.

I sat outside a rural house for an hour, waiting as he administered the final rites to a thirty-five-year-old woman dying of breast cancer. Her husband and weeping teenaged daughter accompanied Padre Constantino back to the street. When we drove off, he sighed, and told me that he had never grown accustomed to this part of his job.

"It is always painful. Even after more than forty years as a priest . . ."

I had come to the Reverend Vincenzo Constantino in fear and trepidation that morning, wondering how to worm my way into the good graces of a tyrant. At the end of the day, I wasn't prepared to break entirely with the village assessment of him; for the most part, he was everything his critics made him out to be: pushy, impatient, surly to the point of rudeness. He was a difficult man, to be sure. But he was also trying his foul-humored best to do a difficult job in a difficult town. Padre Constantino was willing to bend, I thought, if only Terrasini would let him.

HE BENT THE PARISH RULES for me after the errands, albeit so slowly that I wanted to tear out my hair in frustration. It was one thing to have no idea where and when the Monk had died, no idea how to go about unlocking the rest of the story. It was quite another thing to walk past the closed rectory, day after day, in near certainty that it guarded my grandfather's secret.

The rule was that nobody could examine the registries without Padre Constantino himself present. Its flip side was that Padre Constantino hated to be disturbed in his office, except on the most urgent parish business. He resolved that contradiction right away, the evening of the errands: "Be here Friday at 8:00 A.M., when I'm saying Mass."

I would be allowed to enter the office with Signora Notaro and stay there for approximately forty minutes, the time Padre needed to proceed from intoning "I enter unto the altar of God" to "Go in peace, the Mass is ended." But I would be held mortally responsible, in Heaven and on Earth, for any damage to the records.

"These are old, old books, Signore Viviano. Very delicate. My sister and I treat them as though they recall the lives of our own ancestors rather than yours. If they fall apart, nothing can ever replace them."

The initial forty-minute appointment was a disaster. Overcome by a sudden eagerness to help, Signora Notaro's son also showed up at eight and began pulling the *Defunti* registers off the shelves at random, two or three at a time, then tossing them into a heap on the desk.

"Not here, not here, not here. I don't see any Vivianos at all!" he said, rifling through the volumes for 1874, 1875, and 1876, then barging on into the 1880s.

With a sinking heart, I saw that the old records were indeed fragile, thin leaves of brittle paper pressed between cracked leather covers. Two or three had pages askew after *Carabiniere* Notaro was done with them. Opening the 1880 registry to its index, I also saw why he had found no entries under "Viviano."

This was God's ledger, not the municipal government's. It was organized by Christian given name, the allusion to a saint, rather than by family.

In the florid handwriting of the age, all of the Francescos who had died in Terrasini that year were listed together in the index, alongside the dates of their deaths. The funeral entries themselves were arranged chronologically, noting the age of the *defunto*, the first and last names of his parents, the site of the death, and any witnesses who were present. It would be necessary to look up each and every deceased Francesco, in each and every volume, until I happened onto the Monk.

About ten minutes before the end of the Mass—the Sanctus bells were ringing in the church, on the other side of the foyer—I grabbed the discarded volumes, jamming the loose pages back inside, and returned them to the shelf, profusely thanking young Notaro for his help.

OVER THE WEEKEND, the rectory was shut tight. Nobody answered the intercom. On Monday, the door was open, and Signora Notaro was in the foyer. Alone. "Don Constantino says you have to be more careful," she mumbled. She let me in without speaking another word.

I started with the *Defunti* registry for 1864, the last year I could be sure that the Monk had been seen alive, standing at the baptismal font of Maria Santissima delle Grazie as a priest drizzled holy water on my infant great-grandfather, Giuseppe. The inscriptions were faint and written in Latin. It was agonizingly slow, methodical work. When forty minutes passed and Padre Constantino returned to the office, I was just finishing my survey of 1864. It yielded sixteen dead Francescos, five of whom were Francesco Paolos. But there was no Francesco Paolo Viviano.

The Monk had turned thirty-nine that year. He might have been killed in his forties, for all I knew, or as late as my grandfather's adolescence in the early twentieth century. A dismaying number of mornings in the rectory office stretched out before me.

A week passed. I made my way through the deceased of 1865, 1866, 1867. By the decade's end, well into the second week, I had unearthed several Francesco Paolo Vivianos, but not the one I sought. The birth dates and parents' names were always wrong.

It was a ghoulish enterprise, turning the pages of all those departed souls. Between the cemetery, the parish bookshelves, and the municipal ledgers, I had spent half the winter among the dead. One entry in the 1869 parish registry was repeated compulsively, over and over, appearing so many times that I lost count. It was for a baby girl, inscribed simply as "Ioanna," the latinized Giovanna, with no family name. She had died in the year of her birth. The exact date was never specified. Ioanna showed up on dozens of pages, a spectral infant in light brown ink on the brittle paper, the handwriting a bit shaky and a cross always drawn in beside the name. Sometimes, the phrase *"In nomine Patri"* was scrawled below Ioanna's cross. "In the name of the Father."

The inscriptions were a kind of desperate prayer, I thought, either on Ioanna's behalf or that of the priest whose hand trembled when he wrote them. Had he been the infant's unacknowledged father? Had he ever escaped his remorse over her death, before death added his own name to the ledger?

I lifted the pall, occasionally, with brief excursions among the *Battezzati*. One morning, I looked up the baptsimal records of my grandparents and imagined them as babies, crying in bewilderment as water was poured over them at the old marble font in Maria Santissima delle Grazie.

There was my mother's mother, Caterina Cammarata, baptized in January 1900, the future genius of our family kitchen. She died at ninety-one, frail and stone-deaf for twenty years.

Locating my father's mother was more difficult. After a fruitless search through the Angelinas of 1900, the year of birth cited on her 1955 American naturalization papers, I finally discovered her in the ledger for 1899—December 3, my own birth date and the feast of San Francesco. Angelina Tocco was a woman of great vanity, as well as a marvelous storyteller; she must have found it unbearable to be born in a previous century and successfully managed to lie about her age for eighty years.

There was my grandfather, "Paulus Vivianus" at his baptism on November 12, 1897. When I imagined him at the marble font, it was with my infant face, the image drawn from photographs of my own baptism in 1947. I had worn his fifty-year-old christening robes, which my great-grandmother carried to Harlem from Terrasini. She spent the evening before my baptism brushing lint off the lace baby's gown, and carefully ironing it smooth. She died three days later.

There was also the baby who would one day become the Monk, baptized on August 4, 1825. Several days passed before I turned up an entry for Domenico Valenti, his presumed murderer, born March 26, 1802, to Matteo Valenti and Caterina Orlando.

In the *Coniugale* volume for 1848 I found the marriage entry for the Monk and his first wife, Antonina Randazzo. She had been his age, twenty-three, when they were wed, a dozen years younger than my great-great-grandmother, Maria Bommarito, at the Monk's second wedding in 1855.

ON A MILD WEDNESDAY MORNING in the second week of February, I read the death notice of the man who gave me my name. The record, penned into the registry on November 18, 1876, was brief: "Franciscus Paulus Vivianus, age fifty-one, son of Gaetanus, was buried this day in Terrasini."

The parish ledger held no other details.

THE *BIBLIOTECA CENTRALE DELLA REGIONE SICILIANA*, the most important library on the island, is housed in a cavernous eighteenth-century palazzo in the center of Palermo. It fills an entire block of the Corso Vittorio Emmanuele, directly adjacent to the cathedral. The building originally served as a Jesuit seminary; its tranquil echoes survive in a courtyard planted in juniper and palm, and reading rooms with twenty-foot-high ceilings and gilded chandeliers. But the primary impression that the library gives today is one of a barely contained riot. Hundred of students, scholars, and literary hangers-on crush into the ornate lobby, thrusting identification cards and research permits at security guards.

I was altogether too familiar with the vagaries of the guards, who had approved my entry one day only to reject it the next. Fortunately, and in keeping with Sicilian practice, connections came to my rescue. An official of the library was a friend of a friend, with relatives in Detroit. She put me in touch with a librarian, Laura Terranova, who arranged for me to use the rear door of the palazzo, where staff normally entered. Terranova was a godsend; she tapped into the state computers to compile a bibliography for me, studied old manuscripts for anything that might be valuable to my research, and introduced me to the affable curator of the microfilm room.

That was my destination when dawn broke on Thursday, February 15, 1996. I had been unable to sleep all night, jumping in and out of bed so many times that the cat had been spooked and run off to hide. The date of the Monk's death was burning a hole in my stomach. Now that I knew exactly when he had died, it remained to find out how.

The *biblioteca* held the answer in a collection of microfilmed issues of the *Giornale di Sicilia* dating back to 1862. If Francesco Paolo Viviano had indeed been murdered, as my grandfather claimed, there would have been some notice in the *Giornale*. Each issue printed a dreary police-blotter column, the "Chronicle of Public Security," that kept track of killings, assaults, robberies, and arsons in Sicily's endlessly turbulent affairs.

Terranova was waiting for me at the rear entrance when I rang the library bell. I had taken the 7:39 A.M. bus, to be sure of getting to the *biblioteca* just as it opened at nine. On the way into the city, two of my fellow passengers were discussing a proposed civil service strike. I had called Terranova from the station, then run the twelve blocks to the library, when she confirmed the rumor.

"The strike starts at ten forty-five, Signore Viviano. There's no telling how long it may last."

We had one hour and forty-five minutes.

Terranova and I rushed to the microfilm room, where the

curator stood over a projector that was already threaded with the filmed *Giornale* issues for 1876. In twenty minutes, the article swam into focus, an unusually long item in the police blotter of November 24:

> *On the evening of sixteen November, a certain Onorato Evola of Terrasini was returning from a journey to the village of Giardinello in his cart, accompanied by four of his fellow peasants. But when they reached the Contrada of Quattro Vanelle, a voice called out from the roadside hedge, ordering them to throw themselves face down on the ground.*
>
> *They did so, and as the cart suddenly rolled away, out of control, two gunshots were fired, wounding a horse. At this point a man leaped from the hedge to grab the horse by the reins. Perhaps mistaking him for one of their robbery victims, his own accomplices shot him twice. He died immediately.*
>
> *Evola and his companions fled, saving themselves, and the aggressors, three in number, also withdrew in flight. It is believed that the motive of their assault was the robbery and assassination of Evola, and the authorities are on the track of the three malefactors.*
>
> *The policemen who hurried to the scene state that the dead man is an ex-monk of fifty years old from Favarotta, by the name of Viviano, Francesco Paolo.*

PART III

SIXTEEN

The Bandit Kingdom

The Madonie, Sicily
February 1996

WITH MY DISCOVERY of the *Giornale di Sicilia* article, the death of the Monk had burst into the light. But at first, I found even less clarity in his tale than I had when the murder lay hidden under the shroud of a century. He was a riddle buried in riddles. To peel away one layer of questions was only to be confronted with another.

Had my namesake really been a monk, as the *Giornale* article declared? Or was he simply a bandit in priestly disguise? Was he shot by accident in a botched armed robbery? Or was he assassinated by a powerful enemy as my grandfather insisted in his own last days?

What had become of Antonina Randazzo, Francesco's first wife, whose very existence had vanished from our family memory? They were married at Maria Santissima delle Grazie on September 20, 1848, amid the full tumult of that year's insurrection, when the village was in the hands of the rebels. Antonina's death notice never appeared in the ledgers of the *Defunti*. According to Padre Constantino, that meant she hadn't died in Terrasini. The couple must have left the village sometime after the revolt was crushed in the spring of 1849. But where did they go? And how did she die?

Mike said the Monk's story was like a *cacocciula*, the purple

161

artichoke that grows wild in the Palmeto canyons, its leaves tipped with razor-sharp spines that could tear a hand apart. "The heart of the *cacocciula* is protected by a hundred daggers. You can't get to it if you aren't hungry enough, my friend, and you can't reach it without pain."

I needed to think. Away from Palermo and Terrasini, and the archives of the dead. Away from the phone that tied me to my editors and the news wires, to the echoes of distant battlefields. Away from the labyrinth of riddles and the maze of names. So I loaded the car with books and notes, left a large open bag of dry cat food on the terrace for Monacu, and went where the Monk and his bride must have gone—where the failed insurgents of the coast had always gone to escape their pursuers. Into the mountains. Into the kingdom of bandits.

THE MADONIE MOUNTAINS begin their precipitous eastward march, which eventually reaches the lava fields of Mount Etna, in a series of limestone ridges that jut from the Tyrrhenian plain near Palermo. Thirty miles into the march, the ridges break into a dense concentration of peaks, some of them rising above six thousand feet, that overlook a highland plateau. At the plateau's northern edge, the sharp angularity of the Madonie proper yields to the forested glens and alpine valleys of the Nebrodi, a sister range. Together, the two mountain chains cover nearly two thousand square miles of the Sicilian interior.

The Palermo-Catania autostrada, the freeway that links the island's two major cities, cuts directly through the southern Madonie foothills. But I wasn't in a hurry. I took the old Roman road that the Monk and his bride would have used in their flight from Terrasini after the failed revolution of 1848. He was a stablehand and *carritteru,* a horse-cart driver; almost all of the Viviano men were. So I imagined him at the reins of an open cart, his young wife at his side, the wooden wheels churning, as I bumped east in the Peugeot past Corleone and Prizzi.

At Lercara Friddi, the road snaked down into a wasteland of

dry sulfurous canyons before resuming its climb at the drowsy mountain hamlet of Scillato. Beyond lay the immense wilderness, strung with fortified villages of limestone and lava, and brooded over by the volcanic sentinel of Mount Etna.

This is rural Europe as it was in my great-grandparents' day. The villagers' lives have accommodated few changes beyond the installation of electricity and the asphalting of main roads. What tourism there is remains a fledgling enterprise, aimed primarily at urban Sicilians with ancestral ties to the mountains. Hotels are found only in the largest towns, administrative centers that are frequented by itinerant salesmen and bureaucrats.

The rare outsiders who pass this way often find the Madonie strange, even disturbing. Its people are so introspective that they can be mistaken for mutes—Sicilian melancholy carried to a nearly wordless extreme. When they do speak, it is in the formal idiom of an archaic tongue, punctuated by the dialect equivalents of "thou" and "thine" and swept along on flights of poetic fancy. Mike's artichoke image had its origins in the high country; his father was a native of the Madonie who met Nanna during his military service on the coast during World War II and settled in Terrasini. The mountain idiom and extraordinary discretion survived the move. There was a Madonie proverb, Mike once warned me, that applied to anyone who failed to protect family secrets: "If you let dogs into the house, they may drag out bones."

The proverb followed me up the Madonie valleys. Etna's cone, snowcapped yet afire, was soon visible at every eastern twist of the road, smoking into the crystal air eleven thousand feet above a legendary sea—the wine-dark Ionian Sea of Homer and his Greek warriors, lost on their return from the fall of Troy.

The Greeks, Phoenicians, and Romans. The Byzantines, Saracens, and Normans. The Angevins, Aragonese, and Bourbons. The millennial succession of Sicily's foreign rulers, each of them reading their own proverbs and fables into the landscape, was a continuous narrative here, as though the long course of the island's history had been compacted into a single instant of frozen time.

Homer's *Odyssey* shipwrecked its wandering hero on the Ionian shore of Sicily, where his crewmen were eaten alive by Polyphemus, the giant Cyclops of Etna. The Romans used Sicilian mountain oak to build the fleet that destroyed African Carthage, a central drama in Virgil's *Aeneid* and Dante's *Divine Comedy*. The Saracens left their mark all over the map, in serpentine street markets that echo the *souks* of Tunisia and Morocco and in villages with recognizably Arab names: Gibilmanna, Alimena, Calascibetta.

Often, as at the venerable church of San Antonio Abate in the town of Polizzi Generosa, a Muslim minaret had simply been converted into a Gothic campanile. Other churches were grafted onto Greek temples, their austere columns left intact to support eleventh-century Norman towers or to provide maypoles for the seraphim and cherubim who gyrate across Spanish baroque facades.

The town names, the churches, the timeless syncretic jumble: They were all reminders of conquerors who were in turn conquered, of rulers from the coast who were swept aside by their successors and obliged to flee to the mountains. Into Sicily's insurgent heart.

ON MY FIRST PASSAGE through the Madonie, after the Falcone assassination in 1992, I had stopped for dinner at a tiny *osteria* in Polizzi Generosa. The sign over its entrance, on a cobbled piazza near San Antonio Abate, read "Da-da-da Cicciu." One of my fellow diners explained that the proprietor, Francesco Ficile, had stuttered as a boy. He was a gruff and weathered eighty-one now, and announced the day's menu in the level monotone that stutterers cultivate to relax their tongues. It had rid him of the da-da-das, but when he opened the *osteria* in 1950, it inherited the name.

After the mountain fashion, Cicciu was resolutely taciturn, as were the villagers who played cards for hours on end at three tables in the rear of the room, watching his wife, Rosa Di Martino, cook. Their conversation rarely expanded on the *"Bon giu"* that greeted arrivals and the old-fashioned *"a Diu,"* "Go with God," that signaled departures. Rosa, a delicately beautiful woman in her seventies with

soft green eyes, was even more taciturn than her husband and customers.

The reserve masked an infinite supply of natural warmth.
Polizzi Generosa had no hotel, but Cicciu and Rosa offered me the
use of a mill they owned in the nearby countryside when I asked if
there was a room to let. Their son led me to it in his car, descending a mile from the town to a forest clearing.

The mill had been built in 1601, its date carved into a lintel
above a water race that ran full with melted snow from the upper
valleys and gurgled under the building. The grinding stone sat
encased in a huge wooden box at the center of what served as a
living room, with three bedrooms arrayed around it and a simple
farm kitchen at the far end. It looked out into an orchard of chest-
nuts, walnuts, peaches, and cherries that had withstood countless
mountain blizzards. A red terra-cotta stove, scorched from generations of use, burned in the millstone room, fed by cords of dried
pine and oak that were stacked outside beneath a lean-to.

I stayed for a week, eating two staggering meals per day in the
osteria. Everything from the olive oil and tomatoes in the pasta
sauce, to the roast hare, wild boar, pecorino cheese, wine, and
grappa that rounded out the feast, was either plucked by Rosa from
her garden, bottled by Cicciu, or shot in the mountain forest by the
card-table regulars. The bill for my room and board was toted in
half an hour of labored addition. Cicciu looked pained when he
finally arrived at a figure, scribbling the number onto the corner of
a discarded newspaper and pushing it into my hand. The sum was
so low that I left a one-hundred-thousand lire note sitting behind a
vase on the bar, hoping Rosa would find it later. But at our parting,
she embraced me and slipped it back into my jacket pocket; I
didn't realize what had happened until I was home in Paternella.

There was no question where I would sleep this time. When I
called Polizzi Generosa and asked Cicciu if he remembered me, all
he said was *"Aspettiamu."* "We're waiting for you."

THE WORLD THAT AWAITED THE MONK and his bride in these mountains, a century and a half before me, defied the conventions of its age even more thoroughly than it did when I wandered into Polizzi Generosa. It was in every sense a world apart, outside of the law as well as oblivious to time.

The Madonie had sheltered the rebels and survivors of Sicily's violent history for more than a thousand years, offering discreet hospitality, no questions asked. And it had provided the means to a living, the robbery of vulnerable travelers on the torturous mountain roads that linked Palermo to Catania, Sicily's west to Sicily's east. On these roads, deposed aristocrats or failed revolutionaries were transformed into brigands and bandits, generations of highwaymen ambushing generations of wayfarers.

By 1848, when Francesco and Antonina fled Terrasini, the pattern was so fixed that it had become the template of Sicilian history:

A battle rages on the coast between invader and native. Through overwhelming numbers and cunning betrayal, victory falls to the invader. The vanquished retreat to the mountains, and in the pristine wilderness a natural aristocracy of bandit princes takes root. They rule an empire-in-exile.

THERE ARE SCATTERED ALLUSIONS to outlaws in the annals of Sicily's mountainous interior well before the birth of Christ, when the template of conquest and retreat was forged in the crucible of Phoenician, Greek, and Roman invasion. But it is with the brothers Nino and Biagio, "the two bandits of the Partinico forest" celebrated in a fourteenth-century folk ballad, that the recognizable hallmarks of a lasting tradition are established.

The term "bandit," *banditu* in Sicilian dialect, has its origin in the medieval Latin verb "bannire" (to ban or proscribe), which eventually produced the Spanish word *banditos*, literally "banned men." Historians believe that most were tax rebels who refused to pay royal levies on their lands and crops to the island's rulers in Madrid.

Tradition is infinitely more poetic. In the folk ballad of the Partinico forest, the bandit Nino is a chivalric hero who visits Partinico in disguise and catches the glance of a beautiful *contessa*. His brother warns him of the dangers of forbidden passion, but Nino is desperately enamored. Assisted by Biagio, he scales the wall of the amorous contessa's palace. As my grandmother would have put it, that night "they experienced genuine love."

The two brothers fight their way out of the palace grounds the next morning against a force of thirty armed men and escape into the mountains. When the storm winds howl through the forest, however, Nino forever hears in them the distant voice of the *contessa*: "He will return, he will return."

Erotic adventures, stolen nights of forbidden passion between noblewoman and commoner, pervade the bandit tradition. Nino is recognizably an ancestor of Gaetano the Falcon, and the *contessa's* sighs foretell those of the Queen of Naples in my grandmother's fable.

But there is a second, more significant feature of the bandit leitmotiv in the Partinico folk ballad. The fugitive brothers are offered sanctuary in the remote fortresses of lordly Norman families who have been deposed by the island's new rulers and withdrawn into a separate realm with its own history, language, and code. Already, more than five hundred years before the birth of the *sistema*, the Sicilian imagination has taken refuge from the legalistic present in a clandestine past. Justice and morality have assumed multiple, competing definitions.

The die has been cast.

BY THE SIXTEENTH CENTURY, popular support for the bandit underworld is so strong that the Spanish crown feels obliged to make it a capital crime.

"We hereby state, ordain, and command," Emperor Carlos V thunders in 1535, "that anyone who assists these bandits for one day, two, or three and up to ten, shall be penalized at the discretion of the courts; and those who have continued to do so for more than ten days shall be subject to the penalty of death." The bandits themselves may be killed, for a reward, by anyone who succeeds in finding them.

Thirty-five years later, nothing has changed. The viceroy of Palermo issues a proclamation that unintentionally catalogs, in fine detail, the impressive range of services that Sicilians are still providing to bandits. It is also a de facto indictment of the regime, a measure of the profound alienation of its subjects. The proclamation threatens to deport

> all those, including noblemen, who give or offer aid or encouragement to the escape or flight of [bandits], or inform them of judicial charges against them, or see to it that they receive medical treatment or are provided with medicine, powder, or musket balls, things to eat or drink, any type of arms, of horses or other things necessary for the care of horses, or acquire contraband or money that has been given to them by said bandits.

The final clause is telling: bandits are robbing from the Crown and sharing the wealth with the peasantry.

The model is the celebrated Giangiorgio Lancia, who presides over the Madonie from 1570 to 1600 with an army of several hundred brigands. "Lancia principally made war on usurious moneylenders and the rich," writes Salvatore Lo Presti, the chief historian of Sicilian brigandage. "And whatever he took from them, he passed on to his men and to the poor."

Robin Hood has arrived in the mountains of Sicily, the precursor of the line that will lead to Paolo Cocuzza and the Monk. In the Madonie, the latest viceroy concedes, the real government is not Spain but "the kingdom of those known as bandits."

FRUSTRATED, enraged by the popular resistance to its courts and police, Madrid responds to the chronic lawlessness with lawlessness of its own. "Captains-at-arms" are appointed, authorized to form troops of paid vigilantes and undertake any method necessary to fight the scourge of banditry, to establish "order" in the countryside of western Sicily.

The tone is set with the apprehension and execution of Lancia. Each of his four limbs is roped to the stern of a warship in the capital city's harbor. The ships weigh anchor, in plain sight of thousands of Palermitans, and Lancia's body is ripped apart.

Over the following century, the suppression of banditry grows increasingly brutal. When the bandit Antonino Catinella—known in dialect as *Sata li Viti*, "the Vine Jumper," for his astonishing agility and talent for escape—is captured in 1706, he is tortured for four days and decapitated. His severed head is impaled on a spear and mounted on the city wall of Palermo until the flesh rots in the sun and nothing is left but a bare skull.

A similar end awaits Antonio Di Blasi, a bandit so acclaimed for his murders of abusive landlords that peasants refer to him as "the Just Executioner." He is more widely remembered as *Testalonga*, "Long Head," for the narrowness of his face and brow. One imagines him to have resembled a somber El Greco Christ.

Testalonga is born in 1737, in the wake of dynastic struggles that shift control of Sicily from Madrid first to the House of Savoy, then to Austria, and finally to the Spanish Bourbons, in a chaotic two-decade scramble between 1713 and 1734. But the new regime is the old regime, as far as Sicilians are concerned: still foreign, still reliant for "public security" on the ever more brutal vigilantism of the captains-at-arms.

The mountains, too, remain the same: still the lawless kingdom of bandits, with Testalonga as its prince in the first half century of Bourbon rule. In 1767, at the age of thirty, after a brief but sensational outlaw career dedicated to avenging widows and orphans, he and four of his men are ambushed by a captain-at-arms detachment. As is now the usual practice, they are tortured severely and decapitated. Their heads join what remains of the vine-jumper's on the Palermo wall.

CALCULATING AND EFFICIENT, methodically violent to the point of sadism, the Captains-at-Arms set the distant scene for Toto Riina and Giovanni Brusca. For the *sistema del potere*.

But before the late nineteenth century, the *sistema* does not exist. The Mafia, the institution that will evolve from the vigilante armies of the captains, is not even a word when Francesco Viviano and his first wife, Antonina Randazzo, are married.

The Bandit Kingdom is in its prime in 1848. It is a world apart, complete with its own heroes, its own legends. It has its own richly subversive vocabulary, the vocabulary of the conquered employed against the conquerors. Its words are adapted from prison experience, from the coded dialect in which prisoners speak to confuse their jailers. *Lingua furbesca,* in the phrase of the Sicilian anthropologist Guiseppe Pitre. "The language of cunning."

In the Bandit Kingdom, *addurmisciri,* literally "to decorate," means to kill, as does *aggiuccari,* "to put in the chicken coop." To confess is *cantari,* "sing," an underworld usage that will survive immigration and take hold in America. A highwayman's roost is *la purtedda,* the nook. Someone known to be a bandit, a soldier of the mountain kingdom, is *calia,* a hazelnut.

All officers of the criminal justice system, including the police and the military, are *surci,* mice. *Teniri,* to hold on, is to remain silent under interrogation, an especially admired quality as the mice commonly resort to *subbiri,* suffering, the practice of torture.

This is the world of Francesco Viviano and Antonina Randazzo, a volatile brew of savage crime and equally savage vigilantism shrouded in romantic legend.

The legend reaches its full maturity with Pasquale Bruno and Antonino Buzzetta, two bandits who are near contemporaries of the Monk, and whose exploits must have fired my namesake's childhood fantasies.

They pay for their assaults on the Bourbon peace in the now time-honored fashion, with their heads—and in Bruno's case, with both hands, which are severed at the wrist. Following his execution, the hands are presented to the Prince of Castelnouvo, along with the head, encased in an iron box. Depending on the source, Buzzeta was apprehended and executed in 1823, or lived on into the 1830s. The precise criminal records were lost in the Allied bombing of Palermo in 1943, leaving few documented facts on either of these two men. But certain notable details have survived.

In descriptions provided by wealthy robbery victims, Pasquale Bruno's waist is invariably bound in a trademark *cintura di seta rossa,* "a silken red sash." Antonino Buzzetta, whose *'nciuria* was *Fra Diavolo,* "Brother Devil," wore the robes of a monk on his nighttime forays in the Castellammare hills. He was known to make surprise visits to its peasant households, carrying gifts of food and stolen Bourbon gold.

SEVENTEEN

Fable of the Chickpea

→>—<←

LONG BEFORE I SAW THE MADONIE, my grandparents
spoke of the Bandit Kingdom in their fables. The mountains were a
principal setting in Grandma Angelina's tale of the chickpea. In its
awful climax, mastery of a secret language means the difference
between life and death. The tale opens with a beautiful woman
named Santuzza, followed through the streets of a coastal city by
Angelina Tocco's lilting voice: "Santuzza went on a much longer
walk than normal that evening, thinking about some little problem
at home, until she suddenly found herself alone in a piazza she'd
never seen before as the night arrived."

My cousins Donna and Angie sucked in their breath. They
knew what was coming. *"Stupida!"* Grandma suddenly cried, glaring
at them. "Alone! At night! Don't you girls ever do that or I'll kill
you both!"

Then she looked me hard in the eye. From the time I turned
seven, I was expected to escort Donna and Angie, who lived upstairs
in our eastside Detroit duplex, to elementary school and back.

"Maybe Santuzza had important things to do, but nothing is
that important," Grandma continued. "And sure enough, some soldiers of the king came along that night, and when they saw this
beautiful girl alone, they could not control themselves. They dishonored her, *mischina*. They made it impossible for her to think of
having a husband or children, and they defiled the name of the
Virgin Mary."

It would be some years before any of us grasped more than the fact that Santuzza's life had somehow been ruined by the king's soldiers.

News of the dishonored Santuzza flew from the city, carried by travelers into the faraway mountain glen where her brother Turiddu—"Salvatore," the Savior—presided over a band of men. Brigands, to be exact, although their trade was presented to us in a more sympathetic guise.

My grandfather liked to chime in at this point. "Turiddu, he always take from the big people and give to the poor people."

"Grandpa, shut up, I'm telling them the story." My grandmother hated to be interrupted.

"Turiddu cried when he heard what had happened, because he loved his sister," she went on. "He gathered his men together and they decided that something had to be done. The city was ruled by a king from another country in those days. He was evil, and his followers were as evil as he was. The only place anybody was safe from them was the mountain kingdom. There were no foreign soldiers there."

One of Turiddu's men, his closest advisor, asked to speak. There was a problem, he pointed out. "How will we know our enemies? They are strangers, but their faces are like ours."

It was then, Grandma explained, that the Virgin appeared to Turiddu in a dream and suggested the plan of the chickpea. Like the crux of so many of her tales, it too hung on a name. Everywhere in Europe, she told us, people ate these small golden peas, and everywhere they called them something different, "but nobody except a true Sicilian can say the name that we use."

The chickpea in Sicilian dialect is *lu ciciru*. Correctly pronounced, the word resembles the sound of a breeze rustling through a garden. *"Lu shii-shii-ru."* Incorrectly pronounced, it can be confused with dialect terms for the beak of a bird, a tiny fish, or the penis of an infant.

Turiddu called a meeting of all of the mountain bands. Each man was supplied with a *ciciru*. Armed with sharpened knives, the brigands descended on the capital of the evil king. I still feel a slight chill run down my spine when the scenes that follow return to me in daydreams.

"They crept into the city at night, in small groups of four or five men," Grandma said, "and they stopped everyone they saw in the streets. Only the leaders of the groups spoke, and all they said was this."

She held a dried chickpea between two fingers and moved it slowly toward my face: "Signore, please tell me, what are you looking at in my hand?"

The evil kingdom fell that night, the dark city littered with its rulers' corpses.

MY GRANDMOTHER'S *CICIRU* FABLE was her rendition of a classic legend, the folk memory of a bloody revolt that began as the bells sounded for evening Mass in Palermo on Easter Monday, 1282. Known popularly as the "night of the Sicilian Vespers," the uprising soon engulfed the entire island, inspiring terror in the feudal courts of thirteenth-century Europe.

The folk legend also maintained that the soldiers of a foreign army had insulted a Sicilian woman, bringing on their own wholesale slaughter by an outraged populace. As in Angelina Tocco's fable, the insurgents identify their enemies by defying them to pronounce the dialect word for chickpea.

The historic "evil king" was Duke Charles of Anjou, brother of King Louis IX of France. The Angevins came into possession of Sicily in 1266, unseating the island's young hereditary ruler, Manfredi, with the financial and military support of the Vatican. Charles was a tyrannical megalomaniac, and although he is believed to have visited Sicily only once in his sixteen-year reign, his barons ruthlessly plundered the island on his behalf.

Historians differ as to whether the uprising of the Sicilian Vespers was truly spontaneous or a coup d'état engineered by Manfredi's deposed nobles, many of whom had been forced from their coastal lands and into the mountains by the Angevins.

What is clear is that the revolt swelled, almost immediately, into a social explosion that threatened the very concept of feudal order. In a foreshadowing of the slaughter that would so horrify Giuseppe Garibaldi in 1860, thousands of peasants armed with scythes and hand-turned spears swept down on the coastal cities. Through the long night of that Easter Monday in 1282, the mobs took their vengeance on anyone with a French accent. The inability to speak fluent dialect was, in fact as well as in fable, a death warrant.

By week's end, there was not a Frenchman alive in Sicily, except for a few knights who held out in the rocky bastion of Sperlinga, thirty miles east of Polizzi in the shadow of Etna.

For five months after the vespers, a protorepublic governed Sicily, a naïve medieval experiment in democracy that soon descended into anarchy, according to contemporary accounts. The peasant fury was spent by autumn and the experiment faded into oblivion.

The republic was unseated on September 4, 1282, by Pedro of Aragon, the first in Sicily's six-century gauntlet of Spanish and Bourbon rulers. He took the throne with the active help of several fellow monarchs, including former allies of Charles of Anjou. No court in Europe was anxious to see peasants rule themselves.

The Night of the Vespers passed very quickly into the realm of myth, with Charles and his Angevins assuming the roles of evil king and rapacious soldiers in a vast literature of dialect poetry, proverb, and song. They were painted into garish battle scenes on the sideboards of carts, and employed—anonymous but still recognizable—in the fables of Sicilian-American grandparents.

Retold again and again through the generations, the tale of the vespers seized the island's collective imagination. It was the fulcrum of its history, the centerpiece in the Sicilian template.

It was also, it seemed to me, one history imbedded within another, a layering of sensibilities that called to mind those strange syncretic churches with their Doric Greek columns and Spanish Baroque facades. The deeper I plunged into the past, the more I saw the legend of the vespers as another of Sicily's manifold curtains.

Flitting behind it, ghostly but insistent, were the founding princes of the Bandit Kingdom, the Monk's ancestors and mine.

AT CICCIU FICILE'S urging, I drove east to take in the pre-Lenten carnival at Acireale on the weekend before Ash Wednesday. The winter sun cast long shadows on the old Roman road as it snaked through the switchbacks that necklace the Madonie villages. Petralia Soprana, chill and windswept on a ridge high above the tree line, glared down on its temperate valley sister, Petralia Sottana. Gangi poured over the sides of a green hill in cascades of whitewashed stucco. Sperlinga was a troglodyte hamlet, nested with cave houses that had been dug into a limestone cliff under the bleak fortress where the last Angevin knights held out.

At the village of Centuripe, I somehow lost the way and found myself inching upward almost vertically, on a street so narrow that it was impossible to do anything except continue forward. Eventually I arrived at a complete impasse, one wheel on the edge of a stomach-wrenching chasm, the driver's side of the Peugeot scraping up against the wall of a house. Its proprietor, whose own scratched and battered Fiat dangled over the brink on a makeshift wooden platform, came to my assistance. He took the wheel, backed the car up his stone staircase, step-by-step, eased it around in a U-turn, and headed me into a side street that led back to the main road.

After Centuripe, the limestone villages abruptly disappeared, replaced by settlements constructed entirely of black volcanic blocks quarried from Etna. The mountain had erupted half a dozen times in recent years. Rivers of solidified lava crisscrossed the surrounding fields, half swallowing the burned remains of farmhouses in ebony rock. In the patches of soil that remained, grapes had been replanted and vine trellises erected. Etna has been devouring rural villages and farms for four thousand years, but the farmers always return. The volcanic earth is too fertile to surrender.

The distance between Polizzi and Acireale, which lies on the Ionian Sea at the far side of Etna, is less than 120 miles. It took half a day to negotiate the sinuous road, and I arrived at Aci Trezza, the next town down the coast from my destination, at dusk.

"Too many cars in Acireale. Leave yours out on the highway," Cicciu had recommended. I did him one better and left it in Aci Trezza, boarding a narrow-gauge train that wheezed around the base of the volcano.

THE CLAMOR OF ACIREALE reached us before the city itself appeared, a dense blanket of noise that smothered the train as it pulled into a suburban station. As I continued ahead on foot, a continuous human roar filled the air, a single sustained shout exploding from thousands of voices and crashing into a wall of automobile horns.

Locked together bumper to bumper, cars were packed motionless in every street, forming vast lines that converged on a piazza in the town's center. The vehicles closest to the piazza were quiet; their drivers, who now understood that they would be parked where they were for the rest of the night, sat slumped over their wheels or tried to calm antsy children who bounced in and out of the rear seats. Many of the cars had been abandoned.

It was the same every year, Bobby Cortese later told me. He was even convinced that the same Catania and Palermo drivers returned annually with their families, in the inexplicable hope that there would be light traffic this time.

Night had descended fully now, but the center of Acireale was aflame with multicolored lightbulbs that had been strung over the piazza and the city's two principal thoroughfares. Motorized floats wafted slowly along them in a two-mile circuit, carrying gigantic effigies of devils, Italian politicians, ghosts, serpents and dragons, toads and lizards, many of them twenty or thirty feet high, that mechanically raised and lowered their heads. Blasts of music from industrial speakers mounted on the floats rattled the balconies of palazzi and ecclesiastical buildings along the parade route, from which clusters of nuns and priests stared down at the floats with rosaries in their hands.

I was staring back up at one of these little gatherings when an elderly woman suddenly limped out from the crowd and slammed me over the head as hard as she could with a plastic hammer. I ducked as she wound up for a second swing. Laughing hysterically, she hobbled off. Then I was hit again, by a teenaged girl, and a third time, by a thin, bespectacled man whom I took to be her father. The more I ducked, the thicker the blows fell, until six or eight people, an entire family, from grandparents and uncles to adolescent children, were pounding away at me in unison. The hammers were rigged with whistles that produced crude, farting squawks at each blow.

I gave a sharp push to the closest hammerer, a man in his forties, and when he stumbled backward into the street I ran.

The piazza by now was full of small torture circles like the one that had surrounded me, with people of every description beating out their whistling punishment on anyone who tried to leave the area. The only way to avoid them was to stand flat against the wall of one of the buildings. Determined to get out of there, I yanked a hammer out of the hand of a little boy who was pinned to the wall next to me with his mother and began smashing with full force at anybody who stood in my path.

After a few minutes, I fell in with a marching band, goose-stepping alongside a float that featured a monstrous papier-mâché statue of Giuliano Andreotti, the seven-time Italian prime minister who was currently on trial in Palermo on corruption and organized crime charges; it pivoted from side to side on its mechanized legs, lunging forward periodically to bite at a pile of outsized banknotes that sat on the prow of the float. Behind Andreotti, a troupe of heavily made-up adolescent girls in the gowns of Spanish noblewomen danced frantically to an Italian rap song.

In its madness, in its unconcealed fantasy of violence, Acireale was not simply another setting for the carnivals that punctuate Lenten week everywhere in the traditional Catholic world. There was something else being said here, another cry sounded in the riotous night.

THE MARIONETTE THEATER is the principal folk stage of Sicily. Before the dawn of television, itinerant puppeteers carried their props and handmade wooden performers to the most remote villages, where they reenacted many of the same legends that I heard over my grandmother's mangle.

The heart of the puppet repertoire always has been a cycle of heroic sagas from the eighth and ninth centuries featuring the *Paladini di Francia,* the cavaliers of Charlemagne who carried the banner of Christ into battle against Islam on the Iberian Peninsula. This is not surprising, given Sicily's own history as a primal battleground between Islam and Christianity. But the moral ambiguities of that war in its puppet version are often very surprising indeed. And nowhere more so than in the tale of a paladin named Viviano, which would certainly have been known to the Monk in his childhood.

In the puppet tale, the name "Viviano" is presented as Arab, although it resembles no Arab name that I know of, and appears to have no meaning in Arabic. It is given to the hero by Abalante, the emir of then Muslim Portugal, who kidnaps him as an infant. The emir raises the boy as his own son. By early manhood, Viviano is a celebrated Muslim warrior, and Abalante puts him at the head of his army.

One day, when Viviano has been wounded and is near death, an angel comes to him—the echo of Ano's cry must have caught the Monk's attention, as it did mine—and reveals his true origin: He is "Bernardo," the long-missing son of the paladin Buovo d'Agromante.

The warrior heals, accepts Christianity, and secures his rightful place among Charlemagne's knights. Yet he never reassumes the name Bernardo. He remains "Viviano," the source of his heroic identity still rooted in his education and exploits as a Muslim.

Sicily's popular culture is a maelstrom of such unexpectedly subversive currents. There is, for instance, the popular account of *la tarantella,* "the tarantula," the island's frantic folk dance. Its origins, Sicilians believe, lie in the unsuccessful first siege of Arab Palermo by Norman crusaders in 1064. Establishing their camp on a ridge over the city, they fail to notice that it is infested with tarantula spiders, whose stings produce the uncontrollable nervous shivers represented in the dance. Howling in pain and desperately slapping at the spiders, the Normans are forced to withdraw from Palermo. Nature itself, the legend suggests, abhors the invader—even when the invaders are Christian and the defenders Muslim.

The *tarantella* is another exercise in code, a subtext in the island's dreams. The visible surface of Sicilian life, its conscious sensibility, is western and Christian. But in its coded dreamlife, the island is eastern and Islamic.

This is one way to make sense of the violent contradictions that fuel Sicilian behavior and shape the larger pattern of Sicilian history. The disjuncture between reality and dreams—between the visible present and the disguised past—is a proxy war, with the divided heart as its battleground. Not just any war: It is the *war of wars,* the seminal conflict that has raged across half the world since Muhammad's followers swept out of Islam's desert birthplace in the seventh century and seized a huge swath of Christian Europe, establishing a key stronghold in Sicily.

When Norman crusaders reconquered the island at the end of the eleventh century, after 250 years of North African Muslim rule, the vanquished Arabs withdrew first to the mountains, and then into a ghostly universe of dark fantasies, buried names, and hidden motives.

I wondered, when I reflected on it, if one of those Arab ghosts was our ancestral Ano, a man from the desert who is renamed, "saved," and converted, by the intercession of Mary and her angel.

The rebellion of the Sicilian Vespers was stage-managed, like its ritual reenactment in Acireale, into the Christian festivals of Lent and Easter week. Behind the curtain, its followers shouted their resistance to everything that Christian Europe represented, knives thrust into anyone could not pronounce *"ciciru"*—the dialect word is of Arabic origin—hammers wielded in the night against invaders.

IN THE TEN DECADES that preceded the Vespers, Sicily had been wracked by continuous popular uprisings, culminating in the night of Easter Monday, 1282. For the first seven of these decades, the revolts were explicitly Muslim. And as it happens, the greatest of their leaders was from the Castellammare hills.

His Arabic name was Mohammed ibn Abbad, but he was more widely known by his latinized nom de guerre, *Mirabettus,* "the Wondrous." His own preference was a self-bestowed Arabic title, *emir el muslimin,* "prince of the believers."

By the year 1210, Mirabettus and his insurgents ruled a huge expanse of the Sicilian interior, extending from the high valleys of the Madonie to the rich agricultural fields of Alcamo, twenty-five miles west of Terrasini. Medieval sources refer to it as the "Emirate of the Mountains." Its lightly disguised reminders of Muslim Sicily are at every turn. The olive groves of Alcamo were planted by an Arab farmer, "Al-qamah." Cinisi takes its name from the Arabic *cins,* "sanctified ground." The name of the beach at Magaggiari, where the *picciotti* were trapped by the Bourbon army in April 1860, is derived from *margia-el-giari,* "river mouth." And there is spring-fed Favarotta itself, from *fawar,* "the well."

Mirabettus was finally defeated in 1222, by an army of sixty thousand Christian infantry and two thousand horsemen. His followers made a desperate last stand in the countryside just south of Terrasini in 1243, before being exiled to the Italian mainland or withdrawing far into the Madonie. The template had been struck:

A battle rages between invader and native. Through force of arms and cunning betrayal, victory falls to the stranger. The vanquished retreat to the mountains, where a natural aristocracy of bandit princes takes root.

Along with Cinisi and Alcamo, the principal towns of the Emirate of the Mountains were Partinico, Cinisi, Corleone, Montelepre, Prizzi, and Jato—later renamed "San Giuseppe Jato"—where the decisive battle against Mirabettus took place. In short, the topography of his realm corresponds exactly with that of the brigand *squadre* who fought in the failed revolutions of 1820 and 1848, and later alongside Garibaldi. By 1900, it had become a map of the *sistema del potere,* landmarked by the birthplaces of Toto Riina, Tanu Badalamenti, and Giovanni Brusca.

It was the scene of my namesake's wanderings with Antonina Randazzo.

EIGHTEEN

Antonina Randazzo

The Madonie, Sicily
September 1851

THE CANYONS WEST OF POLIZZI GENEROSA are *blinding white in the mountain sun. White as the sulfur pits that honeycomb the Lercara ridge. White as a shroud. The cart heaves and shudders over the creek bed, the horse straining forward under Francesco's whip. Antonina gasps with each jolt of the wheels.*

She knows that it can't be helped. The roads below the Madonie are level, and cooled by gulf winds, but the flatlands belong to the Bourbon police, and her husband is a wanted man. In Terrasini, there will be someone to hide them. In the Lercara canyons, there are the dry riverbeds that pass for trails, the furnace sun, and choking sulfur dust to keep the sbirri at bay.

Antonina Randazzo is twenty-six years old and pregnant. Are she and Francesco driven north from their mountain sanctuary by the sheer attachment to home? By Antonina's longing for her mother's comforting hand? By Francesco's fears for his wife and unborn child? The precise reasons, the arguments for and against this return to Terrasini, will be forever lost a century and a half later. But the naked progression of cause and effect is clear, even from the sketchy records that survive. The cart takes its jarring course past the ruined fortresses of the mountain emirate, along other riverbeds that skirt Prizzi and Corleone, to a mule track that winds around the parched gully between San Giuseppe Jato and Montelepre. By mid-September, Francesco and Antonina are in Terrasini.

The vendemmia has arrived, and the vineyards below Palmeto are a Saracen carpet, woven crimson and gold with ripened fruit. Harvesters crouch among the vines, conical straw baskets strapped to their backs. The Castellammare air is drunken with crushed grape, orange blossom, and salt mist from the gulf.

There is an army of fugitives at large in western Sicily. More than sixteen thousand men—hardened criminals, petty thieves, Bourbon political dissidents—escaped from the prisons of Palermo during the chaos of 1848. Some have accepted the harsh royal amnesty; many have taken refuge in the Madonie. When the need arises, they follow the riverbeds and mule tracks to the coast, under the noses of police and army commanders, who have been bribed to look away. By late 1851, the fugitives are paying regular visits to their families. But pretenses must be maintained and risks shared. Someone must agree to shelter, in secret, these wayfarers from the Bandit Kingdom.

Francesco and Antonina, heavy with child, are turned away at the doors of their parents. However fiercely the mothers plead, the two fathers, Gaetano Viviano and Pasquale Randazzo, will not offer the necessary bribes to the police.

The enmity between these men is bitter. At Francesco and Antonina's wedding in 1848, no Viviano or Randazzo appears among the witnesses noted in the ledgers of Maria Santissima delle Grazie. It is a love match, the fruit of irresistible attraction rather than contractual arrangement, a rare and suspect event in nine-teenth-century Sicily. An event that the families refuse to condone, although they are both viddani, the ledgers proclaim, with manure in their hair and black dirt under their nails.

The couple must find shelter elsewhere. Among friends in the village, when they dare, or in Francesco's rough hut behind the brow of Monte Palmeto when the danger of arrest is too great.

On September 30, Antonina gives birth to a boy. The birth is never officially reported to the municipal authorities. It is instantly apparent to the midwife that something is wrong. She sends for a priest. The infant is christened, given the last rites, and registered in the Church archives as "Francesco Paolo Viviano."

This is an act of love on Antonina's part, mingled with an act of bitter contempt by Francesco. The struggling infant's father, my namesake as well as his, has turned against the family that rejects his marriage and engraved his defiance in a name. His own name, rather than his father's, as tradition demands.

On October 2, 1851, Antonina's three-day-old baby dies. Pasquale Randazzo reports the event to the authorities; for the record, he states that the father of the dead child is Francesco Paolo Viviano. It is the Randazzo family's only acknowledgment of Antonina's husband and child, and the only official evidence that the child ever existed.

No cause of death is recorded in the book of Defunti.

Ninety-six years, four generations of broken tradition, will pass before the Monk's descendants name another infant boy Francesco Paolo Viviano.

That boy is me.

TWO YEARS AFTER HER CHILD WAS BURIED, Antonina Randazzo followed him to the grave. Her death was marked only by the passing reference I'd found in the 1855 marriage certificate of Maria Bommarito and Francesco Paolo Viviano. At first, I hadn't known what to make of this discovery. But as I traveled the Madonie, following the mountain old roads that my bandit-namesake would have known in his years as a fugitive, I began to see that Antonina was the key I had been searching for all along. Before she entered the drama, the Monk himself had been a shadow; the more I learned of Antonina, the more the shadow took on weight and density.

Like Giuseppe Viviano's refusal to name my grandfather "Francesco"—with its evidence of a lasting emotional divide between the Monk and his son—the details of his short, tragic marriage to Antonina helped bring the Monk to life.

I had plunged back into the parish ledgers in the weeks after I returned from the mountains. Every page now carried me further from the simple questions of a reporter. The documentary record was thin and yet articulate in the manner of a Japanese scroll, with meaning and detail expressed in empty space—in what was absent—as well as by the brush strokes that defined it. I came to understand, from the documents' empty spaces, that my namesake had known love and lost it. That he was consumed afterward by a bitterness he could never shake, a despair that would outlive him.

The peculiar indexing of the church archives, by first rather than family name, made it necessary to thumb through lists of all the Antoninas who died in Terrasini between 1848, the year of her marriage, and 1855, when the widowed Francesco took his second wife. At that point, I didn't know the year of Antonina Randazzo's death, much less the fact that it was preceded by the death of one son—and followed by the birth and death of another.

For days on end, the trail led nowhere. Father Constantino was right: Antonina must not have died in Terrasini. Nor, it appeared, was she born there. She had been twenty-three at her wedding; but among the 1825 baptismal records for Antoninas, there was no Randazzo. In frustration, I picked up the parish marriage ledger for 1855. As in the municipal files, there was a brief allusion to Antonina's death, a black footnote to the Mass that joined Francesco Paulo Viviano and Maria Bommarito.

But there was something else, several lines below in the entry— an equally brief allusion to two sons who had not even appeared in the municipal records: Francesco Paolo, *anche defunto*, "also deceased," and a younger brother, Gaetano.

Like Antonina, they were empty spaces, in the public archives and in our family memory. Using the boys' given names, I had quickly located what there was of their parish records. Francesco

Paolo, baptized and gone within three days in 1851. And then Gaetano, born somewhere outside of Terrasini, but declared dead there on July 28, 1855.

The empty spaces pictured the young couple's flight from the village after their marriage and their desperate return to a clandestine childbirth and an infant's burial.

The name of the forgotten child, Francesco, spoke of the controversy surrounding his parents' marriage and the family quarrels it engendered.

The birth of a second son, away from the village and unrecorded by the parish or municipality—but properly named after his paternal grandfather this time—marked another flight into the mountains, and an effort, an act of belated filial piety, to reconcile the elder Viviano and his outlaw son.

In the empty ledger spaces where Antonina's final breath ought to have been registered, a death far from home was written.

The rest must be left to conjecture. A cholera epidemic raced through the Madonie in 1853; in the port of Messina, where it is believed to have entered Sicily, the disease killed fifteen thousand people in six months. But Antonina Randazzo may also have died when her son was born, in a primitive mountain hideaway where the act of childbirth was often fatal.

ALONE WITH A MOTHERLESS INFANT, Francesco seems to have resumed an open life in Terrasini in 1854, a man too shattered to refuse the humiliations of government amnesty and too weak with grief to resist family pressure.

This too is conjecture, but it rests on solid ground. The marriage to Maria Bommarito was swiftly arranged and consecrated in a public ceremony no more than two years after Antonina Randazzo died at the age of twenty-eight. Maria was Francesco's cousin on his mother's side, a thirty-five-year-old spinster who was also an unseemly five years senior to her new husband.

Even the date of the marriage, May 14, suggests haste, a desire to pin the groom down before he could change his mind. *Maiulina non si gudeva la cuttunina,* a Terrasini proverb warns. "The month of May is not suited to the bed quilt."

The implication is that May brides will not produce loyal sons for their husbands.

Eleven weeks after his father remarried, the three-year-old Gaetano Viviano died of unmentioned causes. Two years later, in April of 1857, Maria delivered a second Gaetano, who would one day be called "the Falcon" in Sicily and "Big Tom" in America.

On May 4, 1864, when she was forty-four years old, Maria Bommarito gave birth to my great-grandfather Giuseppe, the last known child of Francesco Paolo Viviano. The cast of my name-sake's immediate family, his two families, could now be completed:

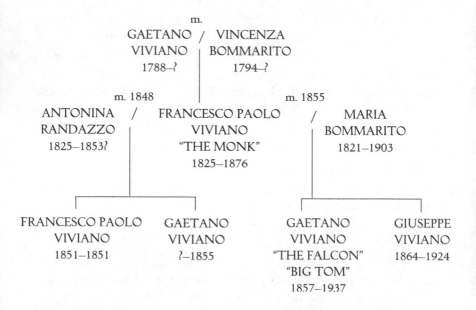

According to the church and municipal records, Francesco was no longer residing in Terrasini when his second son by Maria was born. After that event, the documentary trail in both archives came to a halt. I ran out of places to look for hard facts, the chain of events that would end with four gunshots on a country lane. My namesake had vanished, once again, into the Madonie.

It was then, I believe, that he became the Monk, his very identity defined by loss. By what was now absent from his world, rather than what was present. By the empty space left with the deaths of Antonina and their two sons, and by the inability of Maria and her two sons to fill the void.

NINETEEN

Festival of Bachelors

➤➤◄◄

Jerusalem
April 1996

AS SPRING BROKE in fertile heat over the Castellammare plain, and the ewes began to foal in the old Aumale stables, I was sent back to the Middle East. The assignment came at an opportune moment, another of the many junctures when I felt that the Monk's trail was lost forever and there was no point in continuing the search.

For more than a month after I discovered the article in the *Giornale di Sicilia,* with the date of the Monk's death, the helpful staff of the Tribunale had painstakingly sifted through the archives. They found no files on an investigation of the killing, no record of a trial for the attempted robbery that left my namesake dead on a country lane. At the Biblioteca Regionale, with Laura Terranova's help, I had read my way through every issue of the *Giornale* from November 1876, when the shooting occurred, to the end of 1878. There was no follow-up article on the incident at Quattro Vanelle.

The Alitalia shuttle to Rome passed low over Paternella at take-off. Below the wing, the Villa Fassini and its out-buildings were clearly visible, a tight cluster of amber blocks between the pasture and the sea. Two hours later at Fiumicino Airport, I caught an El-Al flight to Jerusalem.

It was the season of suicide bombings. Four of them in succession, in three Israeli cities. There were still pieces of flesh hanging in the trees of Jerusalem over the charred carcass of a bus. Medical aides and rabbinical students were gently scraping them off for burial.

On the last day of March, I decided to go to Ramallah, a West Bank stronghold of Hamas, the radical Muslim group that was said to be responsible for the bombings. Three of the suspected bombers had been born or educated in the town, which lies about eight miles from Jerusalem. The security was as tight as I had ever seen. The entire West Bank was cordoned off by the military, and hardly anyone made it past the checkpoints. My press card got me in, but it didn't get me back out.

That week, an awful silence hung over the dry hills that separate Jerusalem from Ramallah. It was the speechlessness of human beings reduced to warring symbols. Yet if you stood most Israelis next to most Palestinians, they were hard to tell apart. There were the elegant noses, tawny complexions and tight curls you'd expect on both sides of the divide; but there were also redheads and deep blue eyes among them.

They put me in mind of the Serbs and the Bosnian Muslims and Croats, the Catholic and Protestant Irish of Belfast, the embodiment of our collective end-of-century madness. They put me in mind of Sicily, with its genetic record of endless conquest and bitterness.

A high proportion of the young Israeli soldiers guarding the roads that led back to Jerusalem had no equivalent among the Palestinians, no mirror. They were black Ethiopian Jews who had emigrated to Israel in the 1980s. The Sephards and European Jews in the Israeli Army understood that border duty on the West Bank was unrelieved misery, and they found ways of getting transfers to other postings. But the Ethiopians were new to the tragedy. They could barely speak Hebrew, and few were able to muster more than a sentence or two in a European language.

At 9:00 P.M. on a frigid night, snow whipping over the bare hillsides, one of these kids stuck his Uzi into my gut, unsnapped the safety and shoved me up against a concrete barrier. There was plain, undisguised fear in his eyes.

Two nerve-racking hours passed before an Israeli officer arrived, leaping from his jeep before the driver pulled to a full stop. He had his service revolver out, a precaution that seemed absurdly redundant. The Ethiopian's Uzi was still trained on me, and there were now half a dozen of his comrades standing in a tight circle around us. The officer motioned them away. "Lieutenant Zev Faigen," he said, brusquely saluting, and asked in Hebrew to see my identity papers. I answered in English, as angrily as I dared under the circumstances.

"This is my passport, and this is my goddamned press card. What's going on here?"

The lieutenant looked over the documents. He was American-born, from Chicago. "I guess we've fucked up," he said.

Israeli officers are carefully instructed in the importance of a favorable press image in the United States. The Ethiopian who'd braced me understood "fucked up," and looked uncomfortable. I felt sorry for him.

The lieutenant walked me personally across the border and flagged down a ride for me into Jerusalem. "I've got to ask you," I said. "Why did I scare that kid?"

"The beard," he answered immediately.

I have a closely trimmed beard, black and slightly curly. It was news to me that it might be regarded as incriminating. "Give me a break," I said. "Plenty of Israelis wear beards."

"Not that kind, pal," he answered, gesturing at my face. "Israelis with beards are usually Hassidim, and they keep them long and untrimmed. That's a Hamas beard you're wearing."

He sighed, turned his back on me, and walked away. What can you do with a reporter who doesn't understand the language of symbols, the only vocabulary that Israelis and Palestinians shared?

I RETURNED TO TERRASINI on Easter Sunday. The *Festa di li Schetti,* the annual Festival of the Bachelors, was in full swing in the Piazza Duomo. The young men of the village crowded around an eight-foot-high orange tree that had been cut down at the root and decorated with silk banners. In turn, each of the bachelors raised the tree from the ground and hefted it over his head. The idea was to hold it erect, balanced on the palm of the hand, while tottering toward the home of a prospective bride. To reach her door and drop the tree at its threshold was regarded as a spectacularly promising marriage proposal. The festival was celebrated only in Terrasini, and had been for countless centuries.

A relative of Signore Zucco, a merchant who had a small shop off the piazza, walked up to the *schetti* circle and stood next to me.

The Festival of Bachelors in the Piazza Duomo at Terrasini, with Maria Santissima delle Grazie in the background. Photo by Guido Orlando.

After a few minutes, he said, "Franky, come on over to the *caffè*. We need to talk."

It was the way Terrasinese conventionally approached each other when there was discreet business to be conducted, a sign of how much the distance had shrunk since the previous year, between the villagers and the author of their book. On my part, the sense of separateness, of isolation, had gradually been overcome by the recognition of underlying commonalities. Even beyond the obvious sharing of genetic baggage—virtually everyone in Terrasini was the spitting image of a cousin, uncle, or aunt in Brooklyn or Detroit—I could see, now, how many of my own traits were drawn on theirs: an instinctive mistrust of authority, a quickness to anger at anything remotely perceived as an insult. I could see how much of their universe had remained active below the surface of my American birth and education, germinating in my character and personality.

The merchant and I sat down at Di Maggio's. "About that robbery out in the country," he began. "It was the cops."

When I was in Israel, the wife of a local *carabiniere* had approached Signore Zucco's foreman. The Interior Ministry police were the burglars, she said. "They thought the American was Giovanni Brusca."

The man accused of detonating the explosives under Judge Falcone's car was widely believed to be hiding in one of the Castellammare villages. Not because it was impossible for him to leave Sicily—the honeycomb of small coves on the coast was a fugitive's paradise, ideal for speedboat anchorage—but because he refused to go.

"It is a matter of pride for him not to run," Mike told me.

A rumor that Brusca had been spotted could flood the entire island with police roadblocks and raids. So when a mysterious stranger showed up in a country home that was seldom occupied in winter, the Interior Ministry had sent in a team of their plumbers to check. They lifted my radio to provide a cover motive, however flimsy.

I asked Signore Zucco's relative why the Interior agents had been so suspicious. The Cortese villa at Paternella wasn't the only one occupied this winter.

"Your beard," he said, pointing an index finger at my jaw. "Brusca's face is on posters everywhere in the country. They figure he's probably grown a beard."

He rose from his seat, shook my hand, and walked back into the piazza, lost quickly in the crowd celebrating the *festa*.

A roar went up as another of the bachelors tried his luck at the orange tree. He was a solidly built fellow in his early twenties, a fisherman; I had met him once at a *caffe* on the harbor. The tree was full of fruit and must have weighed sixty or seventy pounds. He raised it waist-high, balanced in his right hand, and shoved it above his head, then lurched forward half a dozen steps and fell headlong to the ground. The tree remained erect a few seconds before toppling flat alongside him, a few oranges rolling into the piazza gutter.

TWENTY

A Parallel Universe

➤➤≺≺

Western Sicily
April 1996

THERE IS A SOOT-BLACKENED SQUARE in the center of
old Palermo, within a fifteen-minute stroll of the Biblioteca
Regionale and the vast hulk of the Teatro Massimo Opera House,
called the Piazza Beati Paoli. It is the site of an ancient monument
in the parallel universe. Two sides of the square are framed by the
high-baroque church of Santa Maria di Gesu and a sixteenth-century convent. But the piazza's true focal point is what the visitor
does not see.

Sicilians are convinced that a monastic fortress lies beneath the
paving stones, a hidden stronghold of avenging monks. I went looking for it soon after I returned from Israel.

I had no illusion that I would be allowed to enter the fortress. If
it is still there. If it ever was.

I walked north to the piazza through the narrow back streets of
the Mercato del Capo, the largest of the old Arab market districts
that wind through the city, engulfed today in stands hawking cheap
underwear, saints' icons, mounds of artichokes, and fresh swordfish
and tuna. A frail elderly woman, dressed in widowly black, sat on a
stool where the market opened into the piazza, boning salted
anchovies from a two-liter tin set on the cobblestones between her
ankles.

The author during a research break in the market streets of Palermo, 1996. Photo by Chiew Terriere.

"Signora," I said, "can you tell me how to find the fortress of the *Beati Paoli?*

She smiled, not at all unkindly, and gently shook her head. A fishmonger a couple of yards away was eavesdropping; I heard him repeat the words "fortress" and *"Beati Paoli"* to a customer. So I asked him too.

"I've never heard of it," he told me. It was what I expected. The wall of polite silence.

According to folktales that date back to the era of the Sicilian Vespers, the *Beati Paoli,* "the Blessed Pauls," were a secret confraternity whose bastion was hidden under the piazza. They were regarded as the agents of popular justice, empowered to settle accounts that the state ignored. Often, as in the legend of the vespers, these accounts involved the wronging of women or the abuses of corrupt and arrogant officials. The confraternity's members were said to gather in subterranean rooms under the piazza after nightfall, to hear evidence and render verdicts. Then, dressed in the robes of the monks of San Francesco di Paola, they set out at the stroke of twelve to execute the sentences.

A similar quasireligious secret order, known simply as "the Avengers," had been active until its forceful suppression by the Normans a century before the vespers. But the *Beati Paoli,* at least by rumor, were never suppressed.

The rumor alone bespoke a significant entrenchment of the moral role-reversal that produced Muslim heroes and Christian villains in early medieval Sicilian folklore. The reversal had come to swamp the entire apparatus of public jurisprudence and law enforcement, installing in its place a shadowy counterstructure of underground sects to determine guilt and deliver popular justice.

"For the Sicilian, the government was never entrusted with educating, guiding, helping, and the institutions of state justice were only administered to bring shame to the just," the historian Antonino Cutrera wrote in 1900, when my grandfather was three years old.

Along with the Avengers and the *Beati Paoli,* the most arcane of Sicily's underground sects revolved around *le anime dei corpi decollati,* "spirits of the decapitated," a macabre army of bandits and other criminals who had been executed by the state. Their worship lasted well into the twentieth century. "Men and women, young and old, all have an offering to make, a prayer to recite, or religious rites to carry out in the name of these occult phantoms," the Palermo anthropologist Giuseppe Pitre wrote in the 1870s. The *decollati,* he explained, "provide an immediate response to prayers for advice or help, and to those who seek to learn something of their destiny."

In cities, the *decollati* were thought to inhabit ancient, narrow streets such as those of the Mercato del Capo; in the countryside, they frequented rivers; at sea, their voices could be heard in the midst of storms, which they sometimes calmed for the benefit of their fishermen disciples. During Garibaldi's sweep through Sicily in 1860, it was widely believed that the spirits of the decapitated could be seen, rifles in hand and red sashes wrapped around their waists, fighting at the sides of the *picciotti.*

The cult's special patron was the martyred St. John the Baptist, who had himself been decapitated. The *decollati,* too, were considered martyrs, but not as a consequence of saintly lives and deaths. Their only credential was to have been enemies of the state.

When the Monk was a young man, the legend of the Blessed Pauls enjoyed a major revival, sparked by the republication of a 1750 gothic novella on the avenging monks, *I Beati Paoli* by Vincenzo Linares. Many Sicilians believed that the confraternity itself had been actively revived on the heels of the unsuccessful rebellion of 1820, to impose midnight justice on the Bourbons, and that it continued its work after the uprising of 1848 and the betrayed revolution of the *Risorgimento.*

It would be impossible to prove, one way or another, that my namesake was a member of the *Beati Paoli.* What I know, all that I know, is that he traveled at night in the robes of a friar. The police who found his body at Quattro Vanelle in 1876 described him as "an ex-Monk of fifty years old." But he couldn't have been a monk in any conventional sense, not with a first marriage at the age of twenty-two and a second less than two years after he was widowed.

So there is only the legend of the *Beati Paoli* to explain his robes and his description by the police, only the language of the clandestine Sicily. That and the fact that his grandson always referred to him as Francesco *lu Monacu.*

RELIGION, IN OUR FAMILY, was always enshrouded in the parallel universe, under a fierce invisible sun that kept the ghosts of Sicily warm through Michigan winters. It was a chasm that separated us from the Irish and Slavic Catholics who sent their children to the parochial schools of Detroit.

Of course, the Irish and the Poles and Croatians had their own invisible worlds; they too had their own underground Church, their own clandestine faiths. At odd moments on the road—in a gilt icon of the Virgin that gazed from the last standing wall of a ruined chapel in Bosnia; in the reflexive bow of an IRA gunman when the name of Jesus was pronounced—I recognized symbols and gestures from the homes of my schoolmates thirty or forty years before.

But I would never fully understand them, just as I never expected my friends to understand the Sicilian Catholicism that we tried our best to keep behind closed doors, out of sight, in America.

Grandma Angelina was its high priestess. In one of my earliest memories of her, she is trembling on the floor of the living room, clutching at a rosary and pleading with the Virgin of Maria Santissima delle Grazie in English and dialect. "Beautiful Mother of God! *Bedda Matri di Diu! Salva mi! Salva mi!* Save me!"

No one could predict what would send Grandma into her fitful trances, or when they might occur. No one could stop them before they had run their course. She had them in the home, in the backseat of my grandfather's car, in the cemetery on visits to the graves of her mother and father. But only when there was no one from outside the parallel universe to watch.

My former wife, Mary, who is Irish, knew Angelina Tocco for twenty years and never witnessed one of these religious seizures. Mary was from the visible, rational, American world of our Detroit neighborhood. The trances were conduits to the invisible topography of Sicily. As they came to an end, my grandmother's screams would ease into a song to the Virgin: "On this day, our beautiful Mother, on this day, we give you our love . . ."

Then she would smooth down her dress and resume preparations for dinner or continue an automobile journey as though nothing had happened.

In calmer moments, Grandma told us stories about the *giuviteddi,* dwarves who lived in caves deep in the earth, where they watched over vast stores of gold and precious jewels. To dream of gold, however, was a negative sign. It meant that the *giuviteddi* felt threatened, Grandma said, and were arranging to swindle you. Dreams of fish or black dogs were announcements of imminent prosperity. But dreams that featured white chickens or snow warned of misfortune and evil.

She believed firmly in the supernatural powers of the *fattucchiera*, a Sicilian witch who practiced white magic and cast spells with the assistance of various saints. The *fattucchiera* had the ability to drive a man or woman mad with love or to render a wandering husband impotent. She also could make nonamorous secret wishes come true, divine the future, and heal the sick. But a *fattucchiera* was no elusive creature of the night; she was a living woman.

We were never sure who, among Grandma's friends, was her own *fattucchiera*, only that there was such a person, and it was necessary that the woman's identity remain secret, even to Grandpa. Sometimes I was convinced that she was a high-strung, widowed Sicilian neighbor of ours in Detroit who incanted strange phrases in dialect when we said hello to her and stared into the street from her living room window for hours on end. More often, I wondered if the *fattucchiera* was Grandma herself, although my suspicions were raised as much by the frenzy of her Catholicism as they were by the cast of witches, spell-throwers, and dwarves in her fables.

Grandma Angelina and her favorite sister-in-law, Ester, were what Sicilians calle *monache di casa,* which roughly translates as "household nuns." Although they belonged to no established religious order and conceived ten children between them, they were thought to possess a secret relationship, a symbolic marriage to Jesus Christ, and thus were regarded as daughters-in-law of Mary.

The Virgin was a primary character in Angelina's fables, dispatching the angel to Ano in the desert and helping Turiddu to avenge his ruined sister on the Night of the Vespers. The rosary that my grandmother squeezed in her trances held a shard of translucent bone in a silver box attached to the crucifix. It was from the skull of a sheephead fish; when she raised it before the light, we were expected to see the form of the Virgin outlined in the bone,

ascending to heaven with one hand on her heart and the other holding a bouquet of roses.

Aunt Ester was even buried in the garb of a nun, to the obvious
dismay of the Irish priest who officiated at her funeral.

For the Irish and other northern Catholics, it was precisely
Mary's virginity that made her holy. For Sicilians, however, it was
her motherhood, the contradiction of virginity. The complex relationships between woman and lover, between mother and child,
were at the feverish crux of Sicilian Catholicism.

Angelina Tocco succumbed to her trances in the presence of
her four sons and two daughters, and as we grew older, her grandchildren. Our role was to witness her agony, to turn our eyes away
from the passion of the crucified savior that preoccupied northern
Christians and toward the maternal passion that Mary suffered at
the foot of the cross.

IT WAS A DECADE after my grandmother's burial that I began
to see her strange behavior for what it was: the expression of a mysticism that reached back to Demeter, to the profoundly maternal
goddesses and their priestesses who ruled Sicily before both
Christianity and Islam, and still survived in the island's rituals.

I had arrived in the port of Cefalu, hard by the Tyrrhenian Sea
east of Palermo, at dusk on Good Friday in 1993, at the end of a follow-up assignment on the assassination of Judge Falcone. To the
sound of trumpet dirges and clashing cymbals, two processions
were winding in opposite directions through the medieval streets.
The processions had been underway since three, the hour of
Christ's death on the cross, a priest explained to me. One procession was led by a terra-cotta Virgin carried in a bower of flowers
upon the shoulders of eight fishermen, the second by a wooden
statue of the dead Christ on a black catafalque borne by eight car-
penters. Half of Cefalu marched behind Christ, half behind Mary,
the priest said.

Many of the older women screamed out prayers like my grandmother's: *"Bedda Matri, Salva mi! Salva mi!"* Orchestras followed

the catafalque and the bower, along with confraternities of hooded men who struck blackened pairs of cymbals or raised oil torches into the night on ten-foot-high poles.

It started to rain around 9:00 P.M., in great sheets that overwhelmed the ancient gutters of Cefalu, sending torrents of water down the cobblestone streets and soaking the marchers to the bone. Heedless, they walked all night. From my hotel room, I heard the orchestras approach, pass under the window, then vanish slowly into the distance.

At seven the next morning, I rejoined the procession behind Mary. The fishermen were moving mechanically forward as though in trances of their own, stooped painfully under the terrible weight on their shoulders. A man ran in front of them, dancing back and forth across the street, then lunging into the Virgin's bower with all the force he could muster after sixteen hours without sleep or food.

I found the priest, trudging along behind the fisherman. "What is that man doing?" I asked him.

"He is trying to keep the end from arriving," the priest answered. "He is trying to stop Mary from reaching what lies ahead."

At noon, the two processions came to a halt, finally confronting each other in the piazza below the stone towers of the cathedral. All of Cefalu was in the piazza, fourteen thousand drenched and exhausted men and women. The crowd parted to form a long open corridor, with the bower of the Virgin at one end and the catafalque at the other. Then for fifteen moments, utter silence fell on Cefalu, but for the sound of weeping, and down that long empty corridor a mother gazed at her martyred son.

WHEN GRANDMA ANGELINA SET OUT on her final procession, my grandfather tried to keep her at home. The rest of us didn't recognize what was happening at first, because Grandma's flights of fantasy had always been peculiar. But Frank Viviano, who had been at her side for more than sixty years, understood very quickly that this was different. So he hid the truth for a long time, just as he still hid the story of his own name and that of the Monk and his murderer.

The descent of Grandma Angelina into hell, which is how I will always think of it, was signaled by ghosts. My grandfather would hear screams in the bedroom and find her wrapped in the sheets, shouting at an invisible tormenter in her own voice and answering in another. After a few months, the ghosts took over the living room, and then the kitchen, so that there was nowhere she—or he—could escape them.

Grandma too understood that these ghosts were different. On Sundays, when the children and grandchildren came for dinner, she did her best to maintain her composure. If the ghosts grew insistent, she paid lengthy visits to the bathroom. In the beginning, we thought she had stomach problems and worried about cancer. But eventually we heard the arguments, the voices, from beyond the closed bathroom door. Whispered arguments with her ghosts, as long as she was able to maintain a semblance of control. Then violent shouting matches later.

Frank Viviano refused to allow Angelina Tocco to be taken from him for two years, until the day that she seized a butcher's knife and threw herself at him, shouting in dialect that he had fucked every whore in Sicily and America and she would kill the next filthy slut who came near him. That she would kill them both.

Where did these words come from? This was what we wondered, in our dumbstruck shock. How did Grandma learn to talk like that?

There was no alternative after the knife incident. The course of Angelina's descent into hell shifted four miles to the east, to a nursing home on Kelly Road in the Detroit suburb of Harper Woods. This was 1980, when my grandfather turned eighty-three.

For the next four years, Grandpa made three trips per day to the nursing home, rising at 5:00 A.M. to shower, preparing his own breakfast before he got in the car and drove over to feed Grandma hers. He returned at lunch, after several hours of work at a West Side produce firm, and again at dinner, leaving in the evening only when the orderly took him by the elbow and led him gently toward the door: "Angelina is going to sleep now, Mister Frank, and it's time for you to get some sleep yourself."

He knew all of the orderlies and nurses by name, and when he wasn't caring for my grandmother—changing her diapers, bathing her, feeding her—he helped with the other patients. I watched him when I was in America and went to see Grandma. Many of the patients were Sicilians from Detroit's old Little Italy on Fort Street. He spent hours with them, quieting them down with his recollections of moments they had shared half a century before.

"Every day is a different day," he liked to tell them. It was his favorite expression, his way of expressing hope in the midst of despair. Some of the patients picked it up; a chorus would greet us as I walked down the nursing home hall with him: "Every day is a different day." Listening to them, I thought of my aunt Grace's story about the arrival of the Depression in Detroit. How Grandpa had learned that he was bankrupt one morning, with six children at home and no way to feed them.

He came home to Angelina with tears in his eyes and said, in English, "Honey, we broke."

She'd answered, "Every day is a different day, Frank," and given him the means to go on, several hundred dollars that she had removed from his wallet since their marriage, dollar by dollar, and hidden in a hatbox.

He was in business another thirty years, until supermarkets choked off the neighborhood groceries that were our customers, and Frank P. Viviano and Sons went bankrupt again. It left a gap in our history, just as surely as the Monk's death and my grandparents' emigration from Sicily. At the age of sixty-six, for the first time since he confronted his uncle Gaetano in St. Louis, Grandpa worked for another man. It was the job he still held at eighty-seven, selling oranges and lemons on the west side. My dad now drove a truck for one of the supermarkets. My uncles had moved on to other jobs and other cities. Nothing was the same as it had been.

Nothing except Grandpa, from whom I had always learned more about strength and dignity than I ever did in a career full of interviews with presidents and prime ministers. And I learned more yet, at the nursing home in Harper Woods.

The first year, Grandma screamed in pleasure at my visits. "Franky! *Figghiu miu, miu cori!*" It was all she said, before falling into gibberish. The second year, there was no greeting. She recognized no one but my grandfather, whose name she shouted with startling clarity: "Frank! *Vieni ca!*" Come here!

Never *Francesco* or *Paolinu;* he was her Frank, her self-named American and only lover.

In the last months before her death in 1984, Grandma Angelina was a featherlike wraith whom my grandfather picked up from her bed and carried to the bathroom, almost seventy years after she had been carried kicking and biting out of her parents' flat. As he lifted her, she spoke only her own name now.

"*Mi ghiammu Angelina. Mi ghiammu Angelina. Mi ghiammu Angelina.*"

She was Ano in the desert.

At the end, her face was thinner than it had ever been in my memory, and her skin almost transparent in its delicacy. Laid out in her nun's habit at the Bagnasco Funeral Home, she once again looked like the teenaged girl in a 1917 photograph taken after her abduction to Canada.

PART IV

TWENTY-ONE

Family Portrait

✦➤◄✦

Detroit, Michigan
September 1973

WHEN I BEGAN SEARCHING for the Monk, I had set out to
solve a crime. Did a man named Domenico Valenti kill my namesake? The reporter in me was determined to unearth the objective
fact, to pluck a clear and documented event from my grandmother's fables and my grandfather's last enigmatic words.

But as time wore on, I recognized that the crime itself, as an
objective fact, could not be the journey's end.

At first, there had only been my own motives, my own story,
the only story I really knew, to propel the narrative. The rest was
obscured in code, hidden in the attic of a chronic dream. Then
my grandfather's story took on shape and depth. And finally, very
slowly, as though the light of conscious recognition was painful,
the Monk began to emerge. He married, fathered two children,
married again, and fathered two more. His murder acquired its
setting.

As the months went on, I plunged much further into the past
than I had expected at the outset, deep into a hidden world that had
held sway for a thousand years when my namesake lived and died. A
thousand years of history, written and unwritten, merged in the
ghostly patterns of family drama, patterns that were as insistent and
unfathomable as those eerie signals that prompt twins who have been

separated since birth to imitate each other across continents and oceans.

Eventually, I had followed the chain that linked me to the Monk and to my grandfather over nine centuries, into remote valleys that sheltered thirty generations of stubborn fugitives. Like Ano, they had emigrated to America in my grandmother's hallucinatory fables.

At every landmark on that long road, I was confronted with the same tug-of-war between rootedness and wanderlust, between the road and the hearth, that echoed in the Monk's two marriages and his relationships with his sons. The same echo that haunted my own life. It was not the pure history, the unadorned solution of the Monk's murder, that mattered most. It was the search itself, the gradual melding of fact and fable in a single truth, a larger tale.

What I never imagined was that the tale had an author, and that his text was me.

THE DAY THE END CAME for my parents' marriage, nobody tried to stop them. They had been fighting a brutal war for twenty-seven years, punctuated by major battles in which my mother screamed that she would kill herself, and my father slammed his fists into the walls until blood ran from his knuckles. The furies ran deep, out of reach of understanding. No other woman drew my father away from us. No romantic interlude with a stranger turned my mother's head. They were simply, and brutally, at war.

It no longer mattered by 1973, as it once would have, that divorce was anathema to Sicilians. The tensions had been so agonizing, for so long, that both families breathed an audible sigh of relief when my mother packed a suitcase for my father on an autumn Saturday and asked him to leave.

My grandparents might have been expected to wage a last-ditch campaign against the separation, as they had when one of my uncles had left his wife a few years earlier. Grandma Angelina had been relentless then, laying siege to her son's flat, telephoning his girlfriend in the middle of the night, pleading with my aunt to take him back. They were hounded into an exhausted reconciliation.

But nobody said a word when my mother packed that suitcase, and nobody made an effort to reconcile her with my father. My grandparents presided over the marriages of six children in the New World. Only one was permitted to founder.

YET OF ALL OF THOSE MARRIAGES, my parents' had been the most traditional. It was the union of a bride and groom who had scarcely met before their engagement, which was formally negotiated in a year of lengthy discussions between their two families. My father's parents played the role of aggressive suitor. They had been extraordinarily insistent about it, my aunt Grace told me, pressing for the match with the same relentlessness that Grandma later brought to bear on reuniting my aunt and uncle.

An arranged marriage was a peculiar fixation to have taken hold of Frank Viviano and Angelina Tocco, whose own sixty-eight years together began with a forbidden courtship and a kidnapping. But it was perfectly in line with the views of Salvatore DiGiuseppe, my mother's father, a Detroit tile contractor with deeply divided feelings about America.

He was a dark, brooding man who never quite mastered English in his fifty-six years in the United States. Like his daughter's, his own marriage to my maternal grandmother, Caterina Cammarata, was arranged. That was Salvatore DiGiuseppe's decided preference, the keystone in an elaborate American recreation of Sicily.

Almost no physical evidence of the old world had made the passage to the new. *Va bene*, Salvatore DiGiuseppe would replace it, superimposing a Mediterranean *campagna* over the concrete landscape of Detroit.

The author's maternal grandfather, Salvatore DiGiuseppe, in Detroit around 1950.

My DiGiuseppe grandparents' home was lit by tile-covered lamps. Tile clocks and tile-framed paintings hung on the walls. There were tile ashtrays on tile end tables in the living room, tile trivets on tile countertops in the kitchen, and tile benches built around the trees in front of the house. A homemade tile fountain, surmounted by spouting mosaic angels, gurgled in the backyard.

Beyond the fountain when spring arrived, Grandpa D. busied himself with the hoe on an empty tract of neighboring land. The owners didn't seem to care. *"'Meddicani,"* he said, shrugging his shoulders, when I asked about them once. They were Americans, which for him was enough to explain their otherwise incomprehensible apathy toward fertile land.

I can see him now in my mind's eye, stripped to the waist if there was the slightest hint of sunshine breaking through the gray Michigan sky, his shoulders rising and falling as he turned the soil. By June, the empty lot was Castellammare. Zucchini vines crawled over the ground into my grandparents' small yard, mounting the

tile basin of the fountain in an explosion of yellow blossoms. Half
of the flowers were left on the vine to produce zucchini, and the
rest were picked to batter and fry in olive oil. Tomatoes reddened
on stakes, interspersed with bushes of marigolds to ward off insects,
and eggplants ripened to a rich purple-black. Grandpa D. grew basil
for marinara sauce, sage for red meat, and flat-leafed parsley to gar-
nish spaghetti with clams.

Twice a day, every day, my grandmother served him pasta—
with garlic and olive oil, with broccoli or cauliflower, with sardines
and fennel, with nine varieties of dried bean, with peas and prosciutto, or with half a dozen green vegetables that appeared to have
no English name and were carried in seed packets to Detroit by vis-
iting relatives from the old country. If Grandpa D. couldn't live in
Sicily, he would eat as though he did.

YET IN HIS OWN HARDHEADED WAY, Salvatore
DiGiuseppe was very much an American, even self-consciously so.
A Yankee tinker without English. He might have been a Franklin
or an Edison with the right vocabulary and accent. His curiosity
about how things worked, and how they could be made to work better, had no place in Sicily. That was why he had emigrated to the
New World, why he had placed that quintessentially American
wager—staking his entire future on hard work and chance—before
he had even set foot on Ellis Island.

He was a man torn by the fundamental paradox of the immigrant everywhere, today as much as a century ago, embracing risk
and fearing change at the same time.

The first thing he had seen when he arrived in New York as a
sixteen-year-old in 1908 was an automobile, idling on the wharfside.
For Frank Viviano that sight had triggered a business idea. It was
the automobile itself that left Salvatore DiGiuseppe dizzy with
admiration. He headed straight for the city that produced it, after
less than a week in New York.

But by nature, as well as by language, he was utterly unsuited to
Detroit's industrial culture. My grandpa DiGiuseppe was an

Andrew Jackson American, not a Henry Ford American, swayed by a Jacksonian-era view of the machine as a work of craftsmanship. Mass production and the assembly line had nothing to do with his interest in the automobile.

He earned his way with the ancient skills he carried westward from Sicily, and the only time he set foot in the auto plants was to install tile in their bathrooms. But he kept his eyes open, watching how cars were assembled as they moved down the line.

Then, in 1921, he built a car of his own, fitting discarded parts that he reconditioned himself into a jury-rigged steel chassis, and finishing off the plywood body with a few choice tiles from Sicily. My mother speaks of it still with the embarrassment of a young girl: "It looked ridiculous. Everyone laughed when we drove by."

But she and her sisters didn't laugh, at least not aloud. If the automobile was Salvatore DiGiuseppe's piece of the American dream, his family's absolute respect was his bulwark against the undisciplined New World nightmare. Even more than the garden and tile work, his wife and three daughters were to be strictly and rigorously Sicilian.

The first two girls were named Provvidenza and Girolama, in pappanomic traditional order, after my grandfather's mother and my grandmother's mother. The third was named Antonina, a feminized version of her grandfather's name, to make up for the fact that there was no son.

They learned how to prepare ravioli by the time they were seven years old, and walked to school in the long black cotton leggings of the Sicilian *campagna* instead of bobby socks. When my mother came down with pneumonia in her teens, she was bled with leeches by an unlicensed healer from the Castellammare hills rather than treated in an American hospital. And neither she, nor her sisters, ever went on a date before their respective marriages— all of them to sons of Terrasini, my grandmother's native village, which was regarded as a slight notch above his own native Partinico by Salvatore DiGiuseppe. They were allowed to go to a single dance, their senior prom at Southeastern High School, on the arm of their cousin Domenico.

The one thing the sisters wanted, their dream, my mother always said, was to be real Americans. To wear bobby socks, saddle shoes, and short skirts, to learn the fox-trot, and to date boys with names like Smith and Miller who ate hamburgers and French fries. But that was Salvatore DiGiuseppe's nightmare.

PROVVIDENZA DIGIUSEPPE WAS BETROTHED to Gaetano Viviano in 1946. To look at my parents in the photograph above my desk, next to the Terrasini studio portrait of my grandfather at three years old, a stranger to this history would not guess at the wounds that lie hidden or the storms that loom ahead.

My mother is twenty-two, radiant in a white summer frock with a brown leather belt pulled tight around her waist. I recognize a slight tautness in her lower lip, a grimace of uncertainty or foreboding, but it's unlikely that anyone who hasn't learned the meaning of that tautness up close would notice.

My father, with his arm planted stiffly on her right shoulder, is a stunningly handsome twenty-six-year-old sailor, with six battle ribbons in his sea chest. The war in the Pacific has just ended, but there is no sign in his open, sunburned face, of the scars it has left on him.

He had been sent into Nagasaki on a reconnaissance mission five days after the atomic bomb was dropped on the city. When my brother, Sam, and I were boys, my father told many stories about the war: about fights in rowdy overseas bars, about the time he was almost drowned when a gale suddenly blew in as he was swimming next to his ship. But he seldom talked about the battles, about the Coral Sea, Iwo Jima, or Okinawa. And for forty-nine years, he never talked about Nagasaki.

Then, one winter evening in 1994, half a century after that

Grandpa and Grandma Viviano with the author's father, Tommy, and his mother, Prudy DiGiuseppe, the week that their engagement was announced in 1946. Ten months earlier, Tommy had been sent ashore by the U.S. Navy at Nagasaki to report on the effects of the atomic bomb.

August in Japan, my phone rang in Paris. It was my father, the first time he ever called me in Europe. He had read a story I'd filed from Bosnia, describing a journey through villages emptied by the war, where the only living creatures were abandoned pet dogs and cats that ran into the road from shattered buildings as our convoy passed, but snarled in terror if a human being tried to approach them. My father had found dogs and cats alive among the corpses in Nagasaki, he told me. Then he spoke, for the first and only time, about what he had seen in 1945, until he began sobbing uncontrollably.

My uncle Pete, who also served in the Pacific, said that he hardly recognized my father when he came home in 1945. Not the face. That hadn't changed. But the mind, the personality. It wasn't

Tommy anymore. He flew into rages nobody could fathom, over discontents that nobody could resolve. He was lost in a desert from which he never entirely escaped.

This is the handsome sailor who rests his arm on my mother's shoulder in 1946, the husband who has been assigned to her by the two people at their left, Angelina Tocco and Frank P. Viviano. My grandmother stares blankly into the camera, perhaps because the sun is reflected in her glasses and imparts an opaqueness that isn't really there. But my grandfather's pose has no ambiguity.

At forty-eight—my age when I take up residence in Sicily, alone and childless—he towers over his wife, son, and prospective daughter-in-law. The big Detroit house full of children stands behind him. He holds an expensive cigar between the fingers of his left hand. A smile of unmitigated self-confidence lights his face. Frank P. Viviano, in the summer of 1946, is a man who has accomplished all that he has set out to do, culminating in this marriage.

For even more than my grandmother, he had been insistent on it, spending hours behind locked doors with Salvatore DiGiuseppe, discussing the future.

THE CAMMARATA / DIGIUSEPPE FAMILY

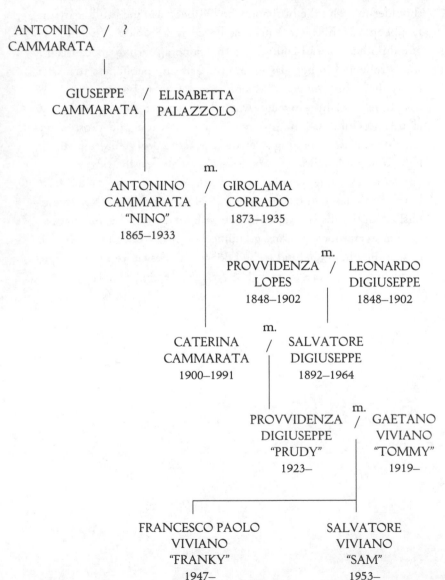

ANTONINO / ?
CAMMARATA

GIUSEPPE / ELISABETTA
CAMMARATA   PALAZZOLO

m.
ANTONINO / GIROLAMA
CAMMARATA   CORRADO
"NINO"   1873–1935
1865–1933

m.
PROVVIDENZA / LEONARDO
LOPES   DIGIUSEPPE
1848–1902   1848–1902

m.
CATERINA / SALVATORE
CAMMARATA   DIGIUSEPPE
1900–1991   1892–1964

m.
PROVVIDENZA / GAETANO
DIGIUSEPPE   VIVIANO
"PRUDY"   "TOMMY"
1923–   1919–

FRANCESCO PAOLO   SALVATORE
VIVIANO   VIVIANO
"FRANKY"   "SAM"
1947–   1953–

TWENTY-TWO

"Mafia"

SINCE THE TRIP TO THE MADONIE, my evenings in Terrasini mostly had been passed alone, apart from early Sunday dinners at the Corteses', which still got me home by 9:00 P.M. Otherwise, it was just me, locked into a solitary regimen that had become so habitual I didn't recognize how strange it was.

At six or so I'd put aside my work, dial in the BBC on my short-wave radio, and pour a glass of wine. Then I made dinner, punctiliously observing Sicilian tradition. There had to be a first course of pasta, followed by meat or seafood with a vegetable on the side, fruit or cheese for dessert, plus the recent addition of grilled liver or fish for Monacu. Several more glasses of wine were poured in between.

The cat learned to wait, purring in encouragement as I kneaded and rolled out pasta dough for homemade ravioli, stuffed as my maternal grandma, Caterina, had taught me, with spinach, nutmeg, and ricotta cheese, or as I sliced wafer-thin fillets of swordfish for *carpaccio di pesce*. Sometimes, I didn't sit down to the meal until midnight, half pie-eyed from Alcamo bianco.

I was used to this routine, bizarrely comfortable with it. At regular datelines in my travels, I made a point of renting studio flats rather than hotel rooms, so that I could cook for myself. So that I'd have something to do after 6:00 P.M.

One night, Bobby and Alice Cortese stopped by to say hello, and found me in mid-preparation, my arms and shirt dusted with pasta flour and dozens of ingredients spread out on the counter. They laughed politely when I told them there were no guests expected, aside from Monacu. But in their eyes, I saw how odd it must have seemed.

From then on, once a week or so, my research days and frantic journeys with Mike were followed by calm evenings at home with Bobby, Alice, and their respective mates. Sometimes one of the women cooked; sometimes I did. When the others were busy, Bobby took me out to dinner, which is how we wound up one evening at the Hotel Castello di Giuliano.

THE HOTEL WAS a turreted, pseudomedieval building in fieldstone and cinder block, set on a rocky hill above Montelepre. It resembled the fairy castle of Disneyland, on a slightly smaller scale. Salvatore "Turiddu" Giuliano, the legendary brigand in whose honor the castle was erected, had been born about half a mile down the hill in 1923.

Montelepre has been a bandit stronghold for more than a thousand years, but Turiddu was its most famous outlaw native son, the subject of Hollywood films, paperback novels, academic studies, and several volumes of poetry. His nephew, Giuseppe Scortino, had not simply built a fairy castle to Turiddu's memory. He had legally changed his own family name to "Giuliano" and taken up the cause that made Salvatore Giuliano more than a brigand: promoting the creation of a Sicilian state.

Naturally, Bobby felt a meeting with the president of *Noi Siciliani,* "We Sicilians"—also known as the Federation for the Self-Determination of Sicily—would be useful for a journalist who covered European politics. He had called ahead, and Giuseppe was waiting to eat with us in the Ristorante di Giuliano, located in the hotel's claustrophobic approximation of a gothic dungeon. Waiters and waitresses, outfitted in thirteenth-century costumes, circled us in the gloom. An armored knight guarded the coat rack, leaning against his eight-foot-long battle-ax.

Giuseppe ordered three pizzas from a waiter in striped tights and tunic, turned to me, and said, "This piece of paper, signore, will show you why *Noi Siciliani* is necessary."

He opened up a map of Europe from which Sicily, the largest island in the Mediterranean, had been entirely erased. It was a full-page newspaper ad, published by the Italian Trade Council, urging closer commercial relations with the rest of the European Union.

"You see what Italy wants?" Giuseppe said. "They want us to disappear. We're an obstacle in their plan to be part of a rich 'new Europe.'"

But the map, which had been republished by *Noi Siciliani* and widely distributed, held a double meaning for the organization's members. A lot of them, Bobby told me on the ride to Montelepre, shared the late Turiddu's enthusiasm for removing Sicily quite literally from the political map of Europe.

At the height of his celebrity, in 1948, Salvatore Giuliano had written a long personal letter to President Harry Truman, proposing that the island become "the forty-ninth star in the American flag" and serve as a Mediterranean bastion in the war against Soviet communism. Shortly afterward, Giuliano established *Noi Siciliani*'s predecessor, the Movement for the Annexation of Sicily to the American Federation, to lobby for the cause. When his raincoat was found after a *carabinieri* ambush, obliging him to make a hasty getaway a few months later, the pockets contained an Italian-English dictionary and a notebook full of English sentences scrawled in Turiddu's labored handwriting.

In his simultaneous embrace of banditry and insurgency, Salvatore Giuliano recalled Paolo Cocuzza, who had also been born in Montelepre. His tactical acumen as a highwayman was matchless in contemporary Sicily. But in the political arena, he was easily manipulated, notably by the dons of the *sistema*.

It was at their instigation that Giuliano joined the crusade against Marxism, with tragic consequences. At 10:30 A.M. on May 1, 1947, his men opened fire with machine guns on a May Day picnic sponsored by the Italian Communist Party at the Porta della Ginestra, about twenty miles south of Terrasini. Eleven people, including several mothers and small children, died in the massacre.

AFTER DINNER, Giuseppe walked us over to the ancestral Giuliano home. It was a narrow three-story building with windows only on one side; the rear wall of the house was backed up against a cliff. No one lived there any more.

"You know, Viviano, I spent the first five years of my life in prison, because of my mother," Giuseppe told me.

He was an intense man, with a nervous tic above one eye and an ex-con's habit of constantly looking over his shoulder. His mother had been found guilty, just after he was born, of aiding criminals and engaging in illegal political separatist activities. She nursed the infant Giuseppe in her cell.

He brought me to his mother's bedroom and showed me a hidden door in her closet that led, through a secret passage, to an exit under the cliff face. "Insurance against the *sbirri,*" he said, then led me upstairs to his uncle's room.

A rusty typewriter, the same machine that had been used to compose the letter to Harry Truman, sat on a wooden table, alongside a camera. Atop a chest of drawers on the opposite wall was his record player and a pile of 78 rpm records. The only label I could read was "Telephone Polka," an American pop hit from the 1940s. There was a drawing mounted beside the record player, a self-portrait by Turiddu. He pictured himself looming over a sketchy map of Italy with a sword, cutting a chain that linked Sicily to the mainland and pushing the island west toward the United States.

By 1950, the *sistema* had no more use for Turiddu and even less for a proposed union with the United States, land of J. Edgar Hoover and the Federal Bureau of Investigation. Under circumstances that remain cloudy half a century later, Salvatore Giuliano was shot dead, no one is sure where or by whom. His bullet-riddled corpse was delivered to Montelepre by the anti-bandit commando unit of the *carabinieri.*

His end could not help but remind me of the Monk.

THE SYSTEM THAT NOURISHED and destroyed Salvatore Giuliano still did not exist when the Monk returned to the mountains, a year or so before the birth of his son Giuseppe in 1864. The word "mafia" did exist by then, but its meaning had little to do with the sinister organization that would emerge, in nearly complete form, a decade later, and evolve into a global power over the next century.

I had been tracking that evolution for months, mining the used bookstores in Palermo, collecting dozens of scholarly treatises on Sicilian customs, history, and dialect. They kept me busy late into the spring nights, trying to pinpoint the origins of the *sistema del potere,* just as I passed my days searching for its architects and victims in the parish and public archives.

In 1863, a Palermo stage actor named Giuseppe Rizzotto had written and produced a two-act play set in the Vicaria, which was at the time the city's central prison. He entitled it *The Mafiusi of the Vicaria,* the first recorded literary use of a term that has since become a standard part of the world's vocabulary.

The play, whose inmate characters dressed, spoke, and fought with each other in the manner of Palermo street thugs, was an immense success. By 1885, it had seen more than fifty separate productions and two thousand performances in Sicily and on the continent, prompting Rizzotto to add two more acts and shorten the title simply to *The Mafiusi.* He was the Mario Puzo and Francis Ford Coppola of his day and more, the father of a genre that has mesmerized audiences for 140 years.

Thousands of plays, novels, and films later, few words carry more accumulated baggage than "mafia," and semanticists are deeply divided over its origins. The two most prominent theories contend that it is derived from the Norman-French *se mefier,* "to beware," or the Arabic *mu'afah,* "exempt from the law." But claims are also made for the Tuscan dialect term *maffia,* ("misery") the Latin *vafer* ("shrewd") and the proper name *Maufer,* which was used by the medieval Knights Templar to refer to the "God of Evil."

Even among those who insist on Arabic origins, there is no consensus on precisely which Arabic word is the root of *mafia.* The alternatives to *mu'afah* include *mahfal,* "a meeting or gathering," and *mahyas,* "boasting or bragging."

But there is general agreement that before 1860 *mafiusedda* was a term of admiration in the argot of the rough-and-tumble Palermo waterfront district known as the *Borgu,* "the Hamlet." According to the anthropologist Giuseppe Pitre, who was raised there before the *Risorgimento,* the Borgu's sense of the word implied beauty, gracefulness, excellence, and talent.

What altered the meaning of *mafiusi,* transforming "beauty" into a universal synonym for criminal violence, was the establishment of the *sistema del potere* in the years between 1865 and 1875.

The Mafia, as it is understood around the world today, was born in these years. Its birthplace was the countryside where I now lived.

THE WESTERN SICILIAN *CAMPAGNA,* dating back to the arrival of the Spanish, had been shared by two ancient institutions, the Bandit Kingdom and the great agricultural estates. Negotiating between them, from the seventeenth century on, were the *campieri*—private rural armies that were retained by the estate managers to guard citrus groves and vineyards. Almost invariably, the *campieri* ranks were filled and led by men with notorious criminal records.

Writing in 1900, when the lexicon of organized crime was formalized, the former public security official Antonino Cutrera flatly declared that the *campieri* of the Castellammare region "are all *mafiosi*." Their power and respect, he said, was derived from three qualities prized by the underworld: *pettu* ("chest," courage), *panza* ("stomach," the ability to maintain secrets), and the power to command an intimate circle of ruthless friends.

The *campieri* were pioneers in the sale of "protection"—from brigand raids on animal herds, from extortion demands, from kidnappings and nighttime assaults on isolated baronial palaces. In short, protection from the very outlaw bands that supplied the *campieri* bosses, the estate overseers. It was a neat, efficient circle.

The relationship between the Duc d'Aumale and his overseer and chief *campiere*, the amnestied brigand Paolo Cocuzza, was typical. Most of the island's vast estates were owned by absentee landlords who preferred to maintain their principal residences elsewhere and who left the management of their properties to the *campieri* and rural leaseholders. The leaseholders, too, were often former bandits; if not, they invested heavily in working ties to the mountain brigand clans, providing food, lodging, and fresh horses to the outlaws. Their properties would otherwise have been indefensible.

The final set of players in the rural Sicilian drama were the presumed agents of official law enforcement. Their first representatives were the Captains-at-Arms who hunted down the Vine Jumper and Testalonga. They were replaced, with the enactment of a new Bourbon constitution in 1812, by "Armed Companies," who were themselves succeeded after 1860 by rural mounted police deputized by the infant Italian state.

Ostensibly, each of these agencies was meant to legitimize government law enforcement in the countryside, to elevate state power over that of the *campieri*. But in practice, the Armed Companies and rural police also recruited men from the ranks of criminals— and viewed their purpose in the same spirit. The rural law enforcement agencies "offer assurance only to those who agree to pay regular bribes," an 1875 Italian parliamentary inquiry reported, "and they abandon others to the mercy of their [criminal] accomplices."

During a rare 1867 crackdown on public corruption in Misilmeri, south of Palermo, twenty-two of the town's thirty-nine local police were found to be involved in blackmail or kidnapping attempts, thefts, and paid assassinations.

The result by the mid-1860s, the onset of what has been called the "Golden Age of Banditry," was a yawning of the historic divide between the Sicilian hinterland and the official Palermo of the state—now Italian, rather than Bourbon or Spanish. The Golden Age opened with a dramatic gesture, a demonstration that the template of Sicilian history remained unchanged.

In September 1866, the *picciotti* who had stormed Palermo under Garibaldi's banner returned in a fierce insurrection against his political appointees. The rebels held onto the city for a week, mobilizing twelve thousand insurgents, before the army of the new Italian state, equipped by Britain and France, was dispatched to Palermo in overwhelming force.

But the point had been eloquently made. Quietly, with few losses, the *picciotti* withdrew into the Madonie and the Castellammare hills, where their supremacy went unchallenged. The Monk—entirely absent from the Terrasini archives from 1864 until his murder in 1876—was almost certainly among them, a robed highwayman of the Golden Age, a legend surrounded by legends.

THE MASTER TACTICIAN OF the Golden Age was a convicted thief and prison inmate named Angelo Pugliese, better known by his *'nciuria,* Don Pippinu the Lombard. Transferred to Sicily by Italian penal authorities from the mainland in 1861, he had promptly escaped into the Madonie. The region was aswarm with military deserters, ex-*picciotti,* recently dispossessed peasants, and other fugitives, and Don Pippinu set out to organize them.

The Italian authorities referred to him as *il capitano della montagna,* the captain of the mountain. He was a brilliant strategist, highly skilled in kidnapping, ambush, and escape techniques.

By 1863, Don Pippinu had assembled a body of two dozen

lieutenants, and had trained scores of others. Technically, his men were brigands, rather than bandits, by virtue of their organization into a structured corps under an acknowledged commanding officer. But the structure was deliberately fluid; one of Don Pippinu's strategic innovations was to break up the group completely for several months following a major action, compelling the frustrated police to pursue their quarry on two dozen separate trails.

The men trained by Don Pippinu dominated brigandage in Sicily, under him until his near capture and flight to Tunisia in 1865, and afterward as leaders of their own bands. The most celebrated of them, Vincenzo Rocca and Angelo Rinaldi, led a gang based near Polizzi Generosa. It was organized on a military model, with Rocca serving as field general and Rinaldi as planning and administrative officer. Extraordinarily well-disciplined, the band even adopted a uniform: blue velvet coats and red caps embroidered with an "R" in honor of their two chieftains.

The Golden Age was to be short-lived, as were most of its flamboyant protagonists, lasting not much more than a decade after the 1866 insurrection that launched it.

In the Sicilian countryside, a new idea was taking hold in the 1870s, inspired by the lucrative protection schemes of the *campieri* and the easy corruptiblity of the police. By mid-decade, the scheme managers had grown ever more efficient, ever more intent on imposing order on Sicily's endless anarchy. The independence of the Madonie's outlaw *picciotti* and brigands made them distinctly uneasy.

Their new idea was the Mafia.

TWENTY-THREE

Domenico Valenti

+>≺+

Western Sicily
1873–1875

MORE THAN TWENTY YEARS *have passed since Antonina's death, but the Monk cannot walk the sun-scorched mountain road to Castellammare without thinking of her. Every rock, every wheel groove, is a reminder of the agonizing journey from Polizzi Generosa to Terrasini in September of 1851. Antonina's moans still echo in his head; they are the metronome of his troubled dreams.*

He doesn't often take this road in the full glare of the sun. It is the realm of his nights, of the brown-robed highwayman whom travelers call "the Monk." The 'nciuria has more meaning for Francesco than it did when he acquired it. His life has grown increasingly solitary, more and more like that of a hermit. The secret visits to Maria and their sons, in the mud-walled hut next to the Frenchman's villa, are rare.

Francesco can't stop himself from comparing Maria, the fifty-three-year-old cousin who is his wife in 1873, and the fragile Antonina, who died in his arms when she was only twenty-eight. He knows it isn't just. Maria, after all, has given him sons—two sons, to replace the two who were lost in the cloud of death that enveloped him twenty years ago.

The second Gaetano is sixteen this year. He is fearless, a con-firmed wanderer who has learned the mountain trails. Maria, when she speaks to her husband, says that the boy spends many nights away from Paternella, sleeping in the shepherd's hut above Monte Palmeto, and that the police have begun watching him. Francesco worries that his oldest surviving son is too fearless, too openly contemptuous of the sbirri.

But in Gaetano's swagger, in the bolt of scarlet cloth he has taken to wearing around his waist, the Monk recognizes himself. The boy who watched Francesco retrieve his hidden gun and march off to join Garibaldi in 1860 is nearly a man.

About their other son, Maria has no complaints. At nine years old, Giuseppe is one of the hardest workers among the children who harvest grapes for the French duke. The boy is fiercely protective of his mother   and wary of the father he so seldom sees.

The distance between Francesco Paolo Viviano and his youngest child is measured in empty space. Giuseppe looks away when the Monk tries to meet his eye; the son renders the father invisible.

Giuseppe could not be more unlike his brother Gaetano, more unlike Francesco. He will never earn an 'nciuria to match "the Monk" or "the Falcon." Giuseppe will repudiate the entire world that these names represent and exchange them for the life of a common laborer in America, gone to his grave from lockjaw in 1924.

When Giuseppe's own first son—and my grandfather—is born in 1897, he will refuse to name him Francesco. The boy is to be called "Paolinu."

Instinctively, Giuseppe recognizes that his father does not love his mother, which might not have mattered if Francesco had not known love before. Most marriages in Sicily are arranged, to suit a code that has governed countless generations. Viddanu cu viddanu, buggisi cu buggisi, marinaru cu marinaru. The code was invoked within months of Antonina's death. And in the interest of a long time family alliance with the Bommaritos, it sent the grieving Francesco to the altar with Maria.

They had married in the darkest moment of his life, with inde cent haste, in the ominous month of May. Eleven weeks later, the first Gaetano followed his mother, Antonina, and his infant brother in death. There could be no peace in his marriage with Maria after that.

Francesco is a wanderer and Antonina wandered with him, far into the remote valleys of the Madonie. In his despondency, he regards Maria as a wife who was forced on him, a wife no one else had wanted. The wrong woman, married in the wrong month.

Francesco Paolo Viviano is a solitary man in 1873, a hermit by choice. He haunts the mountains alone or in the company of other brigands, temporary partners who share the highway with him for a week or so, then move on. The Monk trusts no one. Above all, he does not trust Domenico Valenti.

IN HIS SEVENTY-FIRST YEAR, the patriarch of the Valenti family is one of the most powerful men in Terrasini. His own farmstead lies just across the Bourbon road from the Frenchman's lemon grove and the Viviano hut. On the Valenti side of the road, the land is rocky and uneven, rising too steeply toward Monte Palmeto to hold the winter rains. Oranges and lemons cannot take root in the hard, dry soil. The best the Valentis can manage is a stand of gnarled, ancient olive trees and thick clumps of prickly pear cactus. But the power of Domenico Valenti has nothing to do with the cultivation of fruit.

Valenti is a natural leader. Like his longtime rival, the limping old bandit Piddu Badalamenti, he was born to organize the efforts of others. To order the robberies, extortions and killings that others carry out. The two families, the Valentis of Terrasini and the Badalamentis of Cinisi, are molding a new structure to govern western Sicily, with a clear hierarchy of followers and leaders. A power structure. A system.

The system will decide who is to lose and who is to gain, according to a strict division of labor and the observance of firm, unquestioning loyalties. The system will decide who is a "friend" to be advanced and who is a "problem" to be eliminated, whether the *problem is a troublesome judge or a recalcitrant highwayman. The sistema del potere will put an end to the chaos and liberty of the Bandit Kingdom.*

The system is not to be led by heroes in red sashes or driven by romantic ideas. That was the illusion of the men who killed and died for Garibaldi—and the fantasy of Garibaldi himself. It had evaporated within a year of the Bourbon collapse, when Garibaldi's bankrollers from Turin and Milan descended on Sicily with money, lawyers, and the benign approval of the Italian state. The old aristocratic fiefs were dismembered and sold to the highest bidders. With the notable exception of the Duc d'Aumale, who refused to sell his land, the noblemen were pliant; they parted with their domains and took their exit from Sicilian history.

The viddani, who had made the Risorgimento with their blood and resentment, were of no use to the bankrollers. As much as the Bourbon princes, they were an anachronism. By 1865, tens of thousands of tenant farmers had been expelled from their land. The picciotti who survived the Risorgimento have long since returned to the mountains, to the Bandit Kingdom.

But the sistema del potere will not be about them, any more than the Risorgimento turned out to be. The sistema will be about order.

Domenico Valenti and his allies believe that there must be a war, many wars, before the system can deliver order. A war must be waged against the men who took to the mountains after the failed insurgency of 1848, and again after the betrayal of Garibaldi's revolution. It will be followed by a war for supremacy among those who are creating the system. Then and only then, Valenti believes, will there be order.

The Bandit Kingdom has reached the evening of its extinction. It will stagger forward until 1907, when the Monk's son, Gaetano the Falcon, has emigrated to America, and one of the last celebrated outlaws in the Madonie, Giuseppe Salamone, has been captured and put behind bars. A romantic to the stubborn end,

Salamone spends four years in prison composing and memorizing a verse epic based on his own life.

DOMENICO VALENTI HAS NO SONS, *if the parish records are accurate, but he is rich in nephews and in nieces who have been married off to the sons of other Castellammare patriarchs. Valenti regards them with a cold, measuring eye. He is an organizer, not a sentimentalist, a general preparing for war.*

He likes what he sees in Calogero Corrado, the son-in-law of his cousin Pietro. In his late thirties, Corrado has the mixture of proven loyalty, intelligence, and respect for order that the architects of the sistema *require. Another Valenti cousin, Giuseppe, is married to a girl from the ambitious D'Anna clan; they control two large properties near Terrasini and are linked closely through marriage to the Badalamentis. Giuseppe Valenti and his wife are also godparents to the children of two other local families that must be taken seriously, in Domenico's estimation. They are the Evolas and the Vivianos, his own closest neighbors.*

All of these liaisons are wagers, and Valenti understands that some of the wagers may not pay. Francesco Viviano, for instance, is not a man known for his unquestioning loyalty, and from what Domenico has heard, the oldest Viviano son is cut from the father's cloth. But it is too soon to tell.

The system, in Terrasini, is taking visible shape: a skein of family alliances and obligations that is knotted around the village and stretches beyond Palermo into the Madonie. But the lines of association from one village to the next, the hierarchy of order that will govern Sicily, must be clarified.

THE CLARIFICATION BEGINS *in Monreale, the cathedral town above Palermo where the* picciotti *met the Bourbon army in pitched battle a month before Garibaldi's landing at Marsala.*

Pietro DiLiberto, a man who shares Domenico Valenti's vision, is among several Monreale patriarchs who form a new organization in 1872 called the Stoppaglieri, the Draughtsmen.

Ostensibly, this is a professional association of businessmen, endorsed by several of the town's leading politicians. But in fact, it is the founding institution of the system, the first full expression of the phenomenon that will later be called "organized crime." The association's very name is a play on words, ripe with hidden significance for the architects of the new illicit government; in the argot of Palermo's prisons at the time, stoppaglieri is slang for "saboteurs."

Law enforcement authorities, at a loss to understand the sinister new power emerging in Monreale, refer to the association as "a sect." The description is not wholly inaccurate. The Stoppaglieri veil their organization and its 150 members in elaborate secrecy and embrace mysterious rites said to be inherited from the Beati Paoli.

A prospective draughtsman must pass through a "novitiate," a period of instruction, before he is qualified for "baptism." When the right to baptism is achieved, the candidate is seated before a table in a locked room, under the small wooden image of a saint. He offers his right hand to two senior members of the group, who puncture the tip of his thumb with a needle, drawing a small tumbler of blood and washing it over the saint. Rising to face the image, the candidate now recites an oath of loyalty, during which the "secret words of the ancients" are whispered into his ear. Finally, he picks up a lit candle and burns the saint's bloody image. The oath commits an initiate to an inviolable mandate:

> To come to the aid of fellow members, and to avenge them with blood if they are offended.
>
> To free, by any means necessary, a member who has fallen into the hands of the government.
>
> To distribute among the members, in accordance with the decisions of the group's leaders, the proceeds of blackmail, extortion, and theft.

To maintain the oaths of secrecy and allegiance, at pain of death within twenty-four hours.

The system has already assumed its distinctive identity, a lethal modern business draped in the rituals of medieval superstition.

The Stoppaglieri are organized in sections, responsible for carefully circumscribed districts in Monreale and the Castellammare hills. A capo and sottocapo, a boss and underboss, are named for each section, reporting to leaders who preside over the entire region.

The Mafia now exists.

THE FORMULA PIONEERED IN MONREALE—controlled membership in a secret ruling clique, carefully cultivated political influence, a network of accomplices across the countryside, and a smokescreen of legitimate business interests—is extraordinarily potent.

With cool, deadly efficiency, the Draughtsmen spend the next five years establishing and solidifying their new order. Monreale's senior police official is gunned down by unknown assailants in December 1873. The next victim is the vice brigadier of public security. When evidence points to a Stoppaglieri assassin, rumors of a love affair between the vice brigadier and another man's wife suddenly materialize. A Monreale judge finds that the shooting is a crime of passion, and no one is imprisoned.

A third high-ranking police official promises not to apprehend a fugitive Stoppaglieri member wanted for a crime. When it appears that he is about to break the promise, a tribunal of the association's leaders meets in secret to "try" the official. The verdict is "guilty" and the sentence is death. It is personally carried out in a lemon grove by the fugitive's father, a touch allegedly borrowed from the execution rituals of the Beati Paoli. By now, everyone understands who rules Monreale.

But there are still the men in the hills, the undisciplined Robin Hoods who are no more welcome in the new order than honest officials.

The old-fashioned bandits and brigands on the road above Monreale are held in admiration by the peasants, who weave romantic legends around their generosity and feats of daring. Folk poems extol the virtues of Don Pippinu the Lombard and Vincenzo Rocca. A ballad is sung in the villages, recounting the exploits of a Rocca ally, Antonino Leone: "This valorous man, courageous and overwhelming," the ballad declares, "robbed only from the rich, the merchants, and the land owners."

A few decades later, the dons of the sistema will embrace the legends and claim the old bandits as models. Their code of honor will be borrowed to legitimize the system's internal affairs, and will survive until the violent ascent of Toto Riina a century after the creation of the Stoppaglieri.

But in 1873, the association and its political allies view the bandit romance as a threat to sound, rational order. A second threat is posed by the Giardinieri, "the Gardeners," a primitive extortion gang that has been active in the Castellammare hills since the 1860s. The Stoppaglieri circulate alarming accounts of the Gardeners' crimes, their alleged brutality, and even coin a new name for what some people have begun to call "the old Mafia." The Gardeners and the bandits, in words chosen and carefully popularized by the Stoppaglieri, are scurmi fitusi, "rotting mackerel."

One by one, the mackerel are netted and eliminated, pursued not only by the Stoppaglieri, but by similar organizations that have emerged in Palermo and its outlying eastern villages by 1873. Older men among the bandits find themselves maneuvered into suspicious, fatal duels of honor against opponents half their age. Many more are betrayed to the police, or simply assassinated.

The homicide rate in northern Italy in 1875 is one murder per forty-five thousand inhabitants. In Sicily, it is one murder per three thousand inhabitants.

On January 21, 1875, Vincenzo Rocca is surrounded by pursuers and commits suicide rather than surrender. On May 4, the net sweeps up Nazzareno and Ignazio Trifiro, two brothers who lead the largest band of highwaymen in the canyons above

Terrasini. They are merely the best-known victims of an onslaught that the Palermo newspapers refer to as la mattanza, "the slaughter." By December, 550 bandits and brigands have been hunted down and killed in the Province of Palermo.

Domenico Valenti watches, calculates, from his home at the foot of Monte Palmeto. The new order is almost in place. The mattanza is accelerating toward a climax. The circle of nets is tightening, drawing toward the Monk. He will have less than one year to live when 1875 closes.

TWENTY-FOUR

A Secret Life

>━>━◄━◄

Palermo, Sicily
May 1996

FROM THE MOMENT I learned of Francesco Paolo Viviano's murder, my search for the Monk had also been a search for his killer. My grandfather had been silently haunted by them both for the better part of a century, until the cold November morning in 1992 when he whispered the name of "Domenico Valenti."

Another ghost led me to Valenti, another happenstance discovery, among so many in my search that I began to think of happenstance as a deliberate, if inscrutable, plan. Maybe it was simply another expression of the code that veiled my grandparents' conversations, the workings of the same parallel universe that embraced secret horse races in the *campagna*, Angelina Tocco's fables, and the parable of Adannatu.

Maybe it wasn't happenstance at all, but a twisted deductive trail, full of unexpected signposts and sharp bends like the path etched into the slope of Monte Palmeto.

The ghost who pointed the way to Domenico Valenti was another bandit, hunted down and photographed by the *carabinieri* after the insurrection of 1866.

THE PHOTOGRAPH WAS LOCKED AWAY in a storage cabinet at the Museo Etnografico Siciliano Pitre, an idiosyncratic

Palermo museum founded by a very idiosyncratic man. It had opened in 1909 with the assembly on a single site of thousands of objects collected by the self-educated Palermitan anthropologist Giuseppe Pitre.

There were no limits to what Pitre regarded as worthwhile for his collection. He saved bedspreads, underwear, and hairpins; wooden spoons and tin cups; ox yokes, pig troughs, and chicken coops; magic potions concocted by faith healers; dried-up Easter cookies and the molds that shaped them; religious icons, broken bottles, fishnets, dog collars, musical instruments, masks, puppets and toys, cast-off wheels from farmers' carts, and the gilded carriage of a Spanish grandee. It was all valuable to Pitre.

He was the first determined explorer of Sicily's parallel universe, which he read in the images and symbols that decorate his artifacts, much as a fortune-teller reads palms or tea leaves. Pitre's observations fill hundreds of notebooks and several volumes of commentary, *The Practices and Customs, Beliefs and Prejudices of the Sicilian People,* a work that stands alone in its breadth and penetrating analysis.

In 1934, a university-trained scholar, Giuseppe Cocchiara, undertook the Herculean task of classifying the enormous mass of annotated bric-a-brac that Pitre left behind when he died. Despite Cocchiara's best efforts, the museum remains a curator's nightmare more than six decades later. Yet even in its persistent confusion, it is a matchless resource, a treasure trove installed in a decaying eighteenth-century villa that crosses the architecture of a Greek temple with the ornamentation and roofline of an oriental pagoda.

Formally known as the Palazzina Cinese, "the Little Chinese Palace," the villa was the personal fantasy of Ferdinando III of the House of Bourbon, monarch of Sicily from 1759 to 1815. It was erected in 1799 as the centerpiece of a huge private game preserve and garden, the Parco della Favorita, which sprawled over a thousand acres of northeast Palermo. Today a soccer stadium and racetrack are La Favorita's main attractions, but in Ferdinando's time it was an erotic amusement park for randy Bourbon princes and their celebrity friends. The Palazzina Cinese is where Admiral Horatio Nelson passed his languorous afternoons ashore in the arms of Lady Emma Hamilton, the most flagrant extramarital affair of the Napoleonic era.

The main structure of the complex had been under restoration for years when I pulled into the parking lot on a limpid morning in May. The Pitre collection was crammed into thirty-two rooms of an adjacent service wing that had been originally intended to house domestic workers and supplies. There were no other visitors when I entered the door.

In the ticket office, three middle-aged men sat in a row at a badly warped wooden table, solemnly perusing the day's report on the Riina trial in a shared copy of the *Giornale di Sicilia*. The price of admission to the museum was fifteen hundred lire, a handwritten sign announced, about ninety-five cents. I put a five-thousand-lire note on the table.

"Sorry, no change," one of the men said. His eyes remained glued to the *Giornale*. The clear expectation was that I'd leave a de facto tip that amounted to more than twice the cost of the museum ticket itself. Coffee money for the ticket sellers.

Civil service jobs are regarded as a paid leisure activity in Sicily. There are thousands of applicants for each coveted post. The winners, who invariably have relatives or close family friends in the bureaucracy, often hold "real" jobs in the island's gargantuan black market, to which they promptly repair as soon as the morning coffee and newspaper are consumed. Others lounge in the corridors with little to do and no apparent interest in breaking the monotony of their daily routine. Only with painstaking diplomacy, or outright pleading, can they be prodded into action. But traffic into the city had been especially heavy that morning, and I was on a short fuse.

"No change? What a pity," I said in Italian. "I'll have to go in for free."

All three men finally looked up from the paper. *"Ma signore, non e normale,"* one of them said, his palms held before his chest and fingers extended outward in the gesture that means "I take no responsibility for this." Normal or not, I walked through the door.

THE EXHIBIT ROOMS were arranged around a courtyard, one gallery leading to another, in the rough semblance of scholarly order that poor Cocchiara had tried to establish. The first room, announced a sign over the entrance, was dedicated to "Rustic Dwellings." A peasant hut had been erected in the far corner, complete with thatched roof, oil lamps, and a crude wooden platform on which plaster dummies representing a family of six slept together, angled sideways across the straw-bed pallet.

Further along was the entire apartment of a late Bourbon grain merchant. It was furnished with silk-covered divans, ebony sideboards, and four-poster beds that accommodated one sleeper each in silk sheets. Paintings hung on the walls, bronze statues sat atop marble pedestals, and the salon opened into a fully equipped private chapel. There could have been no more eloquent representation of the chasm that separated *capiddi* from *viddani* than these two reconstructed homes.

Between them was a room stuffed with spindles, needles, looms, woolen blankets, and carpets ("Textiles and Fabrics"), followed by others that ran the gamut from festival ornaments to hunting and fishing equipment, christening gowns, plows and hoes, and a homemade iron-casting forge. Everything was covered in a thick layer of dust that rose in lazy swirls as a breeze tailed me from room to room. Rooms sixteen and seventeen, accorded to "Kitchen and Cooking," lay across the courtyard, next to rooms on "Religion and Magic."

When I stepped out into the sunlight, a large black dog suddenly lunged at me. He looked quite capable of ripping my leg off, had he not just as suddenly reached the end of a chain wrapped around his neck and attached to the "Kitchen and Cooking" door. I opted for "Religion and Magic," and left the half-strangled dog whining in disappointment.

This was the heart of Giuseppe Pitre's attempt to decode the

Sicily that gave birth to the *sistema del potere* in the late nineteenth century, his own adult years, a system that drew on morbid
superstitions and customs reaching back three millennia.

There were scores of grotesque masks on the walls, meant to be
worn by the ill and their loved ones, that mimed the effects of
injuries or fatal diseases—smallpox, syphilis, cholera, malaria. The
mask was a bridge between the dying and various patron saints,
who could accelerate or arrest the course of an affliction. I knew
them well, from Grandma Angelina's incantations during my childhood accidents and bouts of illness: San Lorenzo, barbecued alive
by his persecutors, was to be called upon in the event of burns; San
Biagio, who was beheaded, occupied himself with maladies of the
throat; Sant'Agata, patroness of Catania, died in an eruption of
Mount Etna and protected her disciples from Nature's unpredictable wrath.

Several display cases exhibited *puppi di zucchero,* pastry "sugar
dolls" in the forms of people and the objects associated with them:
sugar priests and crucifixes, shepherds and sheep, fishermen and
boats. They are baked annually on November 2, the Feast Day of
the Dead, and presented as *doni dei parenti morti,* "gifts from the
ghosts of dead relatives," to keep their memory alive. The Pitre
staff, in one of its rare bursts of initiative, had added some contemporary Day-of-Death sugar dolls to the original collection. Among
other things, they represented an Alitalia pilot and his Boeing 747.

Eventually, I wandered into a two-room suite that held nothing
but *ex-votos,* naïve paintings of miraculous intercessions into the
lives of ordinary Sicilians. It was as though I had stumbled into the
very world of the Monk.

In painting after painting, armed men descend on defenseless
peasants, who are redeemed only by the last-minute arrival of an
angel or saint—Ano's tale once again. The victims vomit wildly or
faint in terror, and demonic horns poke through the heads of their
assailants. The Virgin Mary often hovers in the sky, supervising the
timely interventions. A barely literate inscription, probably
scrawled in with the local padre's help, explains: "Romano

Vincenzo and Domenico Crappanzano, assaulted by criminals in the Contrada Runza, and saved by a miracle."

There is no mistaking the agents of evil in one series of *ex-votos,* bearing dates in and around the revolutions of 1848 and 1860, and the uprising against the new Italian state in 1866. The aggressors wear Bourbon army or *carabinieri* uniforms. And when the saints or the Blessed Virgin do not intercede against them, salvation comes with the intervention of mysterious horsemen wearing hoods or masks. Some of them are garbed in the robes of monks.

THE MUSEUM LIBRARY, which occupies the second floor of the Palazzina Cinese service wing, reminded me of my chronic dream. Like the furnishings of that imagined attic in my grandparents' home, Pitre's notebooks, manuscripts, and correspondence lay beyond the last step of a dark staircase, in creaky armoires and trunks that looked as though they hadn't been opened in decades.

But the library staff proved much more energetic than their ground-floor colleagues. I explained my purpose and was immediately ushered to a long oak table by one of the librarians. Ten minutes later, she returned with an armful of manila folders labeled *"Brigantaggio"* and *"Mafia."*

The folders were so dry with age that fragments of paper broke away from the clasps, no matter how delicately I tried to pry them open. The contents were in similar condition. Some of the letters and notebooks that Pitre had laboriously squirreled away crumbled at my touch. But other documents, notably a set of ancient reports on parliamentary investigations of Sicilian banditry, were still firm enough to handle.

Pitre had regarded the mountain highwaymen as expert guides to the clandestine Sicily that his intellectual contemporaries ignored. It was with bandits who had survived the *mattanza* of the 1870s that Pitre studied, and mastered, the arcane concepts of personal honor and loyalty that were eventually adopted by the *sistema.* Thanks to Pitre's work, I acquired a closer understanding of the protocols that had ruled my grandparents' behavior—the rules

that were practiced without being discussed, and passed along to
my parents, and then to me, in the subtle osmosis that preserved
our ties to Sicily.

What I know of the nuances of *'nciuria,* apart from taking its
coded names for granted as a fact of Sicilian life, I learned from
Pitre, just as he had learned its secrets from the old bandits while
the fire burned low in a Madonie hearth or the cries of fishmongers
filled the air outside a Palermo *caffe.*

They had taught him the real meaning of *omerta,* which was
not the fearful, submissive silence that it became in the lurid prose
of popular novels and movies. The word itself was a dialect rendition of the Latin *omineita,* the essential quality of "being human."
For the bandits and brigands who came to trust Giuseppe Pitre, as
he transcribed their comments into his notebooks, to be human was
not to err, although they certainly recognized the frailty of the
human condition in their own lives. It was to transcend that frailty,
to embrace a set of principles and cling to them. To be *omu,* Pitre
wrote, "was not to be humble . . . it was to be *serio, sodo, forte."*
Reliable, firm, strong.

"Lu vucca e traditura di lu cori," one of the old red sashes had
told him. "The mouth is traitor to the heart."

In addition to essays on the ritual underpinnings of the parallel
universe, the Pitre library held what remained of its factual record.
They described the role of the *picciotti* in Sicily's revolutions, the
foundation of the *Stoppaglieri,* the war against the red sashes. The
Badalamenti patriarchs rose, fell, and rose again, as did various
branches of my own family tree. But there was no mention of the
Monk.

MY GREAT HOPE had been to find a portrait of my namesake.
Pitre collected photographs by the bushel, along with everything
else.

Did the Monk resemble my grandfather? My brother, Sam?
Did he resemble me? Pitre's files might tell, I thought.

When a Sicilian bandit was apprehended in the second half of the nineteenth century, he was often photographed by the authorities. So as I examined the contents of a storage case of prison and police photographs that the librarian opened up for me, it was with the peculiar wish that the Monk had known the inside of a jail cell. If he had, I would not only see his face, I would also have a date of arrest to bring to the Tribunale archive in Palermo.

The photos were in a miserable state, even worse than the documents. Many had curled with age and peeled off from the thick album paper to which Pitre or Cocchiara had once attached them. Clots of glue had migrated from the paper to the fronts of some photos, and others had been shredded. The bandits pictured in them were often missing an ear or a leg, which lay in a common grave of photo shards at the bottom of the storage case.

In other instances, the dismemberment was literal; *carabinieri* or army photographers had aimed their lenses at fugitives who were taken dead as well as alive. They were riddled with bullets and propped up against trees in the mountain clearings where they had met their end.

Despite their condition, the portraits were spellbinding, even if they failed to include an image of a monk-robed thief with my Roman nose and thin upper lip. The men in Pitre's mug shot collection were a cross section of the melting pot that was and is Sicily. The Mendola brothers, Antonino and Carmelo, were as fair-haired and pale as the Scandinavian Norman crusaders who must have been their distant forefathers. There were bandits named Salamone and Lopes who had Sephardic-Jewish origins, and a swarthy Pagano who might well trace his lineage to an African village.

Twenty-two of the photographed bandits bore names from the municipal rolls of Cinisi and Terrasini. One of these names, written in blurred ink beside a face with the deep-set eyes and dimpled chin of my mother's uncle Bart, was "Antonino Cammarata."

→><←

The brigand Antonino Cammarata, in a police photo taken after his capture circa 1870. Courtesy Museo Etnografico Siciliano Pitre, Commune di Palermo. (Not to be reproduced without permission.)

BARTOLO CAMMARATA was the youngest of my grandma Caterina's six siblings, her pampered and adored baby brother. He was a native Detroiter, the third and sole surviving American-born child of Girolama Corrado and Nino Cammarata, the grandson of the bandit in the police mug shot.

Their first four children, including my Grandma Caterina, had been born in Terrasini. They sailed for Ellis Island with their mother in March 1910 after Nino earned enough money at the Ford plant in Detroit to buy steerage tickets for all of them. Until then, he rented a single room for fifty cents a day, Grandma Caterina told me, and survived on a diet of crackers and milk. The rest of his pay went into the ticket fund. Six decades later, his daughter still pitied him: "Once, he came back to Terrasini and begged my mother to let him take my two older brothers to Detroit with him. Mamma said no, it was everybody or nobody. He would have to find a way to bring all of us over, or he would die in America alone."

Bart was fifteen years junior to Caterina, but the pampering had more to do with the fact that he was the only American child in the family to live past infancy. Two sisters, both named Ninfa, had died within months of their births in 1911 and 1914. No one was sure what went wrong with the first Ninfa. All Grandma Caterina could say, when she told me the story in 1978, was that the baby had "turned gray and shook and shook with horrible convulsions."

In 1914, Girolama returned to Sicily with the newborn second Ninfa, convinced that the cold winter air of Detroit had killed her first American baby. But she couldn't bear the distance from her older children. On the voyage back to New York, the second Ninfa contracted measles; she was six months old when she died. A year later, Bart arrived, and it was tacitly understood by everyone in the Cammarata house that no risks would be taken with Girolama Corrado's seventh and last child.

Girolama went to work as a seamstress to help buy things that Nino's salary could not put on the table. Meat, fish, cheese. Caterina, then fifteen, became the family's acting mother. It was her principal role for the next seventy-five years.

When I think of my maternal grandmother, I see her in a kitchen, peeling and seeding a bushel of ripe tomatoes; or in a bedroom, where she coos softly over a baby crib. Caterina Cammarata had none of the jagged emotional edges of Angelina Tocco. Physically, the two women were very different fragments of the Sicilian mosaic, Angelina the dark-haired and sultry Mediterranean, Caterina as fair and northern as the Mendola brothers in Pitre's photograph collection.

YET IN HER OWN UNDERSTATED WAY, Caterina also had a secret life. Angelina Tocco surrendered herself to passion, and with a theatrical pretense of resistance, married for love. Caterina may have wanted to do the same thing, but she didn't openly dare.

In 1922, when Bart was a healthy seven-year-old and the other

Cammarata children were gainfully employed and married off, Caterina was selected by a matchmaker for Salvatore DiGiuseppe, a promising young tile contractor. But she was never able to love him, she admitted, long after his death in 1964. I had heard the rumors by then: that in the years just after Bart's birth, when she was preoccupied with her family duties, my grandmother had lost her heart to another immigrant from Terrasini. He couldn't wait, and married someone else.

If Caterina could not have him, she also refused to forget him. The most Salvatore DiGiuseppe could ever expect from his wife was a steady and slightly cool loyalty. Even as a boy, I recognized that this was the chief current passing between them. There was none of the erotic fire that still burned between Frank Viviano and Angelina Tocco when they were both in their seventies.

We knew who the man was, the fellow immigrant who might have ignited a lifelong fire in Caterina Cammarata. He was on the periphery of our extended family, a prominent guest at the weddings and funerals that reassembled the parish rolls of Terrasini in Detroit churches and reception halls. His behavior toward Grandma Caterina always had an unusual tenderness, masked in old world courtesy, that prompted sidelong glances between my mother and her sisters. I won't betray my grandmother's unrequited love by identifying him in these pages, except to say that he was also very well-known to the police in Sicily and the United States.

IT WAS NATURAL that the face of Antonino Cammarata among the photographs at the Pitre Museum would remind me of Grandma Caterina and Uncle Bart. He was their great-grandfather, I established that easily in the ledgers of Maria Santissima delle Grazie. But it was a surprise to find him among bandits. He had almost certainly died before Grandma Caterina's birth, perhaps on the gallows, where bandits usually wound up after capture. In America, the Cammaratas were not as directly associated with Sicily's clandestine universe as the Vivianos and Toccos. They were, in my mother's description, a family of Terrasini blacksmiths who had become factory workers in Michigan. "Our people don't have a complicated background," she liked to say.

"Complicated," in her vocabulary, was a synonym for Mafia connections. The known exceptions to my mother's claim were not Cammaratas; they were the kin of great-grandma Girolama.

I had thought I was writing about the Vivianos, and not my mother's family, until my visit to the Pitre Museum. Now I realized that I had two direct ancestors in the Bandit Kingdom.

The badly faded but still recognizable police mug shot of Antonino Cammarata sent me back to the archives of Maria Santissima delle Grazie.

PADRE CONSTANTINO WAS OUT when I knocked at the rectory door. His sister barked, *"chi e?"* through the intercom, then admitted me when I answered. It took half an hour to follow my mother's family line to the baptismal record of Nino Cammarata, then back to his grandfather, the bandit Antonino.

I transcribed the Cammarata dates and vital statistics into my notebook, and turned to the Corrados. In the 1900 ledger that recorded my grandma Caterina's baptism, her mother, Girolama Corrado, was described as a "seamstress, aged twenty-seven." That placed her birth in the ledger for 1873.

I picked it off the shelf and thumbed through the Girolamas in the index. They were considerably scarcer than the Francesco Paolos, Angelinas, and Salvatores. In less than a minute, I found the page I was looking for and cried out "My God!" so loudly that Signora Constantino dropped a candelabra to the sanctuary floor and came running into the office.

"Corrado, Girolama," the entry read, "was baptized this day at Maria Santissima delle Grazie, in the presence of her father, Calogero Corrado, age thirty-seven, and her mother, Caterina Valenti, age twenty-nine."

The woman who gave her name to Caterina Cammarata, as the Monk gave me mine—the woman who was my own great-great grandmother—was a Valenti.

In the blood, my mother was a Valenti.

The man who killed the Monk was a Valenti.

I am a Valenti.

I sank down into Padre Constantino's chair, his sister hovering over me. "Signore Viviano," she said, "what's happened to you?" But I couldn't find the words to respond. My thoughts weren't in that office. They were on a distant moment in 1911, when a fourteen-year-old boy took possession of a name and a legacy and set out on an eight-decade journey.

The author at four with his maternal grandmother, Caterina Cammarata.

TWENTY-FIVE

Blood Washes Blood

Detroit, Michigan
April 1993

FRANK P. VIVIANO DIED on an April evening, seven months short of his ninety-sixth birthday. It was the middle of the night in Europe, and I was asleep when the hotel operator transferred the call to my room. Jon Stewart, my editor, was on the phone.

"You need to call your brother," he told me.

Jon cleared his throat, and said that I shouldn't file a story tomorrow. "Lots of local news, not much space in the paper anyhow. Might as well take a day off . . ."

So I understood, before I reached Sam in New York, that someone had died. "It's Grandpa," he said.

My grandfather had been ill, but not very. He complained of congestion in the lungs, insomnia, mild dizzy spells. Aunt Grace and Aunt Shirley took him to St. John's Hospital for tests and called Aunt Babe in Brooklyn; she flew into Detroit the next morning. Grandpa was morose when she arrived. He hated being in the hospital, with its cold stainless steel and porcelain, its chemical odors and the groans of pain and incomprehension that reminded him of Angelina's years in hell. Senility was the great terror of my grandfather's last decade. He was distraught every time his memory slipped, every time he had to hunt for a word.

"Don't let me go like Mama," he'd say to my aunts. He forced himself to speak only in English, because he remembered that my grandmother began addressing everyone in Sicilian dialect as her descent accelerated.

On the third morning in the hospital, my grandfather woke from a deep medicinal sleep. The night nurse had given him a shot to calm him down, and he was very confused, Aunt Babe said. "I never saw my father so scared, Franky. It was the only time that Grace and I thought he might go through what Mama went through."

He drifted in and out of consciousness that afternoon, waking briefly when my cousin Betsy arrived to take over from the aunts for an hour. "Betsy, *mi cori,* bring me my pants," he told her. "I got to leave here."

She lied, said they weren't in the room.

My grandfather struggled onto his side, reached into the drawer of the bedstand, and pulled out a twenty-dollar bill. "Go buy me pants, Betsy!" He was yelling now, sitting up. "Buy me pants!"

Then he fell back into the bed, exhausted, and lapsed into a moaning sleep.

But the fourth day, he was suddenly himself again. Clear, even funny. He talked about the old days. There was the time he decided to drive to a wedding in Scranton, Pennsylvania. Angelina sat next to him, lost in her daydreams. My grandfather had no idea how to use a map. Somewhere in Ohio, he took a wrong turn and just kept driving, hour after hour, until the Buick was churning along a rural road and came to a big sign. Angelina read it aloud: "Welcome to North Carolina." It took them three days to find the way to Scranton.

Shirley said they laughed until they were weeping as he told the story. Then they played cards, a few hands of "red dog" poker, which my grandfather loved. When I was growing up, there were always loud, boisterous red dog games around my grandmother's big mahogany table after she and my aunts cleared away the remains of Sunday dinner. Grandpa smoked a Dutch Masters panatela cigar, sipped brandy, and cheated. When he won a pot full of dimes and quarters, legitimately or with a card he'd hidden under the palm of his broad hand, he would call over to my grandmother: "Angelina, buy another Cadillac." Her expensive taste was a running joke between them, like the same silk shirt she presented him with every Christmas for thirty-five years; he held it in the air in feigned surprise, kissed her, and put it back into the box for the following Christmas.

After a few card games at the hospital, Babe told me, "Daddy said he wanted to sleep again, so we went home. The next morning, the hospital called. He had gone into a coma."

Grace and Babe were there at the end. He seemed to recover consciousness, and suddenly sat up, swinging his legs over the side of the bed and crying out, "Angelina!"

The doctors couldn't explain what had happened. But in the family, we all knew that the cause of death was simply and powerfully an act of the will. Frank P. Viviano decided to spend one last affectionate day with his children. Then he left to search for Angelina Tocco.

BEFORE MY JOURNEY to the Monk's death, before I found the courage to enter the dark attic of a childhood dream, I had thought of my grandfather as a man who stood outside of history. He was a man who did not read a newspaper and had never heard of Bosnia or the Persian Gulf. A man whose self-constructed universe was a wholesale fruit business in Detroit and a big, noisy home full of children and grandchildren.

I understood, now, that there was nothing passive about Paolinu Viviano's confrontation with the world that turns so erratically, and often so cruelly, around us all. More than the Monk, more than me, he had been determined to bend history to his own design. To rewrite it.

He waited, building patiently, until the year my father returned from Nagasaki and my mother became the chosen vessel of history's rebirth.

My grandfather couldn't have foreseen the consequences of that marriage, the rage and sorrow. He saw a broken son and a lovely, traditional young woman. He saw an end to one story and the beginning of another. And I believe—I have to believe—that he carried my parents' sorrow as his own terrible burden for half a century.

He kept his silence when they parted. He only broke it, six months before his death, when he whispered a name to me.

Did Domenico Valenti order the murder of Francesco Paolo Viviano, as my grandfather whispered? If there was a trial for my namesake's assassination, its records seem to have been lost with thousands of others in the Allied bombing raids on Palermo in 1943.

In any event, it was unlikely that charges would have been brought against Valenti himself. An underling would have been chosen, indicted and served his time in prison. The sentence would have been minimal. In the eyes of the law, the Monk's death was a settling of underworld accounts. Its net effect was one less bandit in the mountains.

EXCEPT FOR FRANK VIVIANO and Angelina Tocco, nobody knew the truth about my mother and father in 1945.

Caterina Cammarata may have known that she was a Valenti, but she never mentioned it, and if she did, it meant nothing to her.

The Valenti family line had not weathered immigration, or the nineteenth-century struggle for control of the Castellammare hills, as successfully as the Toccos and Badalamentis. Only a few Valentis were left in the Province of Palermo when the twenty-first century dawned.

I thought about looking one of them up in Terrasini; twelve were listed in the local phone directory, none with the first name Domenico. But what would I have said? What would *they* have said, if I'd repeated my grandfather's whisper?

The story was almost lost by my time, along with the name of a man who had been an architect of the *sistema*. The man who ordered the killing of the Monk.

But my grandfather remembered, because as much as anyone apart from the Monk himself, Domenico Valenti had set in motion

the events that propeled Paolinu Viviano across the ocean to the
New World—and transformed him into Frank.

There was no vendetta to end; time had seen to that. But there
was still the blood debt to resolve, *his* debt, from the moment in
1911 that he claimed the name of the Monk, before the old book
could be closed.

He told Angelina what this marriage meant. I'm sure of that,
because he told her everything. But neither of them told Caterina
Cammarata or Salvatore DiGiuseppe, when the proposal was
extended. The Cammaratas never spoke of their own paternal for-
bear, the bandit Antonino, much less a complicated ancestor named
Valenti from their mother's side. The connection was powerful
enough to alter our history. Yet in the vagaries of immigrant memory, it had been utterly forgotten by Domenico Valenti's American
kin. When my parents were betrothed, nobody except Frank Viviano
and Angelina Tocco knew that they had been deliberately chosen to
reconcile violent opposites. To close the old book and write a new
one.

LU SANGU LAVA LU SANGU, the code declared. "Blood
washes blood." It was usually invoked to justify the killing that had
washed Sicily in blood in my namesake's day, and continued to do
so a century later.

But my grandfather, who was a child of the parallel universe,
knew that *"lu sangu lava lu sangu"* had an alternate interpretation.
Short of murdering every male heir of an enemy, as Adannatu and
Toto Riina had tried to do, a vendetta could be ended only by marriage between the warring clans and the birth of an infant.

In bandit lore, the reconciliation is saluted at the infant's christening with a toast by the godparents to San Giovanni, who baptized Christ. They represent the new union between old enemies, a
union that in dialect is called *cumparaticu di San Giovanni.* It is
infinitely weightier than the ceremonial role that godparents play
in a modern American baptism. The *cumpari* are not merely enemies who have reconciled. They are now joined forever as family.

"The birth and baptism of their first child," in Giuseppe Pitre's words, "is also the birth of peace."

This is what my grandfather intended, I now understood: that his blood debt to the Monk be washed away by a union in blood.

THE EMBODIMENT OF THAT UNION, delivered at Providence Hospital in Detroit at the precise stroke of noon on December 3, 1947, was me. The auguries could not have been more remarkable.

It was the feast day of my saint, San Francesco, and the birthday of my grandmother Angelina. The sun, Sicily's primordial god and symbol, was at its apex. The hospital bore the name of my mother, and of the Favarotta madonna who had safeguarded my fishermen ancestors for ten centuries. My grandfather turned exactly fifty the month I was born, the Monk's age in his final year of life.

It is my age as I write this book.

"*Figghiu miu, miraculu!*" Angelina cried, over and over, at the baptism. "My son, my miracle!"

My mother has a photograph of the moment in Detroit's Holy Family Church when an immigrant Sicilian priest pours the baptismal water over me. I am in the same white lace gown that my grandfather wore for his own christening at Maria Santissima delle Grazie in 1897. In the photograph, he is off to one side with Angelina Tocco and my other two grandparents, Caterina Cammarata and Salvatore DiGiuseppe, watching intently.

Grandma Angelina has burst into song. My mother looks at her in alarm. Holding me at the baptismal font are my godfather, Peter Viviano, great-grandson of the Monk, and my godmother, Gerry DiGiuseppe, Caterina Valenti's great-granddaughter. I scream at the frigid sensation of December water on my brow.

I am the first child to be both Viviano and Valenti in the blood. The first in our family to be unambiguously named Francesco Paolo Viviano since the death of a three-day-old infant on September 30, 1851.

TWENTY-SIX

Quattro Vanelle

-+->-<+-

Terrasini, Sicily
June 1996—January 2000

JUNE FLOATED INTO THE CASTELLAMMARE HILLS
on clouds of oleander and honeysuckle. It was past time for Rosalia
and Mike to reclaim their house in the citrus grove, although neither of them spoke of it to me. It was time to leave.

As I began packing up for my departure from Sicily, Monacu
warily circled my boxes of documents on the terrace. Alice had
promised to feed him, but he vanished a few nights later and never
returned.

That week, the Caltanisetta trial of Toto Riina entered its second year. The Beast's right-hand man was in the bunker with him
now. Giovanni Brusca, the San Giuseppe Jato boss who supervised
the assassination of Judge Falcone, had finally been tracked down
and arrested on May 20, 1996, almost four years to the day after
the bomb demolished the judge's car and half a mile of the
Badalamenti autostrada.

The manhunt had ransacked every corner of Sicily, and if
Signore Zucco's relative was correct, it had briefly convinced the
Interior Ministry that I was Giovanni Brusca. But in the end, the
police found their man at his own country villa on the southern coast
of Sicily, watching a television movie with his wife, children, and
brother. The movie was a docudrama on the life of Judge Falcone.

Mike had come out to Paternella the next morning. "I thought you'd like to see this," he said, and handed me the front page of the *Giornale di Sicilia*. Next to the headlines trumpeting the arrest was a photo of two Italian policemen in bullet-proof vests and black ski masks escorting the captured Brusca to jail.

Brusca was heavier around the middle than he had been in 1992. He had grown a thickly curled beard.

A few months earlier, the arrest might have sent a new wave of fear through Sicily, a new wave of anxiety over the possible collapse of the *sistema*, and with it the only form of order that most Sicilians had ever known. But by the summer of 1996, even the Falcone trial seemed likely to join the long list of Mafia investigations that opened in defiance and dwindled into purposelessness. The Caltanisetta hearings had slogged into a swamp of legal motions, objections, and counter-objections so dense with technicalities that the trial was now expected to last as long as a decade. As the proceedings droned on, Riina, a squat man in his late sixties, sat impassively in the steel-barred defendant's box. He was nothing more than a peasant farmer from Corleone, he told the prosecutors time and again, barely able to read, much less run a global empire.

Cynicism over the trial grew with the numbers of *pentiti*. It was beginning to dawn on the authorities that the detailed testimony of self-described turncoats might, in itself, be another curtain pulled over the truth. There were now more than twelve hundred *pentiti* under government protection. By the summer's end, even Giovanni Brusca had offered to turn state's evidence.

It was hard not to believe, as most of my neighbors had come to believe, that the *sistema del potere* would survive. That deep down, Sicily would remain as it had always been. That the code would prevail.

In October 1999, former prime minister Giulio Andreotti was acquitted of all charges in his trial for Mafia collaboration. The chief witness against him, the *pentito* Baldassare Di Maggio, admitted that he had killed twenty-three people as a *sistema* hitman. Three of the murders were committed while he was ostensibly under police supervision, waiting to testify in the Andreotti trial.

"All of this should not last," the Prince of Salina thinks, as the *sistema* takes form in the *Leopard* in the 1870s, painted into the ancient canvas of Sicilian fatalism. "But it will, always. The human 'always,' of course—a century, two centuries. And after that it will be different, but worse."

THE PHONE RANG AT PATERNELLA, early one morning, as I watched the June dawn light the citrus grove. "Are you Francesco Paolo Viviano?" a voice asked. I said that I was.

The caller was a Dominican monk, Father Benedict Viviano. Benedict was his priestly name; he had been born and baptized Gaetano. Like my father. Like the Falcon. Father Benedict was from St. Louis, where the Falcon had run his gambling house under the name "Big Tom."

I had contacted an Italian-American club there months before, in search of someone who might remember Big Tom, might know what had happened to his daughter Maria. The club's president had passed the word on to Father Benedict, who now lived in a monastery in Switzerland.

We spoke for an hour, both of us dizzied by the strange turns of the tale that led to this phone call. He was an erudite man, a biblical scholar, as consumed with the whims of history as I was. There was a chance, I thought, that his father had known Gaetano the Falcon, and a much fainter chance that he would know what had really happened at that deserted crossroads near Terrasini in 1876.

I learned a great deal from Father Benedict about the Vivianos of St. Louis. But he knew nothing of Gaetano the Falcon. He knew nothing of the Monk or his murder.

The evidence, when I left Sicily, was still limited to my grandfather's last words to me—"The boss tell his men to kill him. The boss, Domenico Valenti"—and the description of the Monk's death that I had found in the *Giornale di Sicilia,* based on the testimony of the cart driver Onorato Evola.

I read the article dozens of times, checked and rechecked my translation, mulled over its fatal sentences until I'd committed them to memory:

> Two gunshots were fired, wounding a horse. At this point a man leaped from the hedge to grab the horse by the reins. Perhaps mistaking him for one of their robbery victims, his own accomplices shot him twice. He died immediately.
>
> The policemen who hurried to the scene state that the dead man is an ex-monk of fifty years old from Favarotta, by the name of Viviano, Francesco Paolo.

There was something amiss. I couldn't quite explain what. It might have been the sixth sense of experience, the skepticism bred by three decades as a reporter.

It might simply have been that I refused to believe Evola's account. If it was true, my grandfather's last words to me were not.

ABOUT A WEEK BEFORE I piled my bags into the Peugeot and headed north, Mike took me to Quattro Vanelle. I had told him that I couldn't find it on the map. The name was changed a long time back, he explained. "But years ago, when I was a boy, the old folks still called a place out in the *campagna* 'Quattro Vanelle.' Come on, I'll show you where it is."

"Quattro Vanelle" means "four lanes." Mike said it referred to a point where four small country roads converge in the lemon groves, a mile above the Gulf of Castellammare between Terrasini and Cinisi.

When we arrived there, a dry wind was blowing off Monte Palmeto. Garbage was piled up in rotting heaps against the stone walls that surrounded the groves. Discarded plastic shopping bags blew in fitful gusts toward the sea. A vacation resort, behind walls of its own topped with broken glass, stood no more than half a mile away, yet the place had a remote, deserted feel to it.

"Let's go," I said after five minutes. I didn't want to stay.

LATER, ON A HUNCH, I went to Maria Santissima delle Grazie to make one final survey of the parish ledgers in search of something, anything, that might put flesh on the phantom character of Domenico Valenti. No death record had ever turned up for him. Had he been waylaid by the Falcon? Ambushed in vengeance, somewhere in the mountains, and killed with his body-guards?

Valenti's murder would have filled many of the empty spaces in my canvas: the absence of his death certificate in Terrasini, the departure of the Falcon for America, the broken chain of Domenico Valentis leading from his generation to mine.

An hour crept by, then two. Padre Constantino was used to me now, and I could stay as long as I needed to. In the third hour, my wandering carried me to the Monk's sister Giovanna, born in 1836. Her godfather, the baptismal record indicated, was Giuseppe Valenti.

In itself, that wasn't surprising. Before the *Risorgimento,* before the *sistema* had set them against each other, the Valenti and Viviano families were the closest of neighbors. But Zu Pippinu, as the children would have known him, was not only godfather to a Viviano in 1836. He was also the godfather, that very same year, to an infant named Paolo Evola.

Onorato Evola, the cart driver who provided the only eyewit-ness account of the Monk's death, was his cousin. The ancestral Evola land, on architect Orlando's old military map, was bounded by two of the roads at Quattro Vanelle.

I followed the ledgers to the eighteenth century, into a net of marriages that had tied two Terrasini families together for genera-tions, in the endless entanglements of kinship and blood debts.

They were the Valentis and the Evolas. It was something, a thin cir-
cumstantial thread that tied Domenico Valenti to a man who saw
the Monk die.

The reporter in me knew it wasn't enough.

MORE THAN THREE AND A HALF YEARS were to pass
before I returned to Sicily. Three years on the road. In spare
moments, I wrote the Monk's story, recounting the search that had
carried me so far. I worked, always, in the knowledge that I lacked
a final piece of evidence in my reconstruction of his murder, even if
the larger mystery had been solved.

I had unearthed the secret that lay hidden for eighty years. I
could prove that I was a Valenti—that the murder victim was not
only my namesake, but that I was also the heir to his accused killer.

But the operative word was "accused." The connection between
Valenti and Onorato Evola was too suggestive to dismiss, yet too
ephemeral to qualify as a smoking gun.

History proceeded, shuddering forward on its terrible course.
Bosnia left the front pages of the newspaper and was dropped from
my itinerary. Albania, the Caucasus, and Kosovo replaced it. A mil-
lenium ended. I wrote a book without a final chapter.

THERE WERE OCCASIONAL CALLS from Bobby and Alice
Cortese in Terrasini. Mike had never been comfortable with tele-
phones. Then, for a year, there was nothing at all, until Marianna
Trappeto, the village registrar, called and told me that Mike was in
Ucciardone Prison in Palermo.

The details were sketchy; he hadn't been formally charged with
a crime. The detention was based on "suspicion of Mafia association," invoking a special Italian law that applied almost exclusively
to Sicily. It could land someone behind bars for years without trial.
Mike had been arrested six months before. No one thought he

would be out soon. But no one knew—or said—precisely what he might be involved in. The possibilities, in Sicily, were limitless.

Marianna added, almost as an afterthought, that the new library had finally opened.

I flew to Palermo in the first week of the new century, as soon as I had a few days to spare. Rosalia, Bobby, Flavio, and Alice were at the house in the village. They had lost Paternella and the *salumeria*, selling off everything they could to finance Mike's legal defense. Bobby and Sara were now married; they had a six-month-old baby, a husky little boy. He was named Michele.

Rosalia was somber. "We'll wait as long as we have to," she said. Bobby nodded as she spoke. Alice looked away. Nanna stayed in her bedroom.

Flavio had changed more than anyone. Twelve now, he was very quiet, no longer the karate-kicking whirlwind who had embodied his father's nervous energy. I could only stay a few hours, I told them. We all knew it was just an excuse, that a reunion without Mike was too painful.

MARIANNA WAS IMMENSELY PROUD of the new library, which was installed in a grand baroque palazzo bequeathed to the village by a Bourbon aristocratic family. She had been named its director, and sat behind a large desk in the former ballroom, under a garish painting of tenth-century Crusaders besieging Moorish troops in the Duc d'Aumale's nineteenth-century warehouse.

She took me on a tour. The missing archives had been recovered from their unmarked boxes and shelved in a room of their own. "Not much use to me now," I thought, although I didn't say so to Marianna.

A frail elderly man sat at a table in the corner of the room, in deep concentration, hunched over one of the ledgers. "We call him the *maestro del archivio*," Marianna said. The master of the archives. "He's here every day, from opening to closing. He has your family name, you know."

The old man looked up, and we instantly recognized each

other. It was Giuseppe Viviano, the elusive historian on the bus to Palermo, who had never responded to the messages I'd left at Di Maggio's *Caffe* or in the window of his house on Via Cataldi.

"You," he said. I expected him to bolt.

But he stood up, and walked over to us. "Where have you been, Mister Viviano? I have something for you at home," he said. "Stay here, don't leave until I come back."

He returned fifteen minutes later, and handed me a yellowed sheaf of papers. It was a worn photocopy of a prison sentence, announced by the criminal court of Palermo in December 1879. "Read it," he said, "and please put this in your book."

The master of the archive scrawled a shaky sentence, in English, on the photocopy: "Research carried out by Giuseppe Viviano, son of Gaetano." He hesitated, and crossed out the names. "Make that 'Joseph Viviano, son of Thomas,'" he said.

Then he went back to his ledgers.

THE SENTENCE WAS FOR MURDER, an assassination in Terrasini that had occurred in October 1875, a year before the Monk's death, although the defendants were not indicted and tried until the decade's end. One of them was "Onorato Evola, age thirty-seven." The driver of the cart on that fatal night in 1876 at Quattro Vanelle.

The only eyewitnesss to my namesake's killing.

His accomplice, who had "instigated" the assassination and commissioned it, according to the court transcript, was "Lorenzo Valenti, age thirty-five, son of Pietro."

Domenico Valenti's nephew.

Both men were sentenced to death.

Onorato Evola was a convicted murderer, an assassin for the Valenti family.

I could now write the Monk's final chapter. I could move on with my own life.

Epilogue

Western Sicily
November 1876

FRANCESCO PAOLO VIVIANO *sits alone in a mountain glen,*
staring into the embers of yesterday's fire. It is the final week of
October. The baby who bore his name would have been twenty-
five years old this month.

The Monk tries to imagine his first son as a man. He sketches a
portrait: the broad Viviano shoulders, Antonina's eyes. Maybe the
nose would have been Pasquale Randazzo's. Would Francesco have
resembled his half-brother Gaetano, who is himself about to turn
twenty? If only Antonina's babies had lived, the Monk thinks, some
part of her would still be alive today.

An autumn chill is falling on the Madonie, blanketing the pas-
tures in morning frost, when the distant silhouettes of three men
on horseback appear in the pass. They move slowly in the direc-
tion of his fire, observing the courtesies. In the mountains, an
arrival must be visibly announced or it will be taken as hostile.
These men understand the protocol, and make sure that they are
in his sight long before the trail reaches the forest clearing where
the Monk sits.

He watches. There are fewer and fewer bandits in the moun-
tains, and few days when men come looking for him in the old way,
to talk, and if the talking goes well, to share the dangers and

rewards of the highway. The men disappear as switchbacks carry them behind the ridge, then reappear, closer each time, until he can see their faces. He knows them, but not well. They too are from the Castellammare hills, and like him, they used to walk into Polizzi Generosa or Gangi to buy flour or dried beans.

That was before last year. Before the killers hunted down the Di Martino brothers from Polizzi and drove Vincenzo Rocca into the blind canyon where he took his own life. Before the mattanza, when the Madonie's western passes were ruled by Rocca and his followers. Now they are all dead, or rotting in Palermo cells.

One of the men walks to the edge of the clearing. He stops a polite ten yards from the fire and touches his right hand to his breast. "Salve, Francesco lu Monacu," he says.

The Monk is older than all of them. To be fifty is to be an elder in the Bandit Kingdom, a sage, a survivor. If the men are familiar with his 'nciuria, they are familiar with his story: the two wars against the Bourbons; the years in the mountains; his skill with horses.

The conversation proceeds as slowly, as discreetly, as the men's descent from the pass. They ask about his family. The names of mutual acquaintances come up. Someone mentions Vincenzo Rocca's suicide. "There will never be another one like him. The world is not what it once was," they agree. "Not like the days of the picciotti, Signore Monacu." It is another discreet courtesy, a way of acknowledging Francesco Viviano's red sash.

An hour passes. They are eating olives and cacciocavallo that the three visitors have carried over the pass, when one of them takes the initiative and quietly edges the talk toward its purpose. An opportunity is about to present itself, a valuable shipment from Giardinello to Cinisi. The job will not be simple. It means climbing down to the plain, to the citrus groves east of Terrasini. They will have to strike at dusk, before the full protective cover of night. Without a man of Francesco Viviano's experience, the visitor says, there is not much chance of success.

This final courtesy is the proposition.

* * *

TWO WEEKS LATER, the Monk joins the three men at a pre-
arranged meeting point, and they set out for the Castellammare
plain. The rising wind howls its November warning, and the Monk
pulls the red sash tighter around his cape.

They ride toward the sea in silence. As always on this road,
Francesco thinks of Antonina. The image that comes to him is the
Festa di li Schetti—it will be almost thirty years ago in April—
when his turn at the orange tree came in the Piazza Duomo, and he
lifted it high above his head and walked all the way to Pasquale
Randazzo's house, the crowd following behind in a shouting blur,
until he staggered to Antonina's window and finally let the tree top-
ple into the street.

On November 15, the men camp in a small, rocky canyon
above the Castellammare plain. They must bide time until dusk
tomorrow evening, when a cart from Giardinello is expected to pass
the crossroads of Quattro Vanelle.

The sixteenth arrives. The mountain shadows shorten at mid-
day, then lengthen quickly in the November afternoon. Clouds pile
up over the Madonie. Francesco hopes for a shift in wind that will
push them seaward to cover the Castellammare moon. At 4:00 P.M.,
the men begin their descent.

From the trail that coils down Monte Palmeto, the Monk
watches as the sun flees from the mud-walled cottage of Maria and
his sons and brushes the French duke's villa in amber.

At the base of the cliff, the four turn sharply east, keeping in
the Palmeto shadows, until they reach a walled country road half a
mile beyond Cinisi. In years past, Francesco took this road from
Favarotta to the casa Badalamenti, where Zu Piddu plotted against
the Bourbons in 1848 and again in 1860. He shakes his head at the
thought of all the changes since then, and at all of the things that
haven't changed.

When they reach Quattro Vanelle, the men take up positions
behind a thick hedge of oleander. The wait is brief. As though by
appointment, a heavily loaded cart bounces toward them, drawn by

a team of horses. Two men sit astride the bench of the cart, one of them with the reins in hand. Three others sprawl over the cargo.

"Now," a voice cries.

The Monk hears two shots. A horse rears suddenly and whinnies in pain.

The same voice cries out once more, "Now! Now! Now!"

Francesco finds himself running, furiously, toward the wounded horse. Two more shots ring out. The last thing he recognizes, before dusk tumbles into night, is the face of the man holding the reins.

Acknowledgments

Many names have been changed in *Blood Washes Blood,* for reasons that need no explanation. The people of western Sicily are born to a culture of iron discretion and silence. It took enormous courage to share their knowledge with a distant American cousin.

Fellow journalist Jeremy Stigter and Amy Rennert, my extraordinary agent, were the manuscript's closest readers, unfailing in their encouragement and deeply perceptive in their critical judgments. Without them, the Monk's story may never have reached publication. The patient support of Chiew Terriere nudged the author past a gauntlet of doubts.

My debt to my parents and grandparents and my brother Sam, to the fierce embrace of our family life, is infinite. Sam's maps grace these pages.

Major roles in the drafting of *Blood Washes Blood* were played by Oliver Johnson, Emily Heckman, Tim Neagle, George Lucas and Judith Curr at Pocket Books, Steve Faigenbaum, Sharon Silva, Peter Solomon, and Alane Mason.

Additional thanks to Tony Cartano, Martijn David, Johannes Jacob, Bessie Weiss, Stuart Horwitz, Abner Stein, Christina George, AnnaKaisa Danielsson, Susie Nicklin, Paul Marsh, Polly Hutchinson, Brenda Turnnidge, Jennifer Lyons, Bonnie Nadell, the Deprez family, Jerry Roberts, Jeffrey Klein, Frank Browning, Richard Van Ham, Paul Giurlanda, Diane Bloomfield, Shirley Viviano, Father Benedict Viviano, O.P., Pauline Viviano, Alfonso

Tocco, Pat Cammarata, Mary Viviano, Vince LaMendola, Grace Catania, Lora Fountain, Lisa Greenwald, Anne and Rosa Lechartier, Simone Bocognano, Jacqueline de Harambure, Françoise Mallet, and Francis Christophe.

I was greatly assisted in my research efforts by the Salamone Family, the Biblioteca Regionale della Sicilia, Graziella Moceri, the Biblioteca Communale di Terrasini, the Commune di Terrasini, the Commune di Partinico, the Commune di Cinisi, the New York Public Library, the American Library in Paris, Umberto Santino, Guido Orlando, Giuseppe Viviano, Salvatore Viviano and Susanna Perna, the Giliberti Family, Damiano Zerilli, Father Raffaele Speciale, and Sergio Loj.

For twenty-five wonderful years, Gus LeMendola brought great happiness to my mother and inspiration to her sons. He passed away one week after this book was completed.